Southern Living.

2000
Garden
ANNUAL

Perennial borders wrap a West Virginia mountainside house from front to back in sweeps of changing colors. (See pages 134–136.)

Southern Living®

2000
Garden
ANNUAL

Oxmoor House®

Southern Living
2000 Garden ANNUAL

©2000 by Oxmoor House, Inc.
Book Division of Southern Progress Corporation
P.O. Box 2463, Birmingham, Alabama 35201

Southern Living® is a federally registered
trademark of Southern Living, Inc.

ISSN: 1048-2318
Hardcover ISBN: 0-8487-1937-9
Softcover ISBN: 0-8487-1939-5
Printed in the United States of America
First Printing 2000

SOUTHERN LIVING
Executive Editor, Homes and Gardens: Eleanor Griffin
Garden Editor: Linda C. Askey
Senior Writer: Stephen P. Bender
Senior Photographers: Van Chaplin, Allen Rokach
Photographers: Jean M. Allsopp, Tina Cornett
Associate Garden Editor: Charles Thigpen
Assistant Garden Design Editor: Troy H. Black
Assistant Garden Editors: Liz Druitt, Ellen Riley
Production Manager: Vicki Weathers
Editorial Coordinator: Bradford Kachelhofer
Editorial Assistant: Lynne Long
Production Assistant: Nicole Johnson

OXMOOR HOUSE, INC.
Editor-in-Chief: Nancy Fitzpatrick Wyatt
Senior Editor, Copy and Homes: Olivia Kindig Wells
Art Director: James Boone

SOUTHERN LIVING 2000 GARDEN ANNUAL
Editor: Susan Hernandez Ray
Copy Editor: Cathy Ritter Scholl
Contributing Designer: Carol Loria
Editorial Assistant: Heather Averett
Contributing Copy Assistant: Sally Inzer
Contributing Indexer: Katharine R. Wiencke

Director, Production and Distribution: Phillip Lee
Associate Production Manager: Vanessa C. Richardson
Production Assistant: Faye Porter Bonner

We're Here for You!
We at Oxmoor House are dedicated to serving you with reliable
information that expands your imagination and enriches your life.
We welcome your comments and
suggestions. Please write us at:
OXMOOR HOUSE, INC.
Editor, *Southern Living 2000 Garden Annual*
2100 Lakeshore Drive
Birmingham, AL 35209

Cover: Camellias, pages 20–23
Back Cover: Garden shed, pages 76–78

Contents

purple coneflowers

autumn foliage

paperwhites

violas

$\mathcal{E}$ach of your high school yearbooks holds a year of memories you don't want to lose. All you have to do is pick up the volume and thumb through the pages; it all comes back. We feel that way about the people and gardens we visited during 1999, so we've bound all of our inspiring and informative gardening articles into one pretty book, the *Southern Living 2000 Garden Annual*.

As a gardener, you know that each year abounds with fresh landscaping trends, new plants, and renewed interest in old ones. With your gardening yearbook, you have that information—and more—at your fingertips. Rather than combing your magazines for a flower arrangement to do for a party, an arbor to show your carpenter, or an annual combination to plant, you can find the inspiration all in one place. We've put 12 months of *Southern Living* gardening together with an index for easy access.

We invite you to enjoy the gardens of *Southern Living* in this seasonal celebration of the bounty and beauty a year in the South can bring. And we hope you will make more good memories using the ideas you find on these pages.

Linda C. Askey

GARDEN EDITOR

A breathtaking Arkansas garden that has taken 27 years to create surrounds a New England–style home. (See pages 116–121.)

camellia cuttings (See pages 20–23.)

January

Checklist
for
January

EDITORS' NOTEBOOK

If you've ever had a wound that was slow to heal, be glad you're not a tree. You have antibodies and white blood cells to protect you. A tree has just its bark. When fire, lightning, bulldozers, or Rhonda's runaway pickup truck kills a large section of bark, it exposes the heartwood to termites and wood-boring insects as well as rot-causing fungi. This is dangerous because the heartwood is what supports the tree and keeps it off your head, your car, and your roof. Outwardly, the tree may look fine—not a single brown leaf—and grow normally for years. But inside, it's being slowly hollowed out, just waiting for that final windstorm to bring it down. Don't wait—hire a licensed tree company to evaluate the tree now and decide whether to remove it. True, putting this off might save a few bucks. But it could prove to be a hollow victory.

Steve Bender

TIPS

☐ **Holiday leftovers**—When you take down the garland and haul out the tree, don't overlook the value of these drying evergreen boughs. Cut them into single branches, and place over beds of perennials to create a mulch that doesn't pack down and smother the plant crowns. Just pull them back when new growth begins to appear in early spring.

☐ **Mail orders**—Take time to sit down with the seed catalogs that have been stacking up. Order the flower and vegetable seeds you'll need for spring, summer, and fall gardens. Remember to keep a copy of your order for your records. That's also a good place to note where you intend to plant those seeds and plants. ▶

☐ **Saw palmetto**—Use the fan-shaped leaves of this native shrub for dried arrangements. Cut the leaves from the base of the plant with sharp pruning shears. Leaves will keep for weeks without water.

☐ **Vegetables**—Till this month to prepare for planting next month, in the Middle and Lower South. Be sure to work in plenty of compost, as well as lime if necessary. To be certain of your soil needs, send off a sample to your state lab. Coastal South gardeners can plant this month.

PLANT

☐ **Amaryllis**—After the blossoms fade, plant holiday amaryllis in Middle, Lower, and Coastal South gardens. Give them good drainage and a bed enriched with compost. Plant so that the bulbs are only two-thirds buried; the top third should be above the soil. Take care not to damage leaves and roots.

☐ **Azaleas**—Plant now for spring bloom in the Lower and Coastal South. Indica types such as Formosa and Pride of Mobile may reach 6 to 10 feet tall and wide. Further north, Kurume azaleas are more dwarf and compact in their growth, usually reaching 2 to 3 feet tall. Intermediate selections such as Fashion and Glacier mature to 3 to 5 feet tall. Azaleas prefer partial shade and well-drained, acid soils.

☐ **Blueberries**—The next couple of months are a good time to plant blueberries. Think of them as azaleas that like the sun. They need to be planted in acid soil that has been enriched with compost. Be sure to plant more than one selection for good pollination.

◀ **Glads**—In the Lower South, begin planting gladiolus corms now, and stagger plantings every two to three weeks through February. Plant them in groups of at least 8 or 10 placed 6 to 8 inches apart.

☐ **Peonies**—Plant in well-prepared soil where they are protected from afternoon sun. Choose a spot that's away from competing tree and shrub roots. The peony's eyes or crowns should be set an inch or two above ground level, and then covered with about an inch of prepared soil mix. Early-flowering types such as Festiva Maxima are best for Lower South gardens. Tree peonies are best grown in the Upper South.

☐ **Roses**—Buy now for the best selection. In Florida the longest lived plants will be your favorite selections grafted onto Fortuniana rootstock, so ask at your garden center. Elsewhere roses also benefit from being grown on their own roots. If your soil drains poorly, grow roses in pots of high-quality potting soil. Plant in well-drained soil and at least a half day of direct sun. ▶

☐ **Vegetables**—In the Coastal South, lettuce, kale, cabbage, mustard, turnips, spinach, and other leafy vegetables may be set out now as transplants or seeds. Plant potatoes for harvest in May and June. Cut seed potatoes into 1- to 2-inch pieces that contain at least one eye; plant 2 to 3 inches deep in raised rows.

In the Tropical South, plant tomatoes if you can protect them from frost. If the temperature should plunge to the 30s one night, cover the plants with boxes or blankets. Don't use plastic unless you are able to remove it the next day when the weather warms; otherwise the plants will cook in the sun.

PRUNE

☐ **Liriope and mondo grass**—Mow these two ground covers now to remove browned, ragged foliage before spring growth begins. Set the mower to its maximum height. After mowing, rake away the clippings.

☐ **Perennials**—When frost kills the above ground portions of perennials, remove the unsightly dead portions. Also rake around the base of the plants to clean out fallen leaves and replace them with a neat mulch such as pine straw or bark.

☐ **Petunias**—In areas where petunias grow all winter, keep plants blooming longer by snipping back the stems 2 to 3 inches every two weeks through spring. This keeps plants from setting seed and encourages new growth laden with flowers. Feed with a liquid fertilizer such as 15-30-15 after pruning.

☐ **Trees and shrubs**—Prune now while trees and shrubs are dormant. When the job is complete, the plant should retain its natural form. Remove dead wood first, and then take out crossing limbs and those that are visually unbalanced. A stub of ½ to 1 inch should remain where limbs are removed to allow quick healing.

CONTROL

☐ **Ice**—Avoid pouring salt on slippery steps and walks; it will injure your plants. Use sand or fireplace ashes instead.

☐ **Insects**—Dormant-oil sprays applied to the bare trunks and branches of fruit trees will kill overwintering adult insects, as well as their eggs. You can also spray evergreens to control lacebugs, spider mites, scale, and whiteflies.

☐ **Lawns**—Keeping in mind that a thick, healthy lawn is the best weed control, resolve to fertilize with a slow-release formula, mow regularly at the right height for your lawn, water as needed to keep the grass growing, and repair thin or bare areas. Begin now if summer weeds have been a problem in the past by applying a crabgrass control such as Balan.

FERTILIZE

☐ **Bougainvillea**—Vines will produce more flowers if you don't pamper them. In the Tropical South, keep them dry and fertilize with a bloom booster type of fertilizer such as 10-45-20.

GARDENING
PLANTS AND DESIGN

LASTING
BEAUTIES

Bring home a flower to beat the winter blahs.

Flowering houseplants are key ingredients to warding off the post-holiday blues. While many flowers are fleeting, others have the staying power to see you through winter's dreariest days. Brightly colored anthuriums, cyclamen, phalaenopsis orchids, or bromeliads are instant spirit lifters.

There was a time when these flowers were considered exotic and were available only through selected florists. These days you'll find them in large home-center stores as well as independent garden centers. The sticker price on these plants may be shocking, but weigh the months of perpetual bloom against the cost and they become a good value. Ann Sparkman of Martin Nursery in Greenville, South Carolina, shares some hints on what to look for when you purchase one.

PHALAENOPSIS ORCHID (PICTURED)
Looking like a fragile butterfly, the delicate blossoms of phalaenopsis orchid belie the plant's sturdy nature.

What To Look For: Choose an orchid that has deep green leaves free of yellow spots or damage. The bloom stem should be loosely tied to a plant stake. Ann recommends purchasing an orchid that has only a flower or two open, with the rest of the stem budded. "Look for buds that are fresh and full."

Basic Needs: Place your orchid near an east or west window. Bright light is good; avoid direct sunlight. Phalaenopsis orchids also thrive under fluorescent light. Grow this plant successfully in average house temperature away from drafts or abrupt temperature changes. Water it only when dry. Place the pot in the kitchen sink, and soak the potting medium and

BY ELLEN RILEY / PHOTOGRAPHY TINA CORNETT

Yellow and white Guzmania bromeliads stand tall, while hot pink Tillandsias (right) and green- and pink-striped Neoregelia bromeliad (left) provide complementary colors. Striped prayer plant and lemon button fern have similar water requirements.

CLOCKWISE FROM TOP:
*A phalaenopsis orchid
and maidenhair fern
bring height and grace
to this arrangement.
Miniature pink cyclamen
are tucked along the front
of an old iron birdbath.
The elegant assortment
is completed with pots of
soft pink anthurium and
bright florist cyclamen.*

roots. Allow the container to drain well before returning it to its growing place. In most homes, once a week is just right.

Expect To Pay: A 4-inch pot costs from $8 to $19. A 6-inch pot ranges from $20 to $50, but they can last for months.

ANTHURIUM

This plant will win your affection with its heart-shaped glossy leaves and waxy flowers. Flaming anthurium *(Anthurium andraeanum)* is a tropical jewel that is comfortable in a warm winter home.

What To Look For: Shiny foliage and blooms held upright and high are signs of a healthy plant. Look into the base of the plant for additional buds. Ann reminds, "Buds are almost more important than the blooms you see open right now. They indicate a fresh plant and ensure the longest possible bloom time."

Basic Needs: Anthurium requires bright light from an east or west window, but direct sunlight is not tolerated. Native to the tropics, it appreciates warm temperatures and fairly high humidity. "Keep the soil evenly moist, and use water that

is room temperature. Anthurium leaves should be kept dust free, so mist with tepid water frequently," Ann advises.

Expect To Pay: A 6-inch pot costs between $10 and $16. Blooms last up to three months if properly cared for.

CYCLAMEN

The jewel-colored blooms of cyclamen *(Cyclamen persicum)* look like small fairies dancing on slender stems above lily pad leaves.

What To Look For: Avoid plants with yellow leaves or weak stems. Ann says to "turn the pot on its side and look into the heart of the cyclamen. You should see lots of buds snuggled among sturdy stems."

Basic Needs: Cyclamen is the perfect choice for a cool spot in your home. Bright light is a necessity, but avoid hot sun beaming on it. "It is easiest and best if the plant is watered from the bottom. They do not like their leaves to get wet, and top watering can cause rotting problems," says Ann. When the soil begins to dry, place the pot in a shallow saucer of water and let it absorb all it needs.

Expect To Pay: A 6-inch pot costs between $7 and $15.

BROMELIADS

Bromeliad is the family name that includes many species with very different blooms, all distantly related to the pineapple. Guzmanias, Neoregelias, and Tillandsias provide dazzling flowers.

What To Look For: Choose plants with brilliantly colored flowers and healthy green leaves. "Avoid buying one that has small pups (baby plants) coming from the main plant. This plant has been in bloom for a long time, and will not carry on much longer," advises Ann.

Basic Needs: Bright light from an east or west window is preferred, but they also grow in low light. When in low light the flower will lose color faster. Bromeliad foliage forms a center cup that should be filled with water once a week. At the end of the week, empty the cup and refill it. Water the soil about once a week.

Expect To Pay: A 4-inch pot ranges from $6 to $12. A 6-inch pot at $20 is a bargain. These are long bloomers whose color will fade with age. ◇

Raising Raspberries

Ginny's eyes sparkle as she holds out a basket of sweet red berries. "I think more people should grow raspberries," she says. I know Ginny and her husband, Ed, speak with years of experience from their Indian Springs, Alabama, garden. But I didn't know raspberries grew so well this far south.

Their experiment began about 17 years ago when Ed read an article about Heritage raspberries. The couple recommends this selection for gardens as far south as Columbia, South Carolina; Macon, Georgia; Montgomery, Alabama; and Jackson, Mississippi. Although Heritage will produce a small spring crop and a larger one in fall, the idea is to cut the plants down in late winter and eliminate the spring crop. The plants compensate with a bountiful harvest later in the season.

Ed and Ginny Lusk

Last year, Ginny and Ed began harvesting the last week of June and did not finish until the first week of November. "We picked at least 100 pints," says Ginny.

GROWING TIPS

Ed began by preparing a 12-inch-wide bed in early spring and set his plants about 2 feet apart in a row down the center of the bed. He planted 3 rows that measured about 25 feet each, and left about 7 to 10 feet between the rows so plants could spread to 3 feet wide. That way he can mow a grass path between them.

"When you buy plants, they come cut off about 7 to 8 inches from the ground," Ed says. "Plant them no deeper than they were grown in the nursery. Mulch them; then let them be until they start putting out young leaves."

When the canes start to grow long, Ed buys pressure-treated 1 x 2 stakes and twine. He sets the stakes 1½ to 2 feet from the plants on each side of the row. Then he strings twine between each stake about 1 foot above the ground and at 2 feet. This temporary trellis surrounds the raspberry row, supports the canes, and keeps the garden from becoming a brier patch.

The first summer Ed got a few berries, but it takes a second year for a big harvest. "The second year you have a lot more plants than you set out," he says. That's the other reason for cutting them back and mowing between rows; that way the suckers don't get out of hand.

If frost threatens to cut the season short, Ed is prepared. "I go out before sunup and spray the frost off with a hose," he says. "Then it doesn't bother them. It works."

Linda C. Askey

A RASPBERRY ROW AND TRELLIS

Spacing: 2 feet between plants and 7 to 10 feet between rows

Light: full sun

Soil: loose, well drained, neutral pH, mulched

Pruning: Cut plants back to 5 inches in late winter.

Fertilizer: New plants need 1 cup of 10-10-10 per 10 feet of row in March; established plants need 2 cups. All plants need 2 cups of calcium nitrate (or 10-10-10) per 10 feet of row in June.

Expect to pay: about $2 per plant

Source: Ison's Nursery & Vineyard, 1-800-733-0324

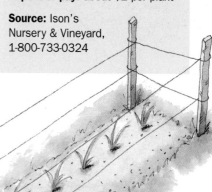

The *Art* of a
BENCH

Placed for impact

as well as seating,

a bench becomes a

garden ornament.

We seldom take time to sit on our garden benches. We spend more time looking at them, walking past them, planting around them. So a bench is more than a spot to rest; it transcends utility to become a garden ornament.

Careful selection and placement can ensure your bench works for the eyes as well as for the body. Durability and style are requisites for outdoor furnishings, although they don't need to be ornate. Sometimes a simple stone slab is best.

The secret to an outstanding bench is where you put it. A settee in the distance becomes a visual invitation to a cozy nook or majestic overlook. It is a device you can use to lead your guests in the direction you want them to go.

A bench used as a focal point, however, is even more compelling. Placed at the center of a view down a path or framed in an arbor, a bench becomes a picture-perfect vista. Rather than a place to sit and enjoy the view, the bench becomes the view.

Most importantly, the location needs to be plausible. Even if you have never slowed down long enough to sit there, your bench needs to look like you could.

That means the bench needs to be accessible, near a path or on a lawn where you can reach it comfortably. Set into a tangle of ferns would be attractive but unbelievable. Likewise, a bench in the middle of a sunny lawn is less inviting than one set beneath a leafy bough.

A slab of stone extends from the garden wall for a natural place to stop and rest. Its presence is an invitation into the garden.

PHOTOGRAPH: TINA CORNETT / DESIGN: BILL NANCE, HUNTSVILLE, ALABAMA

One set in the middle of the front lawn is also uncomfortable because it lacks privacy. On the other hand, a bench may sit alone, looking over an expanse of green pasture. If the setting is solitary, the bench is a welcome sight. Neither the example of lawn nor pasture has any kind of structure or plantings. The difference is in the context.

Benches are an easy way to create a feeling of intimacy. A pair of them on a level area in the woods transforms an undeveloped spot into a secret garden.

If you can't take the time to enjoy sitting on your benches, be sure you like looking at them.

Although the benches shown here are from private collections, *Southern Living* offers plans for three wooden benches you can build—the Board Bench ($4) and the Trefoil Bench ($4), which are both backless, and the Garden Bench ($4). To order, send a separate, self-addressed, stamped, business-sized envelope for each bench to Bench Projects, *Southern Living,* P.O. Box 523, Birmingham, AL 35201. Include a check payable to *Southern Living;* each plan is $4. **Please specify which plan(s) you are ordering.** Allow at least six weeks for delivery. ◇

ABOVE: *This bench enhances its natural surroundings.*

LEFT: *Framed in an arched opening, a bench and urns of white impatiens create a focal point.*

PHOTOGRAPHS: VAN CHAPLIN / DESIGN: PRATT BROWN, BIRMINGHAM, ALABAMA / OWNER: BARBARA ASHFORD

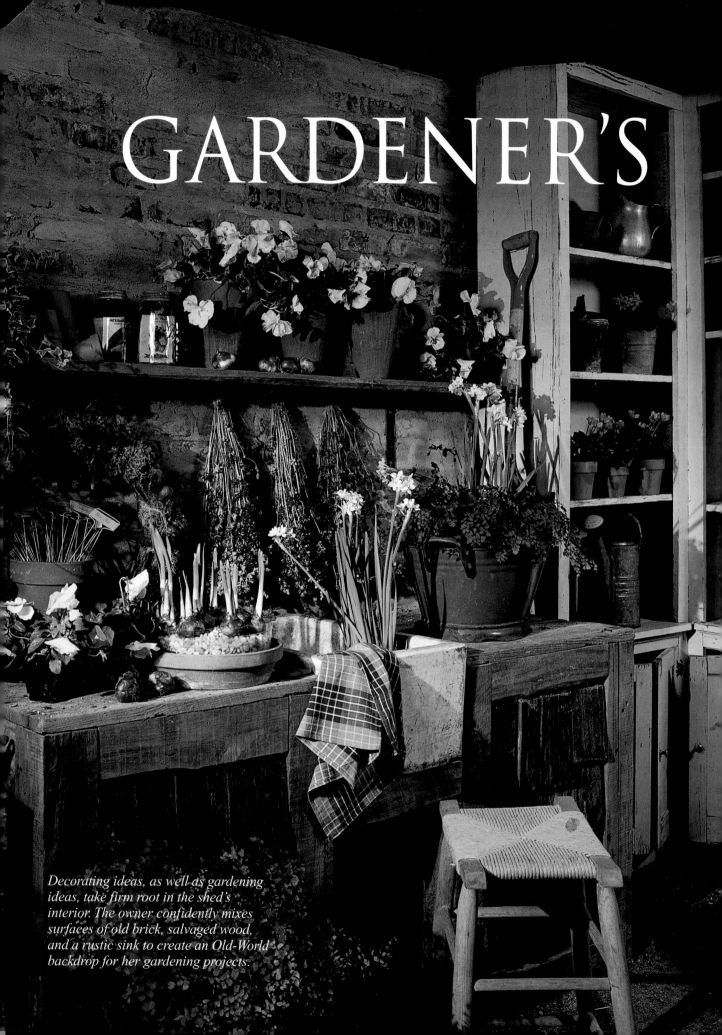

GARDENER'S

Decorating ideas, as well as gardening ideas, take firm root in the shed's interior. The owner confidently mixes surfaces of old brick, salvaged wood, and a rustic sink to create an Old-World backdrop for her gardening projects.

SCRAPBOOK

Working with walls instead of pages, an Alabama gardener creates a living scrapbook of old and new that reflects her singular gardening style.

A friend found the porcelain sink in England. The front door is from a shop in Alabama. The carriage house lantern by the door was a gift. Just like favorite old photos, these treasures bring a smile and a memory to their owner. She displays them with pride on her potting shed, a one-of-a-kind statement of her love for all things gardening. "I'm a collector of old things," says the owner, a noted gardener. "I love old sprinklers and buckets. I guess you could say I've been collecting rust for a long time," she says with a laugh. "When I ran out of space in the house, I had to build something new so I'd have a place for the things I love."

"I'd been thinking about an outbuilding to match the English style of my house," the gardener says. "When I visited England, I fell in love with the cottage style. I knew that cozy, lived-in look would be the model for my shed.

"The shed designed itself," she adds modestly. "All I had to do was add one wall and a roof. I already had existing retaining walls and the one wall from my house."

No humble blue-collar structure, this shed picks up a pedigree with its graceful roofline and cedar-shake facade. A Carolina jessamine leisurely ambles up the front of the cottage, adding to the sense of permanence. The vintage door and window reflect the owner's penchant for collecting things to be used again.

The decor is a mix of gardening odds and ends and essentials that, taken together, meld into "decorator compost." Form, function, and the purely fanciful come together as one in this setting. Old wood and shelving are recycled into work and storage spaces. Weathered, exposed brick walls speak with an English accent.

"This shed reflects my gardening instinct," says the owner. "A garden professional once said that my garden 'reflects a sense of reckless abandon.' That's a compliment to me. There's no rhyme or reason to my garden. I collect plants. I love plants. If I like it, I'll buy it and find a place to plant it. But it all reflects my sense of fun, and so does my potting shed."

And, so often, as all gardeners know, your work is never done. Preparing for a big garden tour one year, the owner labored to get her garden and shed ready for the discerning eyes that would soon be surveying her

A trip to England inspired the owner to design this potting shed with a cottage look. Ornamental kale and pansies survive all but the coldest winter days.

work. "I thought I was finally ready for them," she says, "but the day before the tour, I noticed it looked a little bare under the window box. I just happened to have some creek stones set aside for a 'special occasion.' So there I was, the night before the tour, laying a stacked-stone raised bed to add a finishing touch to my shed."

Creativity has its price—often a good night's sleep. Yet it has its rewards—the pride of creating a space that works and that draws you back time and time again.

It takes a well-trained eye to be so knowledgeable about rust, "reckless abandon," and knowing what works outside in the garden and what works inside on a wall. It just seems right that this gardening enthusiast has created a retreat to display her collections and store her dreams of gardening seasons to come. ◇

BY ELEANOR GRIFFIN / PHOTOGRAPHY SYLVIA MARTIN

The Classic
CAMELLIA

In a camellia garden, Southerners find memories are as fresh as the flowers. The old favorites are more and more prized as time goes by.

BY LINDA C. ASKEY
PHOTOGRAPHY VAN CHAPLIN

Lalla Rookh, 1894

Azaleas aside, no plant of foreign soil has so totally rooted itself in Southern culture as the camellia. Through two centuries, camellias have accompanied Southerners on their journeys through life.

Camellias were the flower of choice for winter weddings and holiday centerpieces. They adorned tuxedo lapels and upswept hair with equal frequency. The faithful brought baskets of colorful blooms to church for the altar. And always you would find a short-stemmed blossom floating in a shallow bowl on a parlor table.

The cherished flower of Northern conservatories, camellias flourish beneath tall pines in Deep South gardens. Here, as in the camellia's native Japan and China, mild winters afford both shrubs and gardeners crisp outdoor days filled with flowers.

Like so much we take for granted until it is gone, many of those old camellias have become scarce, replaced in the nursery trade by the newest and best. While enthusiasts continue to produce exciting new camellias, many of us long to grow the blossoms of old family favorites.

It's good to hear the names again: Lady Clare, Alba Plena, Debutante, Purple Dawn, and Magnoliiflora. They drawl in our memory's ear as they fell from our forebears' lips, bringing not only the recollection of a flower, but a day spent with a beloved parent or grandparent.

They were called "japonicas," referring to the species, *Camellia japonica,* as opposed to "sasanquas" *(C. sasanqua).* The handsome, evergreen shrubs would be desirable if they never bloomed, but they do.

One of the earliest camellias to appear in Southern gardens was Alba Plena. Arriving around 1800, it is still a favorite today. The problem is that, like so many old selections, it is difficult to locate.

The number of selections on nursery lists grew throughout the 19th century. During the 1930s, 1940s, and 1950s, interest in camellias was keen. Every town had a camellia show, and gardeners competed for ribbons.

Meanwhile new selections continually appeared, fueled by widespread enthusiasm and the lust for a prize at the show. But by the early 1960s gardeners' interests had turned to foundation plantings and lawns, rather than gardens. Now Southerners are rediscovering their ancestors' appreciation for the camellia.

"I had never seen a camellia before the winter of 1983," says George Wright of Wintergarden Nursery, referring to the time when he moved to Fairhope, Alabama. "I was in awe. Most of the neighbors could not answer my endless inquiries, but they would direct me to people who could—mostly elderly people, carryovers from the camellia craze. I decided I was going to grow camellias, for I couldn't install a garden in good faith without camellias. It's like serving salad without dressing. And their availability was becoming very limited."

George and business partner Bobby Green began to take cuttings from old garden sites, at times snatching

TOP: *Magnoliiflora (Hagoromo), 1859*

ABOVE: *Coquettii (Glen 40), 1839, received an Award of Merit from the Royal Horticultural Society in 1956.*

RIGHT: *Winter brings big blooms and lots of them. No wonder Southerners' enthusiasm for camellias has spanned the centuries.*

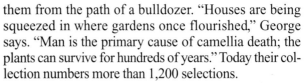

*The camellia
buds are
swelling
and salvation
is at hand.*

George Wright

them from the path of a bulldozer. "Houses are being squeezed in where gardens once flourished," George says. "Man is the primary cause of camellia death; the plants can survive for hundreds of years." Today their collection numbers more than 1,200 selections.

But even in the South, cold snaps are perilous. "I don't think there's anything prettier than Alba Plena," says landscape architect Robert Marvin of Walterboro, South Carolina. "But they were all killed in this part of the world in 1951, when we had the most severe freeze in my life."

Robert grew up with camellias, for his father owned Wildwood Nurseries. "I used to know 40 or 50 of them by their leaf, without having to see the bloom. Professor Sargent and Duchess of Sutherland. Elegans was easy to kill in the cold, but it was a good camellia. Pink Perfection was a wonderful one."

The old-style gardens required enough space to plant 20 to 40 selections beneath trees. Robert recommends creating a camellia walk where you have camellias on both sides of a path. "They ought to be at least 12 to 15 feet apart because they grow pretty big." Gardeners can also plant these evergreens as screens or large specimens in their suburban landscape.

Gardeners in borderline areas can look to the more cold-tolerant selections of the old camellias (see below) or new cold-hardy types (see sources on pages 250–251). It helps to locate them in a sheltered nook such as near a masonry wall. A canopy of trees also offers protection.

The history of camellias in the South reveals an enduring passion. It reaches to the core of who we are.

"I think everybody would be much happier in their life if they had a collection of camellias," says Robert. "There is nothing to equal it in the middle of the winter when little else is blooming." ◇

COLD-TOLERANT CHOICES

Based on 20 years of studies by the American Camellia Society, the following are some of the more cold-hardy japonicas.

- Berenice Boddy
- China Doll
- Coquettii (Glen 40)
- Doncklaeri
- Drama Girl
- Dr. Tinsley
- Governor Mouton
- Imura
- Magnoliiflora (Hagoromo)

Netted iris and violas (See pages 32–34.)

February

Checklist for February

EDITORS' NOTEBOOK

Friends, one thing we desperately need today is a garden design book aimed at animals. Animals just do not grasp the importance of beauty. Instead, they view the garden solely in terms of creature comforts—i.e., "Hey, those flowers look mighty comfortable—I think I'll sleep there" or "Thanks for tilling the soil—now it's easy to dig an incredibly large hole for no discernible reason." But in the absence of such a book, we can take action to nudge animals toward an appreciation of aesthetics. This feline, for example, enjoyed napping in the pot of pansies, until crepe myrtle twigs pressed into the soil made this misguided habit impossible. "Oh, thank you for correcting me," he's undoubtedly thinking. "Well, it's time to get the neighbor's black Lab to chase me through the spring bulb display."

Steve Bender

□ **Bare-root plants**—Roses and fruit trees are often sold this time of year with their roots wrapped in moist peat moss and plastic bags. These plants will do well if you set them out while their tops are still dormant. Avoid ones that have already started to sprout. Get your dormant plants off to a good start by soaking them overnight in a bucket of water, and then plant immediately in the garden.

□ **Houseplants**—Now that your plants have been indoors for a few months, they need rinsing to wash away dust and perhaps a few insects. Put them in the shower or take them outdoors on a day when the temperature's above 55 degrees. Don't let them sit in the sun or they'll get burned.

□ **Water**—This can be a dry month in areas such as Florida. Remember to water the lawn and any new plants. Lawns should turn green as soon as the weather warms, but they may remain brown if stressed by drought. Mulch flowers and plants to help conserve moisture in the soil.

□ **Annuals**—In the Middle, Lower, and Coastal South, set out transplants of hardy annuals such as sweet William, pansies, calendulas, sweet alyssum, violas, poppies, English daisies, and forget-me-nots. Sow seeds of nasturtiums directly in the garden where you want them to grow. Choose annuals that will continue blooming the longest. Madness hybrid petunias, Rocket hybrid snapdragons, and Telstar hybrid dianthus are exceptional for their ability to continue blooming after the weather warms in late spring. ▶

□ **Perennials**—In the Lower South, yarrow, coreopsis, purple coneflower, lantana, Indigo Spires salvia, cannas, and blue plumbago may be set out now in sunny areas of the garden for late-spring and summer color.

□ **Potatoes**—Now is the time to plant potatoes in the Lower South for May harvest. Select a well-drained location, preferably with sandy soil and sun for most of the day. Till the soil to a depth of 8 to 10 inches and make raised rows 2 to 3 feet apart and about 1 foot wide. Cut seed potatoes into pieces that have one or two eyes and allow the cut pieces to dry out for at least a few hours before placing them in 3- to 4-inch holes 10 to 12 inches apart. Cover with loose soil and water.

□ **Trees and shrubs**—Although you can set out container-grown plants any time of year, this is an excellent time. With an early start, they'll get their roots established early and be better able to cope with summer than late-planted stock. When planting deciduous trees, consider arranging them where their summer foliage will cool the house, and their bare winter branches will allow the sun to enter and warm it. Small trees such as redbud, crepe myrtle, Mexican plum, and dogwood may be planted as close as 8 to 10 feet from the house, while larger trees such as live oak, Shumard's red oak, Southern magnolia, and bald cypress should be at least 25 feet or more from a structure.

□ **Vegetables**—In the Lower South, begin setting out cabbage, broccoli, and cauliflower. You can also sow seeds of spinach and lettuce. Continue planting in the Coastal South ▶

PRUNE

□ **Apples**—These trees need a main trunk called a leader with branches radiating from it at different levels. Cut away any competing leaders, as well as branches that cross, grow inward, appear broken or diseased, or rise abruptly from horizontal branches.

◀ **Blueberries**—In the Coastal South, thin old blueberry plants back to four or five main canes. Canes older than four or five years aren't as productive as younger ones. Cut the canes with loppers or a small saw at their base. New shoots will pop through the ground in spring.

□ **Shrubs**—Unless you just can't wait, postpone pruning spring-flowering shrubs, such as azaleas, spireas, forsythias, and weigelas, until they are in bloom. Then you can put the flower-laden branches in arrangements indoors. In fact, you don't really need to prune them at all unless they have outgrown their space. ▶

□ **Trees**—In the Upper and Middle South, it's time to prune trees as needed. Begin by removing dead or weak limbs and those that obstruct views or access. Topping usually results in stunting and unnatural forms. Successful pruning does not severely alter the natural form of the tree.

FERTILIZE

□ **Lawns**—Fertilize lawns or apply weed-and-feed if weeds are a problem. If your lawn is St. Augustine, use a high quality, timed-release fertilizer especially formulated for it. In areas with alkaline soil use a fertilizer that also contains iron to maintain a healthy green color. Water thoroughly after applying to wash the fertilizer into the soil.

□ **Leaf shed**—In the Tropical South, don't be alarmed as avocado, gumbo-limbo, oaks, citrus, and many other evergreen trees shed leaves. This is normal at this time of year and can be a source of additional fertilizer. Simply rake the leaves and add them to a compost pile to create a rich soil amendment for flowerbeds. This is a good time to fertilize with a product such as 12-6-6.

□ **Soil**—A warm weekend is a good time to turn the garden soil and get ready for spring planting. Mix in last fall's leaves from your compost bin. If your soil is heavy or poorly drained, add an extra measure of organic material and some sand as well. If the soil is wet, wait until it dries enough to crumble easily. If adding fresh manure to your garden soil, wait 45 days before planting. The addition of manure raises the soil temperature and releases by-products that may damage seedlings.

Sugar in a snap

BY CHARLIE THIGPEN
PHOTOGRAPHY VAN CHAPLIN

There's no tastier vegetable than a sugar snap pea straight off the vine. The pods crunch in your mouth as sweet flavors delight the taste buds. Not only do these peas taste good but they also look delightful in the garden as they twist and turn, reaching for the sun. Curly tendrils allow them to hug and hold on to a trellis. Small, delicate white flowers mark the spot where pea pods will form.

The sugar snap group of peas is a hybrid of the English pea and the snow pea. They have greater disease resistance and hold their flavor longer than either parent. Although they're easy to grow, timing is critical. Peas planted too late in the season will bloom, but the heat will not allow them to set fruit. Don't worry, young plants will tolerate frost.

In spring, sow seeds as soon as the soil can be worked or six to eight weeks before the last frost. Plants will produce through spring until the weather gets

Loose soil, full sun, and cool temperatures are all it takes to grow sugar snaps.

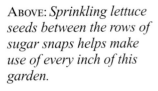

ABOVE: *Sprinkling lettuce seeds between the rows of sugar snaps helps make use of every inch of this garden.*

ABOVE, RIGHT: *Sweet gum branches tied to rebar (steel rods) make a sturdy and attractive trellis. To make your own, bend two rebar poles into horseshoe shapes, and place at either end of the row. Secure a straight piece of rebar on top with heavy-duty wire. Tie sweet gum branches to rebar with twine.*

hot. In the Upper South they can be grown as an early-spring to midsummer crop. In the Lower South they may be grown in fall, winter, or early spring. The ones pictured here were planted in late February and began producing peas in April.

There are many selections of sugar snaps. Some grow tall and need a 6-foot trellis; others are dwarf, needing no support at all. Although the dwarf varieties don't need support, a small 3-foot trellis will keep them from being beaten to the ground during heavy rains and will make it easier to harvest ripe pods.

Seeds should be planted 1 inch deep in heavy clay soils and 2 inches deep in sandy soils. Plant the seeds 1 to 2 inches apart; later thin to 3 or 4 inches. Don't pull up seedlings when thinning because this could disturb surrounding plants. Use clippers or scissors to cut unwanted plants to ground

level. Space rows of dwarf varieties 2 feet apart; taller varieties should have 3 feet of space between rows. The wider spacing for the larger varieties will allow enough room to construct a trellis between rows.

Be sure the site you select receives six to eight hours of full sun daily. Sandy loam soils are best for peas. Heavy soils will work but should be well prepared by incorporating plenty of organic matter such as leaf mold or mushroom compost and loosening to a depth of 8 inches. The pH should be between 5.5 and 6.8.

When picking peas, be gentle; don't rip them from the vine or they may stop producing. A pair of scissors works well to remove ripe pods. To eat pod and all, harvest sugar snaps when the pods are flat. To eat only the peas, pick them once the pods have turned fat and plump. The more mature and developed the pod, the sweeter the peas and the tougher the pod. Pick pods before they turn yellow.

Once sugar snaps have been harvested they should be eaten quickly because the sugar turns to starch after they've been picked. Eat them raw in salads, steamed, or stir-fried. If you've never tasted fresh sugar snaps, plant some now and this spring you'll get a chance to sample one of the garden's tastiest treats. ◇

This clivia still sports last year's seedhead while new flowers rise from the broad green foliage. A clivia that is several years old will offer numerous large blooms, with the number increasing as the plant matures.

One Great Houseplant

Clivia blazes with the colors of a late-winter sunset.

When clivia comes into bloom it is a burst of radiant color unequalled among houseplants. When not in flower it is a handsome plant blessed with an easygoing nature. Clivia *(Clivia miniata),* also known as Kaffir lily, has been a cherished pass-along for generations.

Clivia grows robust in bright light and will grow just as actively in a low-light location. It even tolerates full sun, provided the broad leaves do not get wet when the plant is watered. Drops of water left on sunbathed foliage will burn the leaves, making them unattractive and unhealthy. In summer months clivia will grow contentedly outdoors under the canopy of a large shade tree. Bring it indoors before the first frost.

Summer is the most vigorous growth time, with five or six new leaves emerging from the center of the plant each year. As new foliage emerges, older outside leaves may yellow. Remove them close to the base of the plant. Watering once a week is sufficient this time of year and should always include an all-purpose fertilizer, such as 20-20-20.

During early winter, clivia requires a rest period. Provide cool temperatures, and water only once a month. If foliage begins to wither, water lightly. Do not feed again until summer. By mid- to late January, flowerbuds begin to form. You will first see them snuggled down among the broad leaves. As the plants mature, the stems grow longer and the flowerbuds rise above the foliage.

When the buds begin to open, resume weekly watering. After about a month of bloom, the flowers will fade and drop. Follow the stem down to the base of the plant, and remove it. If allowed to remain, round reddish seeds will form. The mature seeds can be planted to create new plants.

The only maintenance clivia requires is an occasional leaf cleaning. Use a damp cloth to wipe dust from the foliage. This reduces the risk of mealybugs, the only insect to plague clivia. Clean foliage also enables the plant to effectively use all available light. If mealybugs are a problem, spray with SunSpray horticultural oil.

Clivia blooms best if it is potbound. Wait until it is crawling out of the container to repot. Choose a new pot that is only an inch or two larger. Small plants on the edge of the parent can be potted in a small container to establish a new plant.

Clivia is majestic in bloom and one of the hardiest houseplants available. Its long-lived nature makes it a gem to pass along for generations.

Ellen Riley
(For sources turn to pages 250–251.)

CLIVIA
At a Glance

Light: bright light to low light

Water: once a week until early winter; then once a month until bloom begins

Fertilize: Feed plants once a week during summer.

Bloom time: late January and February

These tiny treasures pump life into the garden after a long winter's nap.

Minor

Netted iris rise early in the spring and look great planted randomly around the base of a large tree or topping a planter mixed with violas.

Leaves and pine straw lie flat and matted on the ground. The only sign of life is the shimmer of the neon green moss. The Earth's floor looks monotonous until tiny, strong bulbs wrestle their way through the warming soil and mulch. These diminutive flowers are brave, as they come to life early in the season while larger flowers lie dormant underground, scared to show their faces.

Minor bulbs don't produce big blooms, but they do provide color when there's not much to look at in the garden. These bulbs can be strategically planted along walks, by patios, in pots, or in rock gardens. They're perfect for nooks and crannies. Tuck them beside high-traffic areas where they won't get lost in the landscape.

Netted iris *(Iris reticulata)* is an excellent minor bulb. About 15 years ago, I planted a patch of the one called Harmony that returns each January or February. The striking purple-blue flowers perch atop 4- to 5-inch stems. A small strip of yellow encircled by white marks the center of each flower. There are many selections, with most being in the purple and blue color range. Natascha is a white selection that has a yellow center.

Once the flowers disappear, dwarf iris foliage continues to grow and will eventually stretch to about 15 inches in height. Leave the foliage alone until it turns brown; then cut it to the ground.

Spring-blooming crocuses, the most popular of the minor bulbs, delight gardeners in the late winter and early spring. These little jewels come in a rainbow of colors. Some blooms are striped or veined, some are bicolored, and others are solid. Before the flowers open,

Bulbs

BY CHARLIE THIGPEN
PHOTOGRAPHY VAN CHAPLIN

FAR LEFT: *Greek anemones, or windflowers, sport daisylike blooms and dark mats of green, frilled foliage.*
CENTER LEFT: *The ever-popular spring crocuses are carefree and brighten the garden in early spring.*
LEFT: *Scillas have tiny flowers, but when planted in masses they can be showy.*

the little buds hold tight like little bird eggs balanced on delicate stems.

With more than 80 species of crocuses, it's hard to figure out which ones to plant. There are spring bloomers that range from early- to midspring, and there are fall bloomers that start in late summer and bloom into the winter months.

The spring bloomers are special because they are usually one of the first bulbs to rise and signal the start of a new gardening year. *Crocus tomasinianus,* one of the earliest to flower in the spring, is great for naturalizing. These bulbs will seed and create little colonies.

The Dutch flowering crocuses produce the largest flowers. Although the blooms may be big, the plants still reach a height of only around 5 inches. The Dutch selections work well mixed with pansies in the front of a flower border. An all-time favorite Dutch crocus is Yellow Mammoth.

Galanthus, or snowdrop, is another early surprise. White, bell-shaped flowers appear on 4- to 10-inch stems, the height depending on the selection. These simple little flowers look great in woodland settings. Snowdrops (*Galanthus* sp.) prefer heavy soils that stay damp but not wet.

Greek anemones *(Anemone blanda),* or windflowers, have colorful blooms that resemble daisies. The plants grow about 6 inches tall and can form a clump about a foot or more across. Colors range from white to shades of pink, red, blue, and purple. The anemones look very much at home in a rock garden or massed in large clumps, creating a fine-foliaged ground cover. They'll bloom from four to

ABOVE: *Galanthus, or snowdrops, look almost embarrassed to arrive so early. They always hang their pearl- white heads.*

six weeks under ideal conditions.

Scillas *(Endymion hispanicus),* or Spanish bluebells, look like miniature hyacinths. Numerous star-shaped blooms line the stems. Most of the scillas are in the blue color range, but there are a few white selections. They're inexpensive and multiply freely, so they are good for naturalizing.

All the bulbs mentioned should be planted in the fall. They work well when coupled with annuals such as pansies and violas. Perennials such as hellebores also make nice companions to these early bloomers. Underplant quince, spirea, forsythia, and other shrubs with these little bulbs for an early-spring show.

Before you forget about these tiny flowers, grab a calendar and write "Buy minor bulbs" on the month of October. ◇

(For sources turn to pages 250–251.)

Showers of Flowers

How many shrubs do you know that bloom continuously? Here's one.

Shower-of-gold does two things that Southerners love—it keeps its leaves year-round and blooms almost all of the time. So it's a bit of a mystery why more gardeners aren't growing it.

One reason may be that those who know it still call it "thryallis," a holdover from when the plant's botanical name was *Thryallis glauca*. So when they see it in the garden center labeled with its new botanical name, *Galphimia glauca*, they think the nurseryman is out to lunch and buy a gardenia instead.

That's too bad because shower-of-gold has a lot to offer. True to its name, showers of showy, golden blooms continuously pour from its branches in warm weather. It also features handsome, bright green leaves with reddish leaf stems and twigs. Native to Mexico and Guatemala, this shrub grows 4 to 8 feet tall and wide and suffers no serious pests. It can get a bit leggy with age, but a little pruning restores its bushiness.

Thanks to the blooms, shower-of-gold makes a fine accent plant for focusing attention on a particular part of the garden. You can also mass it to create a big splash of color or use it as an informal screen. Just remember that its brittle twigs break easily, so don't plant it where people will constantly brush against it.

If shower-of-gold has one major fault, it's susceptibility to cold. This semitropical plant isn't winter-hardy north of the Coastal South. If you want to grow it elsewhere, do so in a pot that you can take indoors for the winter. Give it plenty of sun and warm temperatures and watch the flowers come raining down.

Steve Bender

SHOWER-OF-GOLD
At a Glance

Size: 4 to 8 feet tall and wide

Light: full sun

Soil: moist, well drained; tolerates some drought

Growth rate: moderate

Pests: none serious

Salt tolerance: takes mild salt spray if planted well back from dunes

Range: Coastal and Tropical South

PHOTOGRAPHS: SYLVIA MARTIN

Use shower-of-gold in masses to create a big splash of color and an informal screen. The golden blossoms, which attract butterflies, appear nonstop in warm weather atop handsome evergreen leaves.

LONG-LASTING VALENTINE

BY ELLEN RILEY
PHOTOGRAPHY VAN CHAPLIN

Artfully arranged houseplants in a pretty basket
make a thoughtful gift. Add fresh flowers
for a sweetheart surprise that's sure to please.

A Valentine wish lasts longer than a day. Does the gift you give? It should. Create a long-lasting present that will keep your sentiments growing for months.

Find a pretty basket with a handle, and take it with you when you purchase plants. Doing an arrangement is not unlike putting together a new outfit; you will have to try

things on to achieve the perfect look. Select a variety of plants in 3- and 4-inch pots, and assemble a mix of different leaf sizes and shapes to make the collection interesting. Include at least one tall plant and several to cascade over the edge of the basket.

Fresh cut flowers are the heart of a Valentine, but they can be a heart-stopping holiday expense. However, it takes only a few stems to add instant color and freshness to the basket of plants. Our large basket includes only three tulips, three iris, and one Dendrobium orchid stem. It provides great sentiment with a minimal number of expensive flowers. It cost $45 for all materials.

THE ART OF ARRANGING
Line the inside of the basket with foil to contain moisture. Place the tallest plant next to the handle. Arrange the remaining plants so they decrease gradually in height. Place the trailing plants along the basket edges with foliage tumbling over the sides. To snuggle plants more easily into the basket, remove several from their pots and place them in plastic sandwich bags. They will now slip in among rigid pots. If pots or plastic bags are visible, cover with small pieces of green sheet moss.

Once the plants are settled, add your fresh flowers. Determine the length of each stem, and place the cut end into a water-filled florist vial. Gently push them into the soil surrounding the houseplants so the vials are not visible. Cluster the blooms for big impact.

Choose a flower with a long, graceful stem and small blooms to accent the handle of the basket. Heather and Dendrobium orchids are good choices. Push the florist vial into the tall plant's soil, and loosely tie the flower's stem to the handle in several places with a piece of raffia.

CARE AND MAINTENANCE
Check the florist vials every day, and add water as needed. Fresh cut flowers should last from a few days to about a week. As the flowers diminish, remove them from the arrangement—houseplants will still be fresh and attractive.

Learn the water requirements of each plant. A kitchen baster is an easy way to direct water into each pot or plastic bag. Remember that plants in plastic bags don't need to be watered as frequently as plants in containers.

This is a gift that will grow in the

Moisture-loving plants flourish in plastic sandwich bags and fit easily among other pots. Cut flowers in florist vials add sparkle to the arrangement.

heart of your Valentine. And while you're arranging for Cupid's day, do several more small baskets for special friends.

Editor's note: I like to place moisture-loving plants, such as maidenhair fern and creeping fig vine, in plastic sandwich bags. The bags prevent plant roots from drying out too quickly and reduce plant maintenance. ◇

MATERIALS

BASKET WITH HANDLE

FOIL

HOUSEPLANTS IN
3- AND 4-INCH POTS

PLASTIC SANDWICH BAGS

GREEN SHEET MOSS

CUT FLOWERS

FLORIST VIALS

RAFFIA

*Boxwood plantings and pachysandra ground cover
frame the house, yet allow it to be seen.*

ABOVE: *Family parking is located
at the side of the house with a
walk that leads to the porch.*

Simple Symmetry

What was once a farmhouse sitting on the very edge of the road is now a quaint cottage in an established Birmingham neighborhood. After the house was renovated and the city pushed the road away from the house, it was time for the homeowners to replant.

As garden designer Norman Kent Johnson remembers, "The house had the obligatory row of waist high hollies across the front. Because it is a low house, the shrubs were chopping it in half." After the hollies were removed, a low stone foundation was revealed. Consequently, stone was a suitable choice for the front walk.

Laying out the walk was puzzling; a straight path seemed appropriate for the simple house, but it did not work with the way the road curved out front. So Norman used a garden hose to lay out the centerline of an S curve. Then to make it wide enough for two people, he marked off 2½ feet on either side for a gracious walk that's 5 feet in width. Although a 6-foot walk was considered, it appeared stumpy when drawn on the ground, and a 4-foot walk looked like a long, skinny strip. The secret is to mark it off so it can be seen and walked on; that's the time to make adjustments—before it is paved.

Norman kept the plantings simple with two boxwoods at the corners of the porch and two more at the corners of the house. A pair of boxwoods was also placed where the sidewalk joins the guest parking at the front of the walk.

A strip of gravel extends across the front along the edge of the street to allow guests to pull off and access the front walk. The family actually pulls into the driveway, where there are two additional parking places and a landing that leads to the end of the front porch. With the removal of shrubs and the addition of steps, the need for a walk cutting through the lawn from the side was eliminated.

Now simplicity reigns with Japanese boxwoods (chosen for their resistance to pests such as nematodes and leaf miners) and low-growing Japanese pachysandra.

Linda C. Askey

Back Savers

Weekend gardeners know too well the stiffness that Monday morning can bring. Sometimes we need to use our heads more than our backs. Here are a few ideas that do just that.

Getting the lawnmower to the shop is easy if you can get it in your car or truck. These **ramps** can turn a two-person job into an easy load for one. They are made from metal brackets that you can buy from a home-supply store and bolt to 2 x 8 pressure-treated lumber. Rubber pads on the lower side of the brackets help grip your bumper while preventing scratches. Different-size brackets are available for different jobs. Some brackets are made for the ends of the ramps that rest on the driveway. We chose the less expensive option with only top brackets and eased the bump at the lower end by using a circular saw to cut a 45-degree angle (or you can have the lumberyard do it for you). Cost: $20.

Hand trucks are more often seen in the hands of drivers delivering packages than gardeners carrying plants. But they perform the same purpose around the

Ramps can prevent a lawnmower tune-up from turning into an orthopedic incident.

house—allowing us to move large, heavy items with ease. This one has pneumatic tires and can be converted into a four-wheel dolly. Whether you are moving plants indoors for winter, taking a 50-pound bag of lime from your trunk to your shed, or hauling a heavy trash can to the street, a hand truck can be your best friend. Cost: $100.

Garden carts have been around for a while, and they still can't be beat as an effortless way to move heavy loads. The load is balanced over the big bicycle tires so that it is easy to lift and relatively easy to roll, depending on the slope. You can choose from two sizes. The smaller one shown here (labeled Medium by the manufacturer) can carry up to 300 pounds and is ideal for suburban landscapes. Cost: $215. *Linda C. Askey*

(For sources turn to pages 250–251.)

ABOVE, LEFT: *Garden carts hold much more than wheelbarrows do and require far less strength to use.*

ABOVE: *Once you have a hand truck, you'll wonder how you ever lived without one.*

A ROOM WITH A VIEW

Nestled among the shrubs, this backyard garden is a cozy getaway— even in winter.

In the spring and summer, good-looking gardens are a dime a dozen. But having a pretty one in the wintertime when most plants are dormant is a challenge for a lot of homeowners.

This attractive garden in Lexington, Kentucky, shows how design can work through the seasons.

In winter it looks like a room that Mother Nature decorated. A floor of pea gravel crunches underfoot, letting you know you have entered the airy space. Deciduous trees with their gnarly arms create a ceiling. Evergreen yews provide billowy boundaries that form leafy green walls for this outdoor room.

BY CHARLIE THIGPEN / PHOTOGRAPHY SYLVIA MARTIN

The lead statue creates a watery centerpiece. Yellow and orange pansies line the top of the stacked-stone wall.

There's no television set or stereo for entertainment, only a trickling fountain whose raindrops tumble off an umbrella. As you peer at the two sculpted children, you can daydream and remember the days of youth. These children seem delighted to be standing right in the middle of the watery island.

The only colorful painting that decorates the room is a mural of yellow and orange pansies perched atop the stacked-stone wall. From dusk till dawn the sun naturally lights the room. At night the moon and candles set the mood for entertaining and offer just enough glow to experience the garden.

If you think the garden looks inviting in winter, it's even more charming in spring and summer. Ivy in the surrounding beds comes to life with narcissus in the spring and hostas in the summertime to form a lush backdrop for the fountain.

There's nothing complicated about the design of this garden. A small room has been made using natural materials. The water feature is the centerpiece, and its pleasant trickling draws you to the area. A small table and two chairs provide a place to sit down and a reason to stay a while.

If you're creating a garden, think about how it will look during the cool season. It is easy to create a pretty garden during the warm months, but imagine how it will look in the winter. Then envision yourself in that garden throughout the seasons. ◇

a garden accented with Heller Japanese holly and Francis Mason abelia (See pages 70–71.)

March

Checklist for March

EDITORS' NOTEBOOK

You know your lawn is Southern when it starts begging for grits. Actually, this bowl contains corn gluten meal, a by-product of cornstarch. Scientists found that if you spread it on your lawn in spring and fall, it keeps crab-grass, dandelion, annual blue-grass, chickweed, and other weed seeds from germinating. And it's completely safe around kids and pets. (I used WeedzStop from Gardener's Supply Company, 1-800-863-1700. Concern Weed Prevention Plus is available in garden and home centers.) But does it work? It did the job fairly well, al-though I had to apply 20 pounds per 1,000 square feet, and the ef-fect lasted only three months. On the positive side, the earth-worms loved it. But I worry about making them gluten glut-tons. Spoil them on grits and before long they'll start demand-ing hush puppies, pork rinds, and fried okra.

Steve Bender

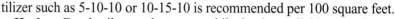

☐ **Bulbs**—Camouflage maturing foliage of narcissus, snowflakes, and oth-er spring-flowering bulbs by interplanting with nasturtiums, snapdragons, violas, or begonias. Let bulb foliage remain until yellowed so next year's bloom is better than ever.

☐ **Containers**—When potting up your spring plants, remember pot feet are far more than an ornamental touch. By elevating the plant, they prevent moisture under the pot from rotting wood or staining any surface. In addition, the pot drains better. ▶

☐ **Garden beds**—Plan and prepare beds for vegetables and annuals. Spade plenty of com-posted pine bark, peat moss, compost, cotton-seed hulls, or other organic matter with fertilizer into the top 8 to 10 inches of soil. A balanced fer-tilizer such as 5-10-10 or 10-15-10 is recommended per 100 square feet.

☐ **Herbs**—Buy basil transplants now while they're available at garden cen-ters. Later they are hard to find and you may have to grow plants from seeds.

☐ **Leaves**—Rake leaves, and add them to your compost pile. You can also collect them with a bagging mower to make mulch or quick compost.

PLANT

◀ **Annuals**—As soon as the last frost date has passed, plant begonias, gerani-ums, impatiens, and marigolds. For those in the Coastal South, it's also time to plant annuals such as caladiums and coleus for color that lasts all season. Or try perennials such as blue plumbago, lantana, and verbena.

☐ **Beans**—Pole beans should be planted before the weather gets too hot; they have the richest flavor but will stop bear-ing when temperatures reach the 90s. Plant beans in soil that is enriched with compost or leaf mold. Drop seeds about 4 inches apart in a furrow along the base of a wire trellis, and cover with about an inch of soil. Keep them watered; in dry weather beans will drop blooms and small pods.

☐ **Bulbs**—After the last frost, plant cannas, dahlias, tuberoses, gladioli, and crinums. All like full sun and well-drained soil. While most bloom in sum-mer, dahlias don't start blooming until late summer and fall. Use dahlias to add life to a flowerbed that will look tired by the end of summer.

☐ **Perennials**—This is a great time to set out new perennials and to divide and replant those emerging from your garden beds. The best candidates for division are clump-forming ones such as perennial phlox, hostas, daylilies, Southern shield ferns, Siberian iris, and old-fashioned chrysanthemums.

☐ **Vegetables**—You don't have to wait until after frost to plant. In fact, some vegetables should go into the ground early. Transplants of cabbage, broc-coli, and cauliflower need about three to four weeks' head start on warm weather, as do onions, collards, kale, English peas, Irish potatoes, sugar snap peas, spinach, and turnips.

PRUNE

□ **Bougainvillea**—In the Tropical South, prune bougainvillea now so that new growth will have time to mature. It will bloom again next winter. ▶

□ **Hedges**—If you have a hedge that is thick at the top and see-through at the bottom, cut it down low enough to prompt new growth in bare areas. This will reduce the size of the hedge. Then shear the new growth several times to encourage branching until it reaches the desired height. Keep the bottom of the hedge wider than the top to maintain healthy foliage all the way to the base.

□ **Shrubs**—This is the ideal time to cut back plants that have overgrown your design. Remove entire limbs where they originate if you can still preserve the plant's natural form. If the plant is becoming a maintenance problem, consider removing it or moving it to a more appropriate location. You may want to prune spring-flowering shrubs after they have bloomed.

CONTROL

□ **Pests**—Black-and-red baby lubber grasshoppers begin appearing in masses on ferns, begonias, crinums, bougainvillea, and daylilies now in the Coastal and Tropical South. Dust plants with carbaryl (Sevin) or another product labeled for their control as soon as the pests appear. The big lubbers are nearly impossible to control, so don't wait.

FERTILIZE

□ **Bromeliads**—In the Tropical South, encourage a ground cover planting to spread and flower by fertilizing with a liquid plant food such as 20-20-20 diluted to half strength. Sprinkle around the roots and into the vaselike cups at the center of the plant.

□ **Camellias**—For deep green camellia leaves in the Coastal South, fertilize now with a formula such as 14-7-7 that contains extra iron. Also rake away old mulch from the base of plants and replace with fresh, especially if flowers have been blighted by a fungus that turns them brown. The spores can live in the old mulch.

□ **Fertilize**—Feed azaleas and camellias as they finish their bloom season. Use special azalea-camellia fertilizers (11-5-5) according to label instructions or an organic source such as cottonseed meal at a rate of 4 to 5 pounds per 100 square feet scattered evenly on the surface of the root areas. Water well after applying.

□ **Lawns**—If you haven't already, apply a quality fertilizer such as 16-4-8 to your lawn this month. Wait until warm-season lawns turn green. If your grass is centipede, apply a product that contains iron and is especially formulated for centipede. Cool-season lawns will welcome the boost at a time when they begin growing rapidly.

□ **Roses**—Apply fertilizer to roses as the first set of flowers begins to fade on everblooming types, or in the case of once-blooming roses, 8 to 10 weeks after planting. Sprinkle a heaping tablespoon of a complete fertilizer such as 6-10-4 or 7-11-9 in an 18-inch circle around each plant. Water well, and repeat every four to six weeks until about September 15.

□ **Vegetables**—Spread 2 or 3 inches of decomposed leaves, well-rotted hay, cottonseed hulls, or other organic matter along with 4 to 6 pounds of cottonseed meal and 2 to 3 pounds of garden fertilizer such as 5-10-10 per 100 square feet of area. Till or spade soil to a depth of 8 to 10 inches, and form rows before planting.

March notes:

TIP OF THE MONTH

Here is a wonderful, inexpensive way to make solar greenhouses for young vegetable plants. Save all of your plastic, gallon milk jugs during the winter. When you plant your squash, cucumbers, and tomatoes in spring, fill the jugs with water. Place four jugs around each plant or hill. The sun will warm the water and protect your plants from cool spring winds. During hot, dry days, you can use the water from the jugs to water the plants. I had the best garden ever by doing this!

LOIS SPENCER
HIGH POINT, NORTH CAROLINA

SPRING *Blues*

When a garden has the blues, the gardener feels like singing.
Soothing yet exciting, it is one color that flatters all the rest.

The aptly named baby-blue-eyes seems only a background for the daffodils. However, the sky blue makes the other colors more exciting.

ABOVE: *The combination of blue phlox with a deeper shade pansy is a winner. The pansies give the border depth; the light blue phlox keeps the darker color from disappearing.*

ABOVE: *Dwarf crested iris grows in carpets of 4- to 6-inch spears of foliage interspersed with diminutive flowers. Best of all, this little charmer is native to the South.*

Perhaps the most treasured flower color in the garden, blue seems the most elusive and difficult to use. Planted alone it disappears, but without it, the garden lacks sparkle. Place blue flowers in combination with other hues, and you will have harmonies of color.

"Blue blends with anything else. You can put it with orange, you can put it with fiery red, and it's a good blend," says garden designer and retired horticulture professor Fred Thode of Clemson, South Carolina. "But if it gets a little bit dark, the color won't carry. Royal blue is rich looking, but it is ineffective. You have to go lighter and lighter until it gets to the point where you can see it. And you've got to get up near sky blue to do that."

Sunny yellow daffodils are pretty, but plant them with the light-colored blossoms of blue phlox, and the combination has far more impact than either color used alone. Blue is like that. It adds zip to any plant around it.

On the other hand, a solid bed of blue flowers needs other colors to perk it up. Texas gardeners see vivid demonstrations of this each spring on the roadsides. A pure stand of Texas bluebonnets is beautiful, but it comes to life when a few orange blooms of Indian paintbrush pop up here and there.

Early spring when the blue phlox blooms in frothy bouquets is a good time to see what blue can do for the garden. Likewise, Spanish bluebells, Greek anemones, grape hyacinths, netted iris, and dwarf crested iris are all bulbs that offer blue in spring.

In the shaded garden one of the most luscious colors of the season comes from the flowers of Virginia bluebells. Buds swell pink, but when they open they turn a clear, penetrating blue. The harmony of the two hues in the cluster is captivating.

BY LINDA C. ASKEY
PHOTOGRAPHY VAN CHAPLIN

blue daze evolvulus

lungwort

TOP: *Normally considered a ground cover, ajuga can also be a showy spring bloomer.*

Clear blue Spanish bluebells (above) and dark blue grape hyacinths (left) are spring-flowering bulbs that multiply.

Lungwort, also known as pulmonaria, has a similar effect.

Among bedding plants, pansies and violas are outstanding sources of blue. When planting a color blend, be sure to include a few blue blossoms. Good choices include Sorbet Blue Heaven viola and Universal True Blue pansy.

As spring progresses you'll enjoy the blue flowers of larkspur, wild blue flax, ajuga, Siberian and bearded iris, veronica, baptisia, and stokesia. Summer blues are fewer, but mealy-cup sage and Russian sage are two of the best for spikes. Blue daze evolvulus is excellent for a mat of dazzling color.

Fortunately, the sources of blue through the season are numerous. Some suggestions are listed at right. Remember, it is not enough to have blue; the key is to use it effectively. For this Fred offers his testimonial: "I've always used blue, but not so much for the sake of blue, but for what it can do for other things." ◇

BLUE OPPORTUNITY

Annuals
baby-blue-eyes
bachelor's-buttons
blue daze evolvulus
forget-me-nots
larkspur
lobelia
love-in-a-mist
pansies
salvia
scorpion weed

Perennials
baptisia
campanula
columbine
dayflower
lungwort
oxypetalum
Russian sage
stokesia
veronica
wild blue flax

Bulbs
dwarf crested iris
grape hyacinths
Greek anemones
netted iris
Spanish bluebells

Vines
clematis
morning glory
sky vine

With plenty of room to grow, this unclipped hedge of forsythia becomes a fountain of gold in early spring.

Mercy for Forsythia

Forsythia is the garden's version of Strom Thurmond. It seems like it's been around forever.

But in fact, it didn't arrive in the South until around 1900 (about the same time as the Senator from South Carolina). That it spread so quickly to so many gardens is due to a trio of factors. First, for most people this shrub grows easier than mildew. Second, rooting it takes no brains at all. Just weigh a lower branch to the ground or—simpler yet—cut off a branch and stick it into moist earth. Third, forsythia, often called yellow bells, is *the* herald of spring. It blooms with the year's first mild weather. Cut branches that are taken indoors bloom as early as January.

Now you'd think something so popular would earn great reverence and respect, but not so. All over the South, otherwise gentle, rational people regularly seize their hedge-trimmers and butcher this graceful shrub into balls, squares, trapezoids, and other bizarre, unnatural shapes. They forget that an innocent-

FORSYTHIA
At a Glance

Size: usually 8 to 10 feet tall and wide; some selections smaller
Light: full sun for best flowering
Soil: moist, fertile, well drained, acid or alkaline
Pests: none serious
Growth rate: fast (up to 4 feet per year)
Prune: Immediately after flowering in spring, if necessary; use hand pruners, not hedge-trimmers
Propagation: cuttings, layering
Range: Upper, Middle, Lower South

looking, 1-gallon plant can grow 8 feet tall and wide in the time it takes to fetch the morning paper. So they plant it in all the wrong places—under low windows, beside the steps, and at the very edge of the driveway. Butchery soon commences, ruining the next spring's bloom.

This heinous practice must end. To look its best, forsythia needs lots of elbowroom. So let it blanket a hillside, cascade over a wall, or form a billowing, unclipped hedge. If your garden is too cramped for this, try one of the new, compact selections that seldom need pruning. Minigold grows 4 to 5 feet tall and wide, while Gold Tide grows a mere 20 inches tall and 4 feet wide. Both feature showy, bright yellow flowers. Please stop the madness of forsythia butchery. Tell your neighbors to stop it too. Then maybe by the time another century passes, we'll have two things we can count on. Forsythia everywhere will be beautiful and golden. And Strom Thurmond's hair will still be red. *Steve Bender*

(For sources, turn to pages 250–251.)

Forgiving Fittonia

Perfectly content with artificial light, fittonia fits right in with a pretty lamp and pictures.

Forgive and forget. For people, this can be easy. Houseplants have a tougher time. Too little water, not enough light, cramped pot—many indoor plants just give up and die. But not fittonia. This is one forgiving houseplant.

Fittonia *(Fittonia verschaffeltii argyroneura)* is a small plant sporting dark green foliage with an intricate white pattern. Commonly called nerve plant, the web of white veins on each leaf gives an indication of this name's origin. Each oval, pointed leaf is the size of a quarter or smaller. For slightly larger leaves and rosy pink veins look for *F. verschaffeltii.*

No matter which type you choose, this bushy, creeping plant is prized for its attractive foliage. It grows 3 to 4 inches tall and produces stems that grow from the side rather than upright. Fittonia flowers sporadically. When it does, the unattractive green bloom spikes should be removed to keep the plant vigorous.

BASIC REQUIREMENTS

Fittonia prefers bright natural light, although it also thrives with artificial light. It is an ideal plant to place under a lamp on a small table. If fittonia is dependent on artificial light, be consistent. Turn on the lamp for at least six hours daily.

Fittonia will flourish in evenly moist soil. In most homes, water about every five days. If forgotten for a day, this durable plant will not curl up and wither. (Editor's note: I forgot to water—for more than a day. My fittonia was flat-out dry and hanging limp. I apologized, watered it, and hoped. A day later, all was forgiven!) Choose a container that has a drainage hole so water does not collect in the bottom.

During winter months when household heat is high and dry, mist fittonia between waterings. Arid indoor air can cause the leaves to curl. If misting is inconvenient, locate the plant in the bathroom or kitchen, where humidity is normally higher.

Keep fittonia controlled by pinching off overzealous stems just above sets of leaves. These small tip cuttings can be rooted by pushing the cut end into a small pot filled with damp potting soil.

The secret to healthy houseplants is consistent care. But if you do occasionally forget, fittonia will be the first to forgive. *Ellen Riley*

Fittonia's fancy leaves are pretty on their own. Choose a simple container to complement the patterned foliage.

Each March the residents of Orangeburg, South Carolina, enjoy the memorable show of cherry blossoms.

An Idea That Grew

Margaret Williams turned a birthday present from her family into a gift to her hometown of Orangeburg, South Carolina. As her 70th birthday approached, her four children were searching for a gift. Daughter Ann Platz of Atlanta called her sister Mary Ashley in Orangeburg to see if she had any ideas. "Mama wants cherry trees," came the response.

Their mother had been saddened by the demise of eight old Yoshino cherries *(Prunus yedoensis)* in Orangeburg's Edisto Gardens. "When I die," she said, "I want you children to plant those eight cherry trees back as my memorial." Her civic accomplishments are as legion as her friends, most of whom fondly call her "Miss Margaret." Five hundred people attended the birthday party.

Thrilled with the presentation of eight cherry trees from her family, she seized the opportunity to suggest that her well-wishers might want to contribute to a cherry tree fund to beautify the city. "We were able to plant 90 large trees instead of just 8," she says with delight.

The city's superintendent of parks, Rotie Salley, helped choose the sites for the trees. Four were planted in front of the First Baptist Church, where Miss Margaret is a member. The Junior Service League, organized by Miss Margaret in 1946, planted four in the town square. New league members sold 509 trees to people around town. The idea was really catching on.

Soon the city bought and planted 60 cherry trees. Not to be outdone, the county planted 60 more around county buildings and at the entrances to the city.

As a memorial after her daughter Mary Ashley's untimely death, Miss Margaret presented cherry trees to every resident on the street where her daughter had lived. More trees were given in memory of her husband, Marshall B. Williams, who served in the senate for nearly fifty years; he died in 1995.

Her late husband, with the help of a cabinet member, got signs put on the highway. "I want people to get off the interstate and come in to see our town when the trees are in bloom. It makes me so happy that this was done while I am alive to enjoy it," she says. If you happen to be driving along I-26 near the end of March, give yourself a treat. Take the short trip into town and see an idea that grew. ◇

Defending Your Garden

When bugs, weeds, and critters invade, the Southern Living Garden Problem Solver *helps you turn them away.*

A Southern garden may indeed be heaven. But sometimes it feels like a whole other place. Maybe yours is saddled with clay soil, or perhaps you live along the coast and must battle sandy soil, constant winds, and salt spray.

You and your family aren't the only ones who love the South. So do bugs, fungi, weeds, and critters. Learning to deal with these pests is part of the fun and challenge of gardening here. *The Southern Living Garden Problem Solver,* a new companion to the best-selling *Southern Living Garden Book,* will help you cope.

Edited by *Southern Living* Senior Garden Writer Steve Bender, the *Problem Solver* addresses the most common dilemmas you're likely to face in your garden. You'll be able to look up a particular plant, use color illustrations to identify the problem, then receive practical advice on how to fix it. In addition,

hundreds of color photographs depict the region's most troublesome insects, diseases, weeds, and animals, accompanied by detailed information on prevention and control.

The result? Once again, gardening becomes a pleasure, instead of a chore.

Here are just a few of the everyday problems this book helps you solve:

■ How to keep black spot from ruining your roses

■ How to foil cabbage-worms without chemicals

■ How to kill poison ivy—roots and all

■ Why tomatoes crack and how to prevent this

■ How to keep powdery mildew off crepe myrtles

■ How to use the spider mite's natural enemies against it

■ How to establish your lawn as a "weed-free zone"

One chapter of the book you'll find especially useful is entitled "A Pound of Cure." It describes the most widely available insecticides, fungicides, and herbicides, both chemical and organic. It lists various brand names for each product, specifies the target pests, and mentions any precautions you ought to take so you'll know what each product does and how to use it safely and effectively.

The Southern Living Garden Problem Solver is more than an informative textbook, however. Sure, it gives you quick answers when you need them. But it's also packed with interesting facts, tips, and humorous observations you'll enjoy during a more leisurely read.

Look for *The Southern Living Garden Problem Solver* at bookstores. Or order a hardcover copy for $29.95 plus shipping by calling 1-800-884-3935. Beginning and experienced gardeners will find this 336-page, full-color book a wise investment. ◇

Welcome to our

Southern Gardener

special section. This

year we focus on a

front-yard makeover.

Our project shows how

an attractive landscape

evolves. Working on it

was like a puzzle. We

PUTTING THE PIECES TOGETHER

put it together one

piece at a time. 🌿

BEFORE

An updated landscape gives this house a fresh new look. We'll take you through the makeover step by step.

WHERE TO START

Landscaping your yard can be a bit intimidating. But by taking on one project at a time, you can achieve the look you want without losing your mind.

This house and yard belong to Joel and Laura Blackstock. Joel is an architect who has a good eye for design and likes nice clean lines. Laura is an artist who loves a colorful landscape with lots of flowers. Their two children, Joel Thomas and Grace, enjoy playing in the yard.

Joel and Laura bought an older house that needed a little work—or so they thought. They soon found out that a little work on an older home turns into a lot of work. First they had to tackle the inside of the house. Once it began to take shape, they turned their attention outside. The landscape didn't enhance the house or fit their needs.

Like most young couples with a family, the Blackstocks live a fast-paced life. Between work and running kids to school and piano and ballet lessons, there's little time for yard work. So the landscape would have to have a nice balance. It would need to look good but require minimal maintenance.

Where do you start when landscaping your yard? First, make lists of needs and wants. Then prioritize your lists, deciding on what must be done immediately and what can wait. Next find a reputable landscape architect or garden designer with whom you feel comfortable. Look at some of the work he or she has done and be sure to check references. A survey is a helpful tool because it shows the footprint of the house and the lot lines.

Joel and Laura had several things they needed to do in their yard and a few things they would like to have-done. We looked at their lists of needs and wants (see below) and drew up a plan. They looked over it, and with a few minor changes, we were ready to start.

Before plants could be purchased or installed, all construction and painting on the front of the house needed to be complete. Excavation for a new sidewalk and parking court would create a big mess, so we wanted all of this wrapped up before setting out any tender plants that could be destroyed.

If you follow this project through the numerous steps, you'll see it's not magic that makes a yard look nice. It takes a good plan, lots of hard work, and money. We tried to minimize cost by using anything they had on-site, such as plants and even some old stone. We also did it in stages so it could be paid for a little at a time. The whole project took about 18 months to complete. As you read through the pages that follow, you will probably find a project that you want or need to do, and we'll show you how. 🌿

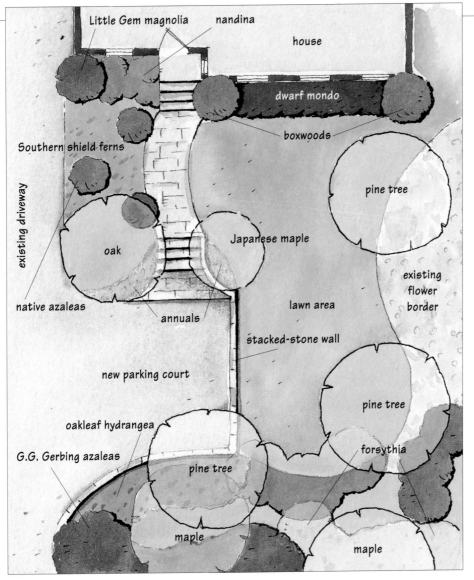

Little Gem magnolia — nandina
house
dwarf mondo
boxwoods
Southern shield ferns
pine tree
existing driveway
oak
Japanese maple
existing flower border
native azaleas
annuals
lawn area
stacked-stone wall
new parking court
pine tree
oakleaf hydrangea
forsythia
G.G. Gerbing azaleas
pine tree
maple
maple

A well-thought-out landscape plan helps make your dreams become reality.

LIST OF NEEDS

- Porch update
- Walkway repaired
- Additional parking or turnaround
- Trees pruned
- Foundation planting
- New grass and less of it

LIST OF WANTS

- Hayrack window boxes
- Flowerbeds
- Shrubs for seasonal color

FIRST THINGS FIRST

Paint your house before you plant your landscape.

A translucent white stain gives this house a fresh new look and allows the natural wood grain to show through.

Every neighborhood has one house that stands out like a sore thumb. You know, the one on the corner that's painted blue and has pea-green shutters. The paint colors just scream ugly. Be sure to be sweet to thy neighbor and paint or stain your home in nice colors that suit your house and are in keeping with the neighborhood.

The Blackstocks painted their house right after they moved in. The new paint began to peel in less than a year. Layers of old paint on top of cedar shingles were beginning to cause problems; the shingles needed to be stripped. Each one was sanded to remove the old paint and expose the cedar. This was a messy project that would have destroyed a nice landscape, so it was one of the first jobs to be completed.

After the cleaning, instead of repainting the house and covering the exposed cedar shingles, they used a translucent stain to allow the wood grain to show through. They chose a white stain because it gave the wood a pickled look.

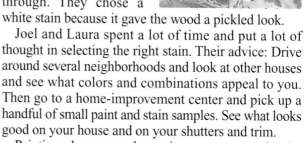

Joel and Laura spent a lot of time and put a lot of thought in selecting the right stain. Their advice: Drive around several neighborhoods and look at other houses and see what colors and combinations appeal to you. Then go to a home-improvement center and pick up a handful of small paint and stain samples. See what looks good on your house and on your shutters and trim.

Painting a house can change its appearance and make it look great. Take your time and don't jump into it. Don't have that blue house with pea-green shutters that all the neighbors talk about. 🌿

Sanding several layers of paint off the shingles created a mess that would have destroyed a new planting.

PORCH WITH PUNCH

This distinctive and welcoming front porch is certainly more than just a step up from its former look.

A large round column replaced a spindly square one for a more stately look. Plant-filled containers soften the steps.

A good-looking porch enhances a home's entrance, setting the mood for what visitors can expect. Minor changes make this one more cozy and inviting.

The old steps leading to the front door were not level and could be dangerous. We built new steps of stone and mortar on top of the old ones and added an extra step to make the risers more reasonable, about 6 inches. Getting from porch to walkway is now safer.

The old square column, shown in the before photo, was not very substantial. The homeowners liked some columns they'd seen on a *Southern Living* Idea House. A few phone calls hooked them up with the manufacturer. They ordered a big round column, more in scale with their house, and installed it themselves.

Large, squatty urns edge the new steps and, because there is no handrail, keep people centered on the steps. The new concrete containers were stark white. To give them an aged look, we created a thick mud with dirt and water, then smeared it all over the pots. These containers, brimming with flowering plants and ivy, look as if they have been a part of the entry for years.

The front door had been painted white and blended into the house. Now dark green, the door contrasts with the house, making it easy to locate. The green color ties into the landscape. It's almost the same shade as the boxwoods used around the yard.

Dress up your porch. It might be as simple as putting up a new column, adding a few flowerpots, or repainting the front door. A new look for your porch will give your whole house a face-lift. 🌿

(For sources turn to pages 250–251.)

NEW WALK, OLD LOOK

Walkways don't always have to be a straight slab of concrete.

The Blackstocks' front walk—made of sandstone that was probably as old as the house—needed to be updated. Many of the stones had settled, making it unsafe. We liked the look of the stone, but the entire walk would need to be relaid.

The new path has gentle curves that give it interest. When laying a stone walk, step back to make sure the layout and pattern are pleasing to the eye.

First we lifted and set aside the stones. Many of them were thick and embedded, so we used a long metal pry bar to get under the rocks and lift them.

We decided to change the straight-arrow walk and make a slightly curving, S-shaped path that would give it movement and character. Although there are a few curves, the walk is still a pretty straight shot to the front door. Curving paths are nice, but you don't want to walk around the whole yard to get to the porch.

To construct the path, we marked the outline with marking paint. For two people to stroll side by side, the walk needed to be at least 4 feet wide. We removed excess soil within the new path lines with a flat shovel and removed exposed tree roots.

Three inches of crushed gravel was used to make a base for the stone. Sand is sometimes used as a base, but it is not as substantial and may sift away during heavy rains.

Chipmunks and moles also have an easy time digging through it. When packed down, crushed stone creates an almost impenetrable barrier for burrowing rodents.

Once all the gravel was spread, we used a tamp to pack it firm. *Tip:* You can make a simple tamp out of scrap lumber. We nailed a 1-foot-long 1 x 6 to the bottom of a 4-foot-long 2 x 4 for our tamp.

Then it was time to lay the stone. We elevated the new walk 1 to 2 inches above ground level, and slightly crowned the center of the walk to make sure water would run off. Then we stepped on each stone to make sure it didn't rock from side to side. If the stone was unstable, we lifted it and sprinkled a little gravel under the low side. Each stone was worked until it fit snug and secure on the new gravel base.

Use a tamp made from scrap lumber to pack down the gravel.

When the stone was set, we swept gravel over the path and tamped it into the joints. After a few weeks of tracking mud and gravel into the house, Laura and Joel decided to mortar the joints for a cleaner finish.

Stone was the natural choice for this house because it was already on-site (in the backyard) and it matched the small strip of stone on the foundation. Another popular choice for walkways is poured concrete, a long-lasting material that can be dyed, edged in brick, or scored to create different designs. Brick is also an alternative, but if you have a long walk it can get expensive. There are also many different colors of pavers available at garden centers that make a nice, easy-to-install walk. Crushed gravel or pea gravel edged in brick or cut stone can be used, too, but be careful if you have active kids. Loose stone will probably be tracked into your house.

Remember that your walkway is an extension of your entry, so make sure it fits the look of your house. 🖋

This new walk looks as if it's been around for years. We achieved this by using old stone. Then we planted ferns that spill onto the walk, softening the edge and helping it blend into the landscape.

PRUNING RULES AND TOOLS

Sometimes trees need a trim. Here are some guidelines.

Low limbs covered the Blackstocks' house. Not only did they obstruct the view, but they also made it difficult to grow plants in the shady areas. An oak tree and two maples were pruned, opening up the yard. Now the homeowners are able to grow plants where previously only moss would thrive.

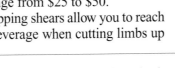
Low limbs made it hard to garden in the heavy shade. Removing a few low branches opened the view and let in more sunlight.

The best time to prune most trees is in the winter, but trees such as maples and birches that sap heavily should be pruned in the summer. Limbs that are very large, difficult to reach, or dangerously close to the house or power lines should be removed by professionals. Before you hire a tree service, make sure it's licensed, insured, and bonded. If the limbs are easy to get and you plan to remove them yourself, make sure you have the right tools.

A pair of clippers can be used for numerous tasks, from grooming the border to removing suckers from trunks. They are also good for tip pruning small trees. Clippers are made to cut limbs no bigger than ½ inch. Good bypass pruners range from $25 to $50.

The long handles of lopping shears allow you to reach high and also give you leverage when cutting limbs up to 1½ to 2 inches in diameter. The cost for a good pair of loppers usually runs $35 and up.

Pruning saws cut limbs that are too big for clippers and loppers. Their compact shape allows you to make neat cuts in tight areas. A pruning saw costs $20 to $50.

Pole pruners cut high limbs (up to about 12 feet) without the use of a ladder. A curved pruning saw blade attached to the tip of the pole helps cut those hard-to-reach limbs. A small hooked pruning blade attached to a rope and pulley can also be used to cut small limbs quickly. Pole pruners cost about $50.

Good-quality tools usually cost a little more, but they're worth the initial expense because they are made with solid materials and will last longer than ones that are cheaply made.

When cutting a limb, always make a small cut on the underside of the limb first. This will prevent the bark on the trunk from being torn from the tree when the limb falls. After you make an undercut, you can cut the upper side all the way through.

SOLVING PARKING WOES

It's important to strike the right balance. Not enough spaces means constant shuffling; too many and your yard looks like a valet lot.

With a single strip of asphalt on the side of the house, the Blackstocks played a game of musical cars every time someone had to leave. Backing out onto a busy road was dangerous, so they added a large parking court. Now cars can turn around before exiting the driveway. The parking area also accommodates guests, so they don't have to leave their cars on the road.

To get a feel for the space we needed, we parked a van in the middle of the yard where the parking court would be built. Spray paint was used to draw the outline. We wanted to be able to park two cars and still have a little room to maneuver. With the newly marked dimensions we could see the shape of the parking court and how much of the yard it consumed.

If you have enough room in your yard, you should build your parking area larger rather than smaller, but don't pave your whole front yard and have asphalt dominate the landscape. Each parking space should be at least 10 to 12 feet wide and 20 feet long. The parking area we designed is 30 feet wide and 30 feet long. The extra room allows the Blackstocks and their guests to open a door without fear of banging the next car. Even with two parked vehicles, they can walk around comfortably and not feel cramped.

A parking court should match the looks of the house and tie into the walk. When previously evaluating the site we noticed a low stone wall in the backyard that was falling down in places. We thought it might be neat to use these large stones on the parking court project. Because we would need to excavate about 3 feet of soil from the front yard, we would have to build

LEFT: Before installing the parking court, we drew out the dimensions on-site to see how it would look. Then we made a few maneuvers with a vehicle to make sure we had enough space.

BELOW: A layer of crushed gravel helps level the site. Tip: Before digging up your yard have all utility lines marked.

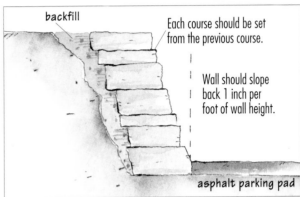

CROSS SECTION OF A DRY-STACKED STONE WALL

backfill

Each course should be set from the previous course.

Wall should slope back 1 inch per foot of wall height.

asphalt parking pad

a low wall around the parking area. The stones from the backyard looked identical to the ones used on the walk and were perfect for the low wall.

Before excavating soil, all the underground utilities were marked. (Call the customer service of individual utilities listed in the phone book and have them mark the lines for you.) A front-end loader and tractor came in handy for excavation work and hauling soil, stone, and gravel.

A low stone wall forms boundaries around the parking court. Stone walls may be built using mortar or may be stacked dry. We wanted a dry-stacked wall because it looks very natural and allows us to tuck small plants in the cracks and crevices for an interesting look. Crevices in the wall also create natural weep holes for drainage.

Before starting on the wall, we pulled twine between two wooden stakes to make a straight line. This is called a layout line. It acts as a guide to keep the rock wall straight.

A bottom row of stone was then set on firmly packed, level ground. Our wall would be 3 feet tall at its highest point, but walls 4 feet tall or higher should have a concrete footing. Larger stones should be chosen for the first course because they will be the wall's foundation.

When building a rock wall, select every stone carefully. Each stone should lean back, so the front side is slightly higher than the back. If a stone wobbles you can either use a small amount of soil under the low spot or use a small thin rock as a shim.

After laying each course, we used soil to backfill behind the rocks. With the butt of a shovel, we tamped soil into all the cracks and crevices. This makes the wall more stable and will minimize settling.

Large level stones were used on the top course. These stones are the most visible, and they make a clean cap for the wall.

The parking area connects to the walkway with a small flared landing that tapers into steps. Flowerbeds on both sides of the landing would be added later for color (see page 68).

Asphalt was selected to surface the parking pad. We liked the dark look of asphalt, and it was a little cheaper than concrete. Concrete is expensive, but it lasts and can be dyed if you don't want the usual white color. Asphalt will last many years, but it's not as durable as concrete and it only comes in black. Bricks and gravel are also popular. Although bricks can be costly, you can create different patterns, and they are appropriate in formal settings. Gravel is cheap, but it only works on level sites.

The Blackstocks' parking court and landing look as if they've been a part of the landscape for years. The

A dry-stacked stone wall allows you to tuck small plants in crevices to make it come alive.

large, moss-covered rocks used on the walls give the new parking area an aged look. If you need more parking at your home, look at the options. There are many shapes and dimensions you can use to solve your parking woes (see diagrams below).

PARKING OPTIONS AND DIMENSIONS

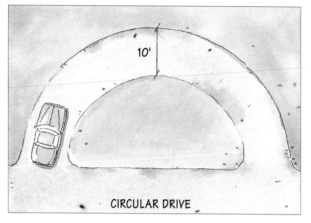

CIRCULAR DRIVE

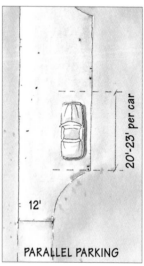

PARALLEL PARKING

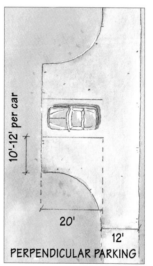

PERPENDICULAR PARKING

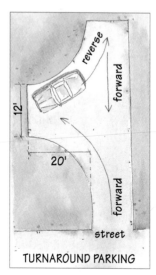

TURNAROUND PARKING

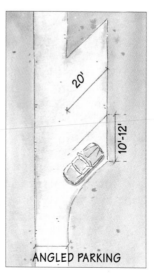

ANGLED PARKING

ABOVE: You can see how ordinary the windows looked before we installed hayracks.
RIGHT: The snapdragons tower above companion flowers and foliage, making the planting more formal.

TIPS FOR INSTALLING AND PLANTING A HAYRACK

- The hayrack should be the same width as your window.

- When mounting your hayrack be sure to leave a half-inch between the rack and the wall. Set a sheet of plastic behind the rack to keep moisture from being absorbed into the wall. Trim the plastic so it doesn't show.

- Fill your coco fiber liner with potting soil, and wet it thoroughly. After the soil settles, add more before you plant. The soil should be level with the top of the liner.

- When planting your window box, don't pack in plants. Give them plenty of room to grow, and space them as you would out in the garden.

- Select flower and leaf colors that contrast with your house so they will stand out.

- Tuck a few plants along the edge so that they will trail over the sides.

- Water, fertilize, and groom plants to keep them tidy.

LITTLE GARDENS ON THE SIDE

This easy idea can give a delightful new effect to your home's exterior.

Window boxes or hayracks are a great way to add charm. The flowers and plants that spill out of them connect the house to the yard. Because this foundation planting is extremely simple, the hayracks really have an impact. Now the house has the appearance of a quaint cottage.

The Blackstocks had installed wooden window boxes on their house when they first moved in, but these rotted in just a couple of years. They found metal-framed hayracks to replace the wooden ones. These nifty planters range from $35 for the small version to $95 for the larger model.

Hayracks have been around for hundreds of years in England. Originally, they were placed in barns and filled with hay. When the farm animals were hungry, they would reach up and pull hay through the metal bars. Because these containers were so attractive and durable, manufacturers began to make them for gardening uses as well.

In order to make the hayracks into usable planting containers, coco fiber liners are slipped into the metal frames, forming a deep and wide pocket. Filled with potting soil, the liner expands and the bars on the racks hold it securely in place. We tucked green moss between the mat and the bars to make the planter look alive and to give it an aged appearance. The coco fiber liners will have to be replaced every few years, but the hayracks will last forever.

During the spring, Rocket snapdragons stand tall in the back of the planter. The spiky plants are topped with burgundy blooms that really show up against the white house. Low-growing Cobbity daisies are nestled in front of the snapdragons. Variegated spider plants anchor the ends of the planter and trail over the sides.

As spring melts into summer, melampodium and New Guinea impatiens take the place of the snapdragons and daisies. The spider plants remain, tripling in size in the summer's sizzling heat and eventually trailing all the way to the ground.

These hayracks are like miniature gardens. Flowers are switched out through the seasons to add color to the landscape.

Each season you can try different combinations for different looks. If you don't want to set out flowers all over your yard, just plant some in a hayrack. Then you can tend to them without ever having to bend over. 🌿

NEW-LOOK FOUNDATION PLANTING

Don't hide your house with a jumble of plants; enhance it with some well-chosen accents.

Boxwoods and mondo grass create a clean, green sweep across the front of the house.

After working on the exterior of the house and ripping up the yard while installing the parking court and walkway, it was finally time to start planting. The first plants installed would be next to the house, wrapping the foundation and separating the house from the lawn. We wanted to keep it simple, safe, and low maintenance.

You keep a planting simple by using minimal material. Too many plants of all shapes and sizes scattered across the front of your house can look cluttered and chaotic. We used two boxwoods and a sweep of mondo grass for a clean look.

It's not often you think about safety when planting shrubs, but you should. Plants should not cover windows because this gives burglars easy access to break in and not be seen. Avoid planting large clusters of tall plants around your front door where someone could easily hide. You hate to have to think about an unwanted guest, but don't let your house be an easy target.

One of the large boxwoods used in the foundation planting was already on-site and growing right in front of a window (see photo at left). It was probably planted many years ago when it was very small and no one could imagine it would get this big. Always find out the maximum height a shrub will attain when selecting plants for your foundation.

An old boxwood planted long ago had grown large, covering half the window. Instead of chopping it down, we moved it.

The boxwood that had outgrown its place in front of the window is right at home just a few feet away at the corner of the house.

The large boxwood needed to be moved from in front of the window, but it was perfect for the corner of the house. Large shrubs work well on the corners, softening the hard edges. We moved the boxwood only about 8 feet, but it made a world of difference.

Another smaller boxwood was dug from the yard and relocated next to the steps. Both the moved boxwoods had been neglected, so we fertilized them and got them on a regular watering program. Because boxwoods grow so slowly, it will take a while for them to flush and get full. They will need to be pampered the next few years to become healthy specimens.

Dwarf mondo grass forms a green sweep between the boxwoods. For this planting, the soil was first amended with sand and soil conditioner and then tilled until it was loose and easy to work. We planted sprigs 6 inches apart. Dwarf mondo grass grows to be only about 2 to 3 inches tall, so it won't cover up the stone. Not many people use a ground cover as a foundation planting, but with this house it worked.

Shredded bark mulch dresses up the planting. The fine bark fits between the mondo sprigs, helping keep the weeds out and moisture in.

The finished planting is attractive and easy to maintain. Slow-growing boxwoods won't require much pruning. The mondo grass will need to be weeded every couple of months until it grows together. The foundation planting is just what we wanted—it's simple, safe, and low maintenance. Best of all, it was inexpensive because we already had the two boxwoods. 🌿

TIPS FOR MOVING SHRUBS

- First find some help. Large plants are heavy and cumbersome. It will take at least two people to lift a large shrub.

- Have a sharp ax, round-point shovel, and a long-bladed spade. If your tools aren't sharp, use a flat file to sharpen them.

- If the shrub is wide and grows low to the ground, use twine to wrap around the plant. Tie one twine end close to the ground onto a strong main trunk. One person can squeeze the plant while the other wraps.

- Use ribbon to mark the good side of a shrub (see photo below). A large shrub growing close to the house will usually have a flat side.

- To keep a tight root ball, dig a 12- to 14-inch-wide ring around the plant. Then use a spade to dig under the plant. Don't try to rock the plant with the spade until you have undercut all the way around the shrub.

- Once the root ball is free, one person can tip the shrub to one side while the other slides a tarp under it as far as possible. Then lay the shrub down in the opposite direction and pull the tarp all the way under the plant. Now slide the shrub out of the hole.

- Once the plant is out, use the shovel handle to measure the depth and width of the root ball to determine how big to make the hole.

- Plant the shrub so that the root ball is a few inches higher than the surrounding soil grade. Most large heavy plants will settle after being watered.

- Backfill around the plant; with the butt of the handle, tamp the soil to make sure the dirt is settled around the root ball.

- Water the plant thoroughly, making sure the root ball and surrounding soil are completely wet.

SMALL, CLEAN, AND GREEN

A beautiful lawn can make the landscape glisten.

BEFORE

This glowing green patch of fescue is the centerpiece of the landscape. It's small, neat, and easy to maintain.

There's nothing like walking on cushiony soft sod. The only problem is grass can be difficult.

The Blackstocks didn't want to spend all weekend cutting the lawn. So we greatly reduced the amount of turf by turning a large area under two maple trees into a natural bed (see "Planting a Screen" on opposite page).

We rolled out a carpet of Emerald Zoysia grass late in the summer only to watch it go dormant in fall and rot in winter. The area we sodded was the sunniest on the site. We thought it would get enough sun to establish Zoysia, but a wet winter left the turf area wet and the grass never greened up very well in the spring. Instead of trying Zoysia again, we seeded the yard the following fall with a shade-tolerant fescue blend.

One of the reasons we lost the Zoysia was that the soil stayed damp. So before sowing the fescue seeds, we tilled a few loads of sand into the topsoil to help it drain better. The loose soil also allowed the newly seeded grass to establish deep roots.

A drawback to the fescue is that it needs to be seeded each fall, and the summer's heat makes it look tired around August. But a little overseeding and fertilizing in September will quickly give you a fresh lawn.

Don't make the same costly mistake we did; check with a local turf expert in your area or a county Extension agent before you plant.

SOUTHERN LAWN GRASSES AT A GLANCE

Bermuda (hybrid)—Zones CS, LS, MS, TS
Less drought tolerant than common Bermuda; the improved type is just as wear resistant but has a finer texture and requires more maintenance, including heavy fertilizing. Does not thrive in shade. Establish by seed, sod, or plugs; mow from ½ to 1½ inches.

Centipede—Zones CS, LS
Although fairly shade tolerant, centipede grass cannot tolerate much wear. It prefers poor, acid soil, and needs little fertilizer. Establish by seed, sod, or plugs; mow from 1 to 2 inches.

Kentucky Bluegrass—Zone US
High-maintenance turf; requires average feeding and plenty of water. Will tolerate moderate traffic and light shade but not too much of either. Establish by seed or sod; mow from 2 to 3 inches.

St. Augustine—Zones CS, LS, TS
Shade tolerant and able to withstand salt spray by the coast; also moderately drought resistant. Requires average fertilizer. Establish by sod or plugs (spreads quickly); mow from 2 to 4 inches.

Tall Fescue—Zones LS (upper half), MS, US
Can grow in shade or full sun, fairly drought tolerant and able to resist wear. Medium feeder. Good alternative to bluegrass or ryegrass. Establish by seed or sod; mow from 3 to 4 inches.

Zoysia—Zones CS, LS, MS, TS
Extremely drought tolerant and tough, this dense, slow-spreading turf can be established by sod or plugs. Tolerates some shade and requires regular watering; mow from 1 to 2 inches.

CS=Coastal South, LS=Lower South, MS=Middle South, TS=Tropical South, US=Upper South

PLANTING A SCREEN

If you want carefree shrubs and less grass to cut, create a natural area that also provides seasonal color.

In order to eliminate some of the turf, we created a large natural area under two big maple trees. First we sprayed a couple of times with a nonselective herbicide, then we added a thick layer of pine straw to keep the weeds down.

We wanted to plant shrubs, but they would have to tolerate the shady location. The maples were limbed up and thinned out to get more sunlight around their bases. Now there was enough dappled light to keep the shrubs happy. We selected ones that would grow large and wide because we wanted to plant as few as possible to save money.

The large sweeps of shrubs were staggered and set out in a random fashion. By using large, flowering shrubs and massing them together, we produced big blocks of seasonal color and also screened the road in front of the house.

We set out oakleaf hydrangeas along the edge of the parking court. They will eventually spill over the stone wall. These native plants produce year-round interest. In the late spring, bunches of tiny white flowers appear. In summer, the flowers fade pinkish red, and in the fall, they will turn a transparent brown.

Behind the hydrangeas, we planted Mrs. G. G. Gerbing azaleas. This mounding evergreen is great for screening. The large white flowers have yellow and green splotched centers.

Forsythia, or yellow bells, were planted along the road, where their flower-lined stems form golden arches in the early spring. Although these shrubs aren't evergreen, when planted en masse they make a nice woody thicket in winter.

If you create a natural area, select shrubs that will bloom at different times. (See the chart at right for ideas.) 🌿

ABOVE: Oakleaf hydrangeas are native to Southern woods. These showy, loose-growing shrubs have also become quite common in residential settings.

SHRUBS FOR COLOR

Shrubs	Size	Comments
banana shrub	15' x 10'	yellow spring flowers
common camellia	15' x 8'	red, pink, white or variegated—fall through spring flowers
sasanqua camellia	15' x 8'	white to pink—fall to winter flowers
Florida anise	10' x 10'	white or red spring flowers
forsythia	8' x 8'	yellow early-spring flowers
Japanese anise	10' x 10'	creamy to yellow-green spring flowers
fuzzy deutzia	8' x 6'	white spring flowers
flowering quince	8' x 8'	scarlet, pink, white, orange, salmon winter flowers
gardenia	(varies)	white summer flowers
G. G. Gerbing azalea	10' x 10'	white spring flowers
large fothergilla	8' x 5'	white spring flowers
Japanese kerria	6' x 6'	orange late-spring flowers
oakleaf hydrangea	8' x 6'	white late-spring flowers
wintersweet	12' x 6'	yellow winter flowers

ADDING COLOR

The pansies on the left side of the walk were planted in the fall, but spring's when they really show their stuff. On the right, sweet William blooms with strawberry geranium.

Once all the foundation plants were in place, it was time to add flowerbeds that would frame the front walkway. These will put on a show, providing color throughout the seasons. Now when guests step out of their cars and approach the walk, they have something nice to greet them.

To begin, we decided exactly where we wanted the beds by outlining the area with a garden hose until we got a shape we liked. Then we tilled soil conditioner and sand into the soil to make it loose and porous. Loose soil is easier to dig and gives the plants a good start.

Annuals, which should be switched out two to three times a year, paint the landscape. Buying transplants in cell packs gives quick color, and there's little downtime between plantings.

In the fall, pansies and sweet William fill the garden. Pansies bloom sporadically throughout the winter and become very showy in the spring. Sweet William forms thick mats of green in the winter and then sends up flat multicolored clusters of blooms in spring.

Late in spring, the pansies were becoming leggy, so out they went. Trailing torenia was planted along the top of the stone wall so its tiny blue flowers cascaded over the edge. Torenia blooms aren't terribly showy, but they are continuous from spring till fall. Behind them, caladiums were massed for a white, leafy delight. White and blue are cool colors that work well in summer heat.

Pink impatiens took the place of sweet William after it had finished blooming. The impatiens would grow well in the shade under the small Japanese maple. Impatiens are a top-selling, shade-loving annual because they are easy to grow and come in so many different colors.

In the summer we used shade-loving plants because all the deciduous trees in the

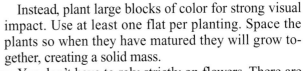

Caladiums and trailing torenia produce a nice blue-and-white combination. A slow-release fertilizer sprinkled under the plants keeps them fed through the season and into the fall.

yard leafed out and created a dappled-light setting. In the fall, we were able to plant annuals that needed more sun because all the leaves were falling. In the winter, the yard received much more sun. Before you plant, track the sun and see exactly how much your yard receives; then choose plants accordingly.

If you use different annuals in the same flowerbed, make sure they are compatible. They should require the same amount of water, sun, and fertilizer. Some people plant flowers with opposite needs, only to find one plant thrives, while the other struggles. This makes the whole bed look ragged.

Also, if you mix plants, make sure the colors don't clash. Flower color should also be compatible with the house color. Don't plant too many different-colored plants or you'll have a cluttered and chaotic look.

Instead, plant large blocks of color for strong visual impact. Use at least one flat per planting. Space the plants so when they have matured they will grow together, creating a solid mass.

You don't have to rely strictly on flowers. There are many attractive annuals that have striking foliage. Plants such as caladiums, coleus, and dusty miller may not have showy blooms, but their colored leaves are stunning. These leafy annuals can also be mixed with flowers for an attractive alternative.

Try to use white flowers or foliage. Many people think white isn't colorful or showy, but it gives a garden a pure, clean look. It also blends well with other plants and helps tone down bright colors such as red and orange. Whites are also visible under low-light conditions.

No matter what color annual you choose, plant a few in front of your house. It will take some work and maintenance, but beautiful flowers will reward you and enhance your landscape. 🌿

Impatiens, caladiums, and torenia took summer's heat and never missed a beat.

The Southern Gardener special section was written and coordinated by Charlie Thigpen and photographed by Van Chaplin; graphic design by Amy Kathryn Rogers.

KNOT PERFECT

The heart of the garden is formed of twig and leaf,

twisted into an intricate puzzle.

Small boxwoods are planted in pots at the corners of the garden. Containers enhance the impact of small shrubs.

BY LINDA C. ASKEY
PHOTOGRAPHY
VAN CHAPLIN

Sue and Donald Pritchard's knot garden fills a tiny nook in their Birmingham landscape with spring delight. The symmetry and pattern tie it to the formal architecture of the home, while separating it from the woodland area beyond.

"Originally I had a rose garden down there," says Sue, "and it needed too much loving care. I wanted something that was pleasing to look at and required very little maintenance." She called garden designer Mary Zahl to help her achieve her goals.

"It's a garden that is viewed from an upper terrace and an intermediate terrace," Mary explains. "So it needed to look good from above, and it needed to be formal."

The solution was to create a small garden that is framed by hedges and walls. Mary created the symmetrical pattern of a knot in sheared hedges to fill the center of the 20- x 30-foot area with year-round impact. Two-foot-wide borders of seasonal color fill the two long sides. At the far end, a love seat–size bench becomes the focus of the view while serving as an invitation to stroll out and enjoy the garden.

PUTTING IT ALL TOGETHER
Sometimes it's difficult to see all that went into a garden when it comes out looking right. Here are a few design techniques Mary employed.

■ The area was small, so she started by making the garden as big as it could be

and then adjusting the proportions. Actually, it was too long, so Mary moved the bench in about 4 feet.

■ Materials used in the garden repeat those used elsewhere on the property to make the garden seem as if it has always been there. The brick was existing on

the property, and the cobblestone landing at the top of the steps matches the cobblestone parking court in front of the house.

■ The bench sits on a limestone pad that echoes the limestone steps (not pictured). The firm surface makes the bench more secure than it would be sitting on gravel.

■ In order to reduce maintenance and keep down weeds, Mary laid landscape fabric over the soil before the pea gravel for the paths arrived.

■ Mary incorporated perlite into the soil to make the beds drain better. It doesn't deteriorate like organic matter, and it's lighter than sand. Weight was a concern because an old railroad tie retaining wall holds up one side of the garden.

■ Boxwoods planted in pots anchor the four corners of the garden. "That's a way of giving impact," Mary says. "A small boxwood in a pot has a similar or greater effect than a large boxwood in the ground, and is more economical." ◇

ABOVE: *Designed to be viewed from above, this tiny garden features a formal pattern for year-round appeal and a border that changes with the seasons. The knot is planted with the dark green foliage of Heller Japanese holly and the lime-green of Francis Mason abelia.*

LEFT: *The downhill side of the garden would be open and feel vulnerable without the wall of foliage created by Nellie R. Stevens hollies.*

Lavender-pink sweet rocket, Pink Meidiland roses, and pansies (See pages 94–99.)

April

Checklist for April

EDITORS' NOTEBOOK

Please don't think me hateful because I promote beheading annuals. But sometimes it's simply the right thing to do. Say you've been distracted lately by such matters as convincing the IRS that tuition to Beer School qualifies you for an Educational IRA. You forgot to plant your packs of impatiens and now they've gotten leggy. No problem—just take some clippers and lop off their heads. (And look sad, lest you incur the wrath of the annual rights crowd.) Sure you'll lose the first few blooms. But with less foliage to support, the plants won't be as heat- or water-stressed. And you'll end up with more flowers. While this doesn't work for all annuals, it helps wax begonia, floppy coleus, narrowleaf zinnia, and melampodium plants. Now excuse me, I must resume my search for IRS form #8706CP—Reimbursement For Expenses Incurred During The Consumption of Domestic Cheese And Cheese-Related Products.

Steve Bender

☐ **Azaleas**—Buy shrubs in bloom to be certain that the color complements your home and garden. Keep in mind the ultimate size of the plants; there is a wide range in size among azaleas. ▶

☐ **Daylilies**—If you want specific colors, shop while they are in bloom. That's now in the Tropical South. Look locally for evergreen types. Daylilies sold through catalogs may not do well because most need a cooler climate.

☐ **Gardenias**—If you want to keep blooms fresh, store them in the refrigerator. Place the cut stems in a vase with

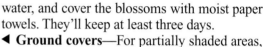

water, and cover the blossoms with moist paper towels. They'll keep at least three days.

◀ **Ground covers**—For partially shaded areas, choices include English and Algerian ivies, ajuga, common periwinkle, or liriope. For open, sunny sites, consider purple leaf honeysuckle, creeping junipers, or Asian Jasmine.

☐ **Houseplants**—Take tired foliage plants outdoors for the summer, but be careful to put them in the shade. Their leaves are as sensitive to sunburn as a person's skin after a long winter indoors. Repot, spray, and prune as needed to encourage new growth.

☐ **Sprayers**—Before putting pesticide in your sprayer for the first time this season, fill it up with water and pressurize it. Leaks and clogs are safer to deal with when it's only water running up your arm. Replacement parts such as hoses, O-rings, and nozzles are available where sprayers are sold.

☐ **Staking**—Support tall flowers such as delphiniums and foxgloves, as well as heavy-headed ones such as peonies before they bend and break in a spring storm. Use single stakes of bamboo or metal, or use prunings from trees and shrubs. Push the cut end in the ground and let the ends of the branches stick up to give effective, but almost invisible, support.

☐ **Tags**—Remove tags around the trunk or limbs of trees and shrubs when you plant. If allowed to remain, they will tighten as the plant grows, cut into the bark, and kill it.

☐ **Vegetables**—Cherry tomatoes, hot peppers, and eggplants tolerate heat and humidity. Cherry tomatoes will bear fruit all summer. Most hot peppers do better than sweet bells. Dependable eggplants include long, tender Oriental types such as Ichiban. ▶

☐ **Annuals**—Plant zinnias now for summer arrangements. Choose long-stemmed selections such as Big Red, Royal Purple, Canary Bird, Envy, or Scarlet Queen. Pick a sunny spot and sow seeds directly into the soil. You can start planting early this month in the Lower South, late in the month in the Middle South, and next month in the Upper South.

☐ **Easter lily**—Plant your Easter lily in the garden 4 to 6 inches deep after it blooms. Give it a sunny spot and well-drained soil.

☐ **Fall perennials**—Plant Mexican bush sage, autumn asters, Mexican mint marigolds, and mums as soon as the first frost has passed so they will form masses for late summer and fall bloom. Plant them in drifts or groups of at least three to five plants of each type for maximum effect. Space individual plants 1 to 2 feet apart.

☐ **Herbs**—In all areas but the Tropical South, wait until two weeks after the danger of frost to set out transplants of basil. Plant perennial herbs, such as chives, oregano, mint, fennel, horseradish, lemon balm, parsley, sage, thyme, and tarragon in a permanent location. Place tender, woody herbs, such as rosemary and bay in a sheltered spot or in a container if winter cold is a threat in your area. Tropical South gardeners will have better luck planting herbs in fall. ▶

☐ **Tomatoes**—As soon as the last frost date in your area has passed, set out healthy plants of locally recommended selections an inch or two deeper than they were growing in containers. Water well. Be prepared to provide temporary cover during late cold spells. Tie the vines to stakes or surround them with wire cages soon after planting.

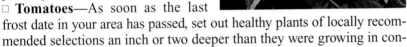

PRUNE

◀ **Spring shrubs**—Prune spring-flowering shrubs soon after they flower. Climbing and once-blooming roses such as Lady Banks, climbing Cecile Brunner, and climbing Don Juan are also pruned after spring bloom. Keep the natural shape in mind as you trim and avoid excessive cutting except to control size.

FERTILIZE

☐ **Annuals**—Rejuvenate pansies, violas, and snapdragons by removing spent flowers and applying fertilizer at the rate of 2 to 3 pounds of 5-10-10 or similar for every 100 square feet of bed area. Water well.

☐ **Azaleas**—Leaves that remain yellow in spite of regular fertilizing may not have enough iron. To darken the leaves use an iron supplement such as liquid iron or iron chelate or a product called Ironite. Don't spray it on foliage (as may be directed) if the weather is hot—above 85 to 90 degrees; it could burn the leaves. Apply to the soil instead.

☐ **Citrus**—In the Tropical, Coastal, and Lower South, fertilize with a formula such as 12-5-8 especially made for citrus. Plants that drop too many blossoms may need extra phosphorus. Apply 1 cup of superphosphate around the base of trees, if blossom drop is substantial.

April notes:

TIP OF THE MONTH

Before planting tiny seeds, spread them on a baking sheet, and press a wet piece of string over them; the seeds will stick. Then stretch out the string, place it in a shallow planting trench in your garden, and cover with soil. Few seeds are wasted, the string eventually decomposes, and the seeds come up in straight rows.

SANDY FOSTER
RIVERDALE, GEORGIA

SCOTT'S GARDEN

Growing vegetables and growing up

Even before the word "garden" was part of his vocabulary, Scott Chappelle was growing vegetables. Now 14, he possesses the seasoned wisdom of an old-timer and a sense of the soil to carry him into a lifetime of gardens. "My dream is to live on a farm. I'll grow all my own vegetables and have horses, cows, and chickens," Scott says.

The Chappelles live in Mountain Brook, Alabama. Scott's mom, Lyn, grew up gardening in the shadow of her grandfather, and at her mother's side. "Mom grew vegetables and flowers in a real garden," says Lyn.

"The vegetables were part of every summer meal." Scott is gladly following family footsteps.

Every spring, he and his mom visit local garden shops and decide what to plant. A few selections are repeated from year to year, and an experiment or two is also added. Scott's standard fare includes Sweet Million cherry tomatoes, Black Beauty eggplants, and zucchini. Scott plants something for everyone, including Cracker and Sparky, his two pint-size pets. Originally, the eggplants were destined for the dinner table. But Cracker and Sparky

BY ELLEN RILEY / PHOTOGRAPHY VAN CHAPLIN

took a shine to the deep purple produce and claim it as their own.

"I like to start every spring with small transplants," Scott says. "The year we planted only seeds, the birds ate them all. With transplants, the garden goes from small to big pretty quickly." Scott plants in late April or early May, after danger of a late frost has passed. In early June, the family leaves for their annual trip to the beach. "When we leave, my garden still looks pretty small," says Scott. "But when we get back, I go straight out and check on it. It seems to have doubled in size and there is usually something ready to harvest."

Harvest is a word that keeps cropping up with Scott. "The best part of gardening is getting to harvest what you grow. I love to pick my Sweet Million tomatoes. Only about three make it into the house. I eat the rest right out there in the garden," he confesses.

When asked whether any of his friends share his green thumb, he comes back to the harvest with a pinch of teenage appetite thrown in. "They don't like to grow things, but they like to pick tomatoes out of my garden. Most of them have to weed for their moms, so it's more fun to pick out of mine. They usually end up eating something out of the garden."

SWEET SUCCESS

Most gardeners have at least one plant they're especially proud of, and Scott is no exception. "My best gardening success is my mint. I was at a friend's house, and his family had a big patch of it that they didn't like. They were going to pull it all out, so I took a piece home and stuck it in the ground. The next summer I had about 10 plants. Last year the mint was everywhere."

In recent months, the Chappelles have moved to a new home, and Scott hopes to begin his new garden with a sprig of rescued mint. And, when he finally gets that dreamed-about farm, a piece of that mint will surely follow.

LOOKING AHEAD

Next year Scott plans to grow some of his zucchini in soda bottles. "When the squash are real little, you slide them into Coke bottles. When they've grown enough to fill up the bottles, you harvest them. Carefully break the bottles, and you've got Coke-shaped squash."

Scott has gained much more than tomatoes and corn from his vegetable plot. When asked what he loves most about gardening, his answer is almost sage. "Whenever I go into my garden, there's always something there waiting for me." Gardening is secure for another generation.

CHILDREN AND THE HARVEST

"Children who garden quickly learn the joy of sharing. They learn responsibility, nurturing, and productivity. Let a child harvest his first tomato or bunch of zinnias, and you will see pride beyond compare." These words of wisdom come from Dr. Tommy Amason, a pediatrician and gardener in Birmingham who believes in the benefits of encouraging children to garden. Dr. Amason, a past member of the American Horticultural Society, helped develop extensive materials on gardening with children for this organization. He is also involved with the American Horticultural Therapy Association. He suggests both organizations as good sources of information. The American Horticultural Society can be reached at 1-800-777-7931. The American Horticultural Therapy Association can be reached at 1-800-634-1603. ◇

Jubilant Spring Table

Dressed in heather and daffodils, this topiary bunny seems to say "Hooray for spring."

PHOTOGRAPHS: JEAN ALLSOPP / STYLING: BUFFY HARGETT

This is a season full of celebration. Be it a family Easter dinner or a shower for baby or bride, the attitude is joy and playfulness. So throw your arms wide and greet our flowery bunny surrounded by sunny daffodils.

There are two projects in this simple tablescape. The bunny topiary takes a bit of time, but the results are long-lasting. The daffodils are cut from the garden and assembled in just a few minutes. The result is a doable combination fitting any occasion.

HEATHER BUNNY

Our flower bunny is a wire topiary form that ordinarily would be filled with sphagnum moss and planted. But we wanted bright colors. A trip to the florist produced vibrant cut heather that stays fresh for several days and then dries. Our form required two bunches for good flower cover.

Begin at the bottom. Cut several stems of heather the length of the rabbit's leg, and wire them to the form in clusters using paddle wire. This wire allows you to keep winding in a continuous strand rather than cutting many short pieces. Attach enough heather to cover the wire leg. Cut the paddle wire, and secure it to the form. Repeat the process for the other leg, and then continue on to the rest of the body until the form is completely hidden with flowers.

Anchor the finished form in a terra-cotta container. Add gravel to the container to provide weight and stability to the tall topiary. Hide the gravel with green sheet moss.

As heather begins to dry, it will shed slightly. Spray with clear acrylic sealer to diminish dropping flowers. If kept out of direct sunlight, the heather bunny will retain good color for about a year.

MATERIALS

HEATHER BUNNY

WIRE TOPIARY FORM

BUNCHES OF HEATHER

CLIPPERS

PADDLE WIRE

TERRA-COTTA POT

GRAVEL

GREEN SHEET MOSS

CLEAR ACRYLIC SEALER

DAFFODIL SUNBURST

8 CUT DAFFODILS

RAFFIA

SHALLOW CONTAINER WITH PINHOLDER

GREEN SHEET MOSS

CUT VIOLAS

DAFFODIL SUNBURST

Tie the flower heads in a cluster and daffodils provide a sunburst of color. Our container is a shallow pinholder that requires water to be added on a daily basis.

Step 1: Cut eight daffodils with long stems. Cluster three together, and add the others around the outside, facing the trumpet of each one out. Tie the bundle with raffia close to the flower heads. Secure the stems at the bottom with another piece of raffia. Trim stems to the same length.

Step 2: Push the stems into the pinholder. Add water to the container.

Step 3: Place moss around the container base. A few violas tucked in will finish the arrangement. *Ellen Riley*

(For sources turn to pages 250–251.)

PHOTOGRAPHS: VAN CHAPLIN

The addition of vertical elements gives a low ranch-style house a lift.

BEFORE

Suburban Update

A trio of columns gives weight to the entrance where formerly a row of spindly columns obscured views.

All of these ranches are just so horizontal," says architect Bill Edwards of the home he shares with his wife, Laurie, and two young children in Atlanta. Having worked with landscape architect Dan Franklin on several other projects, Bill called upon Dan to help with his renovation. The pairing of professionals—landscape architect and architect—gives outstanding results. As Dan says, "It's the way it should be done."

"As an architect, living in a split-level was on the bottom of my list of things I thought I would do," Bill says. "But that's where we ended up."

Dan and Bill worked to shorten the long appearance of the house by breaking up horizontal lines and introducing vertical lines wherever they could. "It's like trying to dress when you are overweight," Bill says. "You do everything vertically that you can."

BEFORE
short windows

long line of shrubs along the foundation

long, uninterrupted walk

Four columns made porch appear longer.

horizontal siding

Dark brick and light siding created a horizontal line.

AFTER
windows lengthened with panel and shutters

foundation planting lowered so house appears taller

walk partitioned by new row of hollies

Columns on corners give emphasis to entrance.

Paint eliminates the line of siding against brick.

Darker color makes house recede.

THE FACADE

Vertical additions include lengthening the windows with a wooden panel, molding, and long shutters. Adding heftier columns and moving them to the corners of the porch kept it from looking so long and framed the entry for emphasis. The view from indoors through the bay window was improved as well.

Painting eliminated the line across the two story wing between the light siding and the dark brick. Because Bill and Laurie chose a dark color, the house recedes. The light trim color helps emphasize the porch and entry.

Tall shutters, added to the two-story wing, create an illusion. "We were trying to mask the split-level feel of the house," Bill explains. "Pulling those windows up aligned them with the main floor and kept the small windows above almost like transoms."

And finally, new steps and a low wall were added. "Where you have walks

Wooden panels and long shutters lengthen the windows with minimal expense.

from the driveway," Bill says, "you can pull out the steps as far as you can toward the walk in order to make the distance feel shorter."

THE LANDSCAPE

Because Bill and Laurie were on a budget, Dan rearranged many of the existing shrubs. The azaleas were pulled away from the foundation and grouped in a mass of a single color. Heller Japanese hollies were transplanted to form a line perpendicular to the foundation, creating a sense of entry between the small lawn area and the beds of pachysandra.

A conical evergreen cryptomeria in front of the last pair of windows on the two-story wing serves a dual purpose. It stops your view as you head for the front door and visually shortens the house from the street. "That's a bedroom window," Bill explains, "so on the front of the house it's nice to have a little more privacy."

Linda C. Askey

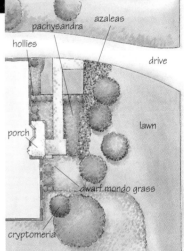

To save money, Dan used many of the shrubs that were already on-site, rearranging them in a more suitable fashion.

Whiskey begonias edge the front, salvia fills out the middle, and coneflowers and ornamental grasses tower in the back.

Order in The Border

Whether you were short or tall growing up, you knew where to stand when it was time for class photos. The tall children stood on the back row while the medium-sized children were stuck in the middle and the short kids were always kneeling up front. Well, if you want to see all the pretty faces of flowers when planting a border, remember this arrangement.

If you're not sure how tall your flowers will grow, you should try to find out. Just because a plant is only a couple of inches tall in the spring doesn't mean it won't grow to be 4 feet by summer's end.

When purchasing plants from a nursery look for the small plastic tags or labels that usually accompany each container. These tags tell if the plant likes sun or shade, if it's an annual or perennial, and the approximate height it will reach. County Extension agents and gardening books are also good sources of information.

If you are still not sure about a plant you purchased or received as a gift, put it in a pot or plant it in the back of your border. This way you can keep an eye on it and move it once you've learned its characteristics. ◇

The Ivy Challenge

Ivy as a houseplant is alive—but not always well. It can be found hugging topiary forms of all shapes and sizes on mantels and windowsills or gracefully climbing over the edge of a container on a coffee table. Indoors, ivy is a haven for spider mites and a challenge to keep healthy. That is, until you learn a few secrets.

The question is not whether your ivy will get spider mites, but when. The key to controlling these pests is prevention. Once spider mites become visibly evident they have won the battle.

Ivy requires a bright location. It does not thrive in direct sunlight or very low light. It should be watered only when dry. In most homes, this is about once a week. The less light that the plant receives, the less water will be needed to maintain it. When it is time to water, take the plant to the kitchen sink and moisten the soil thoroughly. After watering, turn the container on its side. Using the spray attachment or a gentle stream of water, wet the foliage. Be sure to wet the underside of the leaves also. This is the first step in preventing spider mites.

Use a household insecticide spray or insecticidal soap routinely, once a week. If spider mites do make themselves at home, more drastic measures must be taken to solve the problem. Move the plant outdoors to a shaded location. Hose it off with a strong stream of water. Then, spray with a systemic insecticide, such as Orthene. Allow the chemical to dry before returning the plant indoors. If the temperatures are above freezing, consider leaving the plant outdoors in a shady place for a week or two. Repeat the spray treatment within a week.

If all of this seems like a lot to do, don't despair. This routine takes less than five minutes a week and is certainly worth the effort. Your ivy will stay healthy and insect free. ◇

A Beastly Beauty

Roll up your sleeves if you plant this wildflower. You could be in for a tussle.

PHOTOGRAPH: VAN CHAPLIN

Hundreds of showy blossoms decorate pink evening primrose in spring. Despite its name, the flowers open in daytime.

Adding a beautiful perennial to your garden doesn't usually require inordinate courage. But pink evening primrose isn't like other perennials.

Consider that this native wildflower grows happily through cracks in the pavement. Consider it flourishes in any well-drained soil, from the parched caliche of West Texas to the red clay of Georgia to the sands of South Florida. Consider that planting it in good soil among well-mannered perennials is akin to leaving your Pekingese in a pen with a hungry wolverine.

So why plant it? When it blooms from April to June, it's an unquestioned joy to behold. Also known as showy primrose, Mexican evening primrose, and in some parts buttercups (because if you playfully shove a flower onto the end of someone's nose after asking him to smell it, the pollen leaves a yellow smudge), it bears hundreds of pink or occasionally white blossoms. With a unique, cruciform style (female reproductive part) in the flower's center, each magenta-veined blossom reminds me of a satellite dish. Well-informed ants reclining below are probably tuning in to CNN.

Despite its name, pink evening primrose *(Oenothera speciosa)* blooms during the day. The 1½-inch-wide blossoms appear atop a sprawling mat of foliage that's 10 to 12 inches high. The plant spreads rapaciously both by seeds and underground stems. Poor, rocky, or highly acid soil slows its progress to a saunter. However, in loose, fertile soil, it attains warp speed. After finishing blooming, it dies back a bit and appears to rest. But don't be fooled—those innocent-looking seeds and stems have ideas.

The safest spot to grow pink evening primrose is where it can spread to its heart's content without hurting anything—for example, a wildflower meadow, naturalized area, or informal lawn. Near my home, it prospers in a parkway median, despite the efforts of insightful highway workers, who interpret its flowers as an urgent signal for emergency mowing.

But if you prefer this plant in a traditional border, beware—it will insinuate itself between bricks and stones and devour finicky flowers. One solution, says garden designer Edith Eddleman of Durham, North Carolina, is to combine it with tall perennials it can't engulf, such as Russian sage or Siberian iris. Or we suggest planting it among other perennial thugs, such as hardy ageratum, obedient plant, or common yarrow, and let these bad boys duke it out. "Even then, on the whole, *Oenothera* will win," she warns.

Unfortunately, hungry wolverines won't triumph either. They will just wind up with funny little yellow smudges on their noses.

Steve Bender
(For sources turn to pages 250-251.)

PINK EVENING PRIMROSE
At a Glance

Size: 10 to 12 inches high
Light: full sun
Soil: any well drained
Pests: none serious
Propagation: seed, division
Range: throughout the South
Expect to pay: $4 to $5

Perfect Planters in Sun or Shade

Try these techniques for knockout containers.

ABOVE: *In a sunny location, this plant combo can't be beat. Pentas, lantana, and Provence lavender provide color, while sedum, sage, and ivy add texture.*

RIGHT: *Geraniums, cape plumbago, and Blue Wonder fan flower thrive in sun or part sun. Variegated Swedish ivy falls gracefully over the sides of its container.*

A perfectly planted container should be a seamless mix of foliage and flowers," says Jeremy Smearman, owner of Planters Nursery in Atlanta.

"A container should be the crowning touch of the garden. It's the very last thing you do to complete your landscape," he says. Choose a simple container that will hold large annuals and tropical material. "You want your planter to look like it has been growing at least two months the day you plant it," he says.

Also, plan your container's contents to complement the garden, not compete with it. If the flowerbed bordering the patio is a riot of color, plant containers using only one color. In a landscape of green trees and shrubs, your container plantings can run wild with color.

Whether you're planting in sun or shade, another key is compatibility. Jeremy stresses the importance of using plants that have similar light and water requirements. But it goes further than that. "Colors must be compatible, as well as textures. Pair large, coarse leaves with smaller, more delicate leaves for pleasing texture." Avoid planting flowers that all have the same shape or have foliage with the same texture. Visual depth is achieved by varying the size and shape of both flowers and foliage.

HOW TO START

First, the container must have a large drainage hole in the bottom. If the pot has a tiny hole, carefully enlarge it using an electric drill and masonry bit.

Next, put a layer of gravel or broken pottery in the bottom to help keep the drainage hole open. Fill the container with lightweight potting soil. Trickle water into the container to settle the soil prior to planting. Jeremy prefers to layer soils in containers that will be placed in full sun. "Use lightweight soil in most of the pot, and top it off with a layer of heavier potting soil. I like to use a soil that

PHOTOGRAPHS: JEAN ALLSOPP

RECIPE FOR SUN

rose color pentas
(Pentas lanceolata)

purple sage
(*Salvia officinalis* Purpurascens)

Lemon Drop lantana
(*Lantana camara* Lemon Drop)

Provence lavender
(*Lavandula intermedia* Provence)

Gold Baby English ivy
(*Hedera helix* Gold Baby)

October Daphne sedum
(*Sedum sieboldii* October Daphne)

RECIPE FOR SHADE

Pink Cane begonia
(*Begonia* x Pink Cane)

Japanese painted fern
(*Athyrium goeringianum* Pictum)

Pixie Dixie English ivy
(*Hedera helix* Pixie Dixie)

RECIPE FOR SUN/PARTIAL SHADE

Pink Camellia geranium
(*Pelargonium* Pink Camellia)

cape plumbago
(Plumbago auriculata)

Blue Wonder fan flower
(*Scaevola aemula* Blue Wonder)

variegated Swedish ivy
(*Plectranthus coleoides* Variegatus)

contains expanded shale as the top layer. This heavier soil forms a crust on top of the pot, helping retain moisture."

PLANT IT BIG

Scale is the relationship between the size of the planting and the size of the container. Put another way, it's how to keep your container from being skimpy. Jeremy has simplified this idea and developed a rule to ensure the scale of plants to container is correct. "The volume of plants should be equal to or greater than the volume of the pot," he says.

Choose mature plants that are already blooming or are close to it. Many garden centers sell annuals and tropical plants in 1-gallon pots. This is the perfect size to give your newly planted container an instant finished look.

Begin planting in the center of the pot with the dominant plant. This is the focal point, or where your eye goes first. Then plant toward the sides, "knitting the plants together with color and texture," Jeremy advises. Remember to loosen the roots of each plant before placing in the container.

KEEP IT FRESH

A pot filled to the brim with vigorous plants requires vigilant care. Keep in mind that a container in full sun needs more water than a shady pot. Expect to water a sunny container once a day during the hottest summer months. Water-retaining polymers can be added to the soil at planting time to help hold moisture. If taking time to water is a problem, a flexible irrigation system can be put into most containers. In shade, water more sparingly.

To keep your container in peak bloom from spring through first frost, feeding is essential. At planting time add a well-balanced (14-14-14) time-release granular fertilizer to the soil. In addition, feed with a liquid fertilizer high in potassium (15-30-15) on a monthly basis. Remove old flowers, and trim any plant that becomes greedy for space.

View your container as a tapestry of flowers and foliage. Follow these time-tested rules and you are sure to succeed.

Ellen Riley

TOP, LEFT: *Pink Cane begonia, Japanese painted fern, and Pixie Dixie English ivy are good companions for a shady container.*

ABOVE: *When moisture is added to water-retaining polymers, they expand to keep extra water in the pot. As the soil dries, the moisture is released.*

They'll Grow Out of It

Tall and awkward plants are sometimes like children.
They need a little guidance and time.

The plant was too tall, the pot was too small, and insects infested the upper limbs. After we pruned the limbs, new growth appeared in a few weeks.

A tough houseplant is a treasure, persevering in spite of our busy lives. But when we realized that our old friend (shown at far left) had struggled too long with nothing but an occasional dousing of water on its hard-packed soil, we decided to give it a chance or give it up.

Like dumb canes, dracaenas, and Chinese evergreens, our tropical yucca *(Yucca elephantipes)* has a bamboolike trunk that can be cut off at any height. We knew that one or more shoots would arise just below the cuts, giving a thick head of new growth atop a tall stem. But we had other challenges.

The upper portion of each stem was infested with scale, little brown bumps that suck the life out of a plant and wear an armor that insecticides can't penetrate. We cut back the plant to a height we would enjoy in our home, and, fortunately, this also removed most of the scale.

Using fresh potting soil, we repotted the plant in a larger container. To clothe the bare soil we bought a 6-inch pot of silver-leaved Rex begonia, divided it, and planted the divisions around the yucca trunks. Then we sprinkled a scoop of timed-release fertilizer (such as 18-6-12 or 10-15-10) on top of the soil and began watering weekly.

We decided SunSpray Ultra-Fine Oil was our best defense against scale. This horticultural oil acts by coating and suffocating insects. We chose this particular product because it is lighter and less likely to damage the plant during warm weather. We mixed the oil in a spray bottle and coated the leafless stubs that remained, letting the excess run down the trunks and into the crevices in the bark. We sprayed again two weeks later to catch any of the little varmints that had escaped.

Left outdoors in the shade for the remainder of the summer, carried indoors for the winter, and then taken back outdoors the next summer, the yucca and begonia have grown into a lovely combination we now point to with pride. *Linda C. Askey*

BEFORE

Stealing the show with its frosted foliage, silver plectranthus is surrounded by white lantana, Purple Wave petunias, pink Waterlily colchiums, and annual purple fountain grass.

Add a Little Silver to Your Garden

Plectranthus argentatus. Wasn't that the name of those cute little dinosaurs in *Jurassic Park?* No, it's actually an elegant, if underused, garden plant.

While it hasn't hired a publicist to give it a spiffy common name, don't let this stop you from adding silver plectranthus *(Plectranthus argentatus)* to your garden.

This tender perennial's silvery leaves look as if Tinker Bell has sprinkled them with stardust. Under the overlay of silver hairs, the leaves are a light, fuzzy gray-green, 2 to 4½ inches long, with scalloped margins. Both leaves and stems are suffused with purple. In summer it produces slender clusters of lavender salvia-like blooms. But this plant is grown for its beautiful foliage. The flowers are just a bonus. It makes a fine companion for roses, salvias, and buddleias.

Nancy Goodwin at Montrose Garden in Hillsborough, North Carolina, says they use silver plectranthus in urns, in the aster border, and anywhere they need its color.

It can be grown in sun to partial shade. It grows fast, making a small shrub 1 foot tall and 3 feet wide in about three months. Grow it in moderately fertile, well-drained soil.

Although heat and drought resistant, it will not make it through the winter. But you can save it for next year by taking stem tip cuttings at any time and potting them up.

Silver plectranthus is available at most large garden centers. So step up, take a deep breath, and ask for it by name. ◇

SILVER PLECTRANTHUS
At a Glance

Size: 1 foot high and 3 feet wide

Light: sun to dappled shade

Hardiness: perennial in frost-free areas

Soil: well-drained, but able to hold moisture

Pests: can be susceptible to mealybugs, spider mites, leaf spot, and root rot

Expect to pay: $6 for a 1-gallon container

PHOTOGRAPHS: VAN CHAPLIN

This shapely azalea puts on a stunning spring show.

New-Look Azaleas

With a little pruning, this most popular flowering shrub can also be an attractive little tree.

Azaleas drape the Southern landscape each spring with clouds of pink, red, white, and lavender blooms. Most azaleas naturally have a billowy, mounding form, although some overzealous gardeners feel the need to clip them into tight rounded balls or boxy squares. I have found that with minimal pruning, some can be shaped into small, attractive, evergreen trees.

A few years ago I noticed three azaleas growing in my side yard. They had been planted several years ago by the previous homeowner. They were growing too close together and were rather leggy, but the larger inner trunks were sturdy with sculpted shapes. I had been looking for some small specimen trees

for my front yard, and I thought these azaleas—with a little pruning—just might work.

I pruned some of the lower branches halfway up the plants, exposing the nice lines of each trunk. Then I took out some of the inside growth, removing any cross branching. This made the plants more open and airy. Because azaleas have shallow roots, they were simple to dig and relocate to the front yard.

I placed them in a location on top of a low stacked-stone wall. The spot was perfect as azaleas need a well-drained soil. They would receive good morning light, but large trees would shade them from the hot, western sun. They were in a location where they would be viewed

ABOVE: *Because this large George Lindley Taber azalea needed to be moved, I dug it up and set it in a large pot. After limbing it up, I underplanted with ivy, lettuce, and columbine for a colorful spring combination.*

BELOW: *This $6 azalea was purchased at a local nursery. It was selected because of its upright form. I removed the small suckers from the main branches and then thinned out some of the top growth to make it look more treelike.*

as you walked up to the house. I even put in small spotlights to illuminate them at night.

Most azaleas become a solid mass of color when in bloom, but tree-form azaleas have a layered look. Clusters of flowers appear on the end of graceful stems. Each plant has a distinct appearance. Even when not in bloom, they look right at home in the flower border or growing in a large container.

In locations across the South where the soil has too much lime, azaleas should be grown in pots. Growing the plants in pots is simple, as long as well-drained acid soil is used. They prefer a soil with a pH between 5.0 to 6.0 with lots of organic material. They need some shade and perform best under tall trees where they receive dappled sunlight.

An azalea/camellia fertilizer can be used immediately after plants bloom to keep them healthy and give them a boost during growing season. They should also be pruned quickly after they bloom. Any tender young suckers that appear around the trunk may be broken off with your fingers as needed to keep the trunk clean.

Azaleas are relatively easy to grow. They come in an assortment of colors and are available at a reasonable cost. You can buy a large established plant from a garden center and shape it into a tree yourself (see photos at right). Select plants that have an upright form and three to five nicely shaped main stems.

A common azalea doesn't have to look common. By removing a few lower limbs, you can turn this shrubby plant into a specimen. Try this trick this spring, and people will ask where you got that neat little tree with azalea-like blooms.

Charlie Thigpen

ABOVE: *Set into the existing slope, this nearly new waterfall appears much older, thanks to large, weathered stones and skillful planting.*

BEFORE

PHOTOGRAPHS: ALLEN ROKACH

Watery Solution

You can't live without water, but sometimes you're tempted to try. Just ask Darshan Mehta and Lynda Maddox of Rockville, Maryland. The old patio in back of their house directed water into the basement. And a gully at the base of the slope was always soggy with runoff. Fortunately, garden designer Wade Weaver had an idea—take something negative and make it positive.

The result? A beautiful new terrace and waterfall that fixes the drainage, adds privacy, provides a place to relax or entertain, and makes the neighbors wish they had a water problem too.

ABOVE: *Large rocks and river stones line an old gully, making it look like a natural streambed. A pipe carrying runoff from the terrace and downspouts empties out beneath the large rock at the bottom.*

It's hard to believe, but the waterfall in these photos is little more than a year old. Carefully chosen plants tucked into niches, as well as handpicked, weathered native stones, help it appear much older. "Wade's idea," Darshan explains, "was to use natural, earthy materials to make the waterfall look as if it had been there for years and the house had been built around it."

Though an adjacent stone retaining wall is reinforced and mortared, the waterfall isn't. Its heavy stones are simply wedged in place atop a flexible rubber liner that encloses the waterfall's sides and bottom. Not using mortar allows any leaks to be fixed without breaking the stones. Water collects in a pre-formed, fiberglass basin nestled among the rocks at the base of the falls. Then a hidden pump recirculates it to the spillway above.

Up top, Darshan and Lynda enjoy a larger, refurbished flagstone terrace, complete with a fishpond and bubble fountain. This pond has its own pump. Its water is kept separate from the waterfall. This makes it easier to keep the fish's water clean. A previous broken pump left an oil slick that killed the fish. So Lynda recommends using more expensive, oilless pumps in fishponds.

Heavy rain no longer ends up in the basement. Drains collect runoff and pipe it beneath the waterfall to the gully below, where it empties out beneath a large rock. Lining the gully with rocks and river stones gives the look of a natural streambed.

Wade continued the natural theme by choosing plants that flourish near ponds and streams, such as ferns, loosestrife, cattails, and iris. Lynda had wanted lots of flowers, but shade from large trees made that a challenge. "So we tried to find compromises to get more color— water lilies, plants with colorful leaves, and so on," she says.

The entire setup takes much less upkeep than you'd expect. The fish live off of bugs and algae and need very little attention. The waterfall runs year-round. Cleaning the pumps is the only consistent chore.

Darshan and Lynda give all the credit to Wade. Not only did he design the garden, but he also built and planted it. His insight took what was a nightmare and turned it into a dream. *Steve Bender*

A fishpond and bubble fountain in a corner of the terrace have their own water and pump. Evergreen shrubs and ornamental grasses screen the terrace from neighbors, while preserving a view of the nearby golf course.

MATERIALS

12" WIRE
HANGING BASKET

I-LB. BAG GREEN
SHEET MOSS

I FLAT IMPATIENS

POTTING SOIL

TIME-RELEASE
FERTILIZER
(I4-I4-I4)

This basket of white impatiens complements the trim color on the house for a cool summer accent.

Step 2: Fill the inside of the basket with soil up to the edge of the moss. Sprinkle a small scoop of timed-release fertilizer across the soil.

Step 3: Add moss up the sides of the basket for another 2 to 3 inches, working it around the stems of the impatiens. Repeat the planting process. Place plants 3 inches apart, staggering them between the ones on the lower layer. Add soil and fertilizer.

Step 4: Finish mossing the basket up to the top wire. Along the edges, place the impatiens on their sides with foliage and flowers facing out. On the inside of the top layer, stand the plants upright. Add potting soil and fertilizer to finish planting.

Hang the basket in a shady place before watering. It will become heavy when water is added, so a sturdy hook is essential. Gently trickle water into the basket to moisten. Add extra moss on the sides where water pushes through and makes a hole. Tuck moss between the wires from the outside to fix any leaky places on the sides. Water should run from the basket's bottom.

During summer months, the basket will require water every day, or at least every other. The pros know that constant watering quickly diminishes the supply of time-released fertilizer. So fertilize once a week with a liquid fertilizer such as 15-30-15 after the basket has been growing for about a month. This keeps the basket in constant bloom throughout the summer.

If you would like to hang your planting in the sun, impatiens are not practical. Use begonias instead. They will fill out nicely and grow into a rounded, flower-filled ball. Begonias are especially good if you would like identical baskets in sun and shade. Begonias will grow happily in either light situation. The basket in the shade will require less water than the one in sun. Be careful not to overwater. *Ellen Riley*

Hanging Around
With Annuals

W hen you're traveling on vacation, you have time to slow down a bit. You notice little things, such as hanging baskets dripping with color. These are the baskets for which resorts become famous. "How do they do that?" you wonder. Here are a few tricks of the trade to give you that luxuriant look you thought only professional nurserymen could create.

Step 1: Line the bottom and 2 to 3 inches up the sides of the wire basket with green sheet moss. Place the green side facing out. Gently push the roots of a small impatiens through the wire sides of the basket, so only the stem and leaves are outside the basket. Repeat with additional plants in a ring around the base of the basket. Place the plants about 3 inches apart.

Prickly Pear

Spineless prickly pear is a natural for Texas gardens. Among its attributes are bold texture, bright yellow summer flowers, and fall-ripening purple fruit.

Its ability to thrive in very hot and dry conditions makes it a logical choice for containers and low-water-use landscapes. The more common spiny forms of prickly pear may be useful where traffic control is desired, but spineless types are much more garden friendly. Although mostly void of long spines, even spineless types usually have clusters of short hairlike barbs that can be sufficiently irritating to suggest handling with gloves.

Few other plants provide the bold textural contrast for borders or container groupings. Companion plants with similar water requirements include yuccas, agave, skullcaps, autumn sage *(Salvia greggii)*, sedums, ceniza, and red yucca *(Hesperaloe parviflora)*. Some of the native grasses such as Lindheimer's muhly and Gulf muhly are also visually pleasing and culturally compatible.

Various types of prickly pear are cold hardy, but the most attractive ones come from Texas and Mexico. During times of drought, native stands of prickly pear on Texas ranches were sometimes used as cattle feed. Flamethrowers burned off the spines, and the pads were then quickly consumed by hungry cattle. Humans also find young tender pads to be edible, with a flavor similar to green beans.

Although new plants may be started from seed, by far the easiest and surest method is to take cuttings. First choose a sunny area with well-drained soil. Then cut an entire pad and cover it about halfway with soil. Roots will soon sprout, and flowering usually occurs the second year. If even this simple method

Bright yellow summer flowers are followed by purple fruit.

sounds too complicated, take the advice of Jerry Parsons, Extension horticulturist in San Antonio, who suggests, "Break off a leaf, then throw it like a Frisbee into your garden, and where it lands it will grow."

Cold hardiness varies among the types, but unprotected plants are common throughout the Lower South. Gardeners in colder areas may wish to plant them in containers where they may be protected during spells of extreme cold. *Bill Welch*

PHOTOGRAPHS: VAN CHAPLIN

Spineless prickly pear combines beautifully with other low-water-use plants such as agave, sedum, ceniza, sotol, and pink skullcap, providing bold texture and seasonal color.

Once threatened with
disaster, Liz Tedder's
garden weathered a
storm to become a treat
that is long remembered.

Unforgettable

BY STEVE BENDER
PHOTOGRAPHY VAN CHAPLIN

Certain images stick in your mind like gum to your shoe. I'll never forget the first time I laid eyes on Liz Tedder's garden.

Jane Bath, a friend and garden designer in Stone Mountain, Georgia, had told me of a new garden near Newnan, about 40 minutes southwest of Atlanta, that I just had to see. So I called Liz that spring and drove out for a visit. As I pulled up to the house, I feared my call had been a harbinger of doom. A huge tree lay sprawled across the garden, crushing peonies and irises beneath its limbs and splintering a section of fence.

Liz walked across the grass, calmly stopping now and again to tidy the destruction. "A tornado hit last night," she said matter-of-factly. "Fortunately, it didn't damage the house. Oh well, I'd been meaning to take that tree down anyway. I guess God did it for me."

As Liz calmly surveyed God's handiwork, I carefully surveyed her borders. She had the prettiest tornado-ravaged garden I'd ever seen.

In the decade since, the garden has blossomed like a debutante, growing lovelier with each passing year. Every time I visit, I can't wait to stroll the length of its borders, admire their composition, identify heirlooms that I'd like starts of, and marvel how a single peony plant in bloom can make you forget the rest of the world. But to truly appreciate the scope of Liz's accomplishment requires some elevation. Looking out from a third-floor window between twin brick chimneys reveals the essence of her creation.

Formal mixed borders of perennials, shrubs, and seasonal annuals extend 100 feet from a terrace on the house's south side. Between them, a rectangular fescue lawn, chosen for its green winter color and acceptance of sun or shade, serves as a stage.

> "Fortunately, it didn't damage the house. Oh well, I'd been meaning to take that tree down anyway. I guess God did it for me."

Like a doorman waiting to greet you, pink wood sorrel pokes its head through the gate, while a red climbing rose clambers along the fence.

Planted in groups of three, Liz's peonies came by mail as an unnamed assortment of three different colors. This double pink one is probably Sarah Bernhardt.

Flanking the borders, white picket fences and rows of Yoshino cherries direct the eye to a dramatic focal point—a hexagonal gazebo directly in line with that same third-floor window (see photo on page 94). It's a perspective that only friends, family, and birds get to see.

Liz credits an elderly friend named Agnes Newton with the idea. At Agnes's house, the formal rooms had a formal garden planted outside their windows for the purpose of capturing the beautiful view. Agnes has since passed away, but her spirit lives on in Liz's design. It survives, too, in the iris, naked ladies, and other heirloom perennials she happily shared with Liz.

Except on winter's coldest days, this garden blooms. Highlights include blossoming cherries, flowering almonds, pansies, tulips, daffodils, candytuft, money plant, irises, peonies, and roses in spring; daylilies, salvias, phlox, coneflowers, roses, balloon flower, veronica, and obedient plant in summer; salvias and asters in fall; and pansies during the winter. Reseeding annuals, such as sweet

One advantage of such sumptuous borders is plentiful cut flowers.

rocket *(Hesperis matronalis)* and love-in-a-mist *(Nigella damascena),* fill gaps between plants and carry on the show long after the supernova of peonies, irises, and other brief bloomers burns itself out.

Great gardens spring from good soil. Yet the clay soil Liz started out with was redder than the face of a swimmer who's lost his trunks. By constantly working in copious amounts of organic matter, such as leaves, bark, and wood ashes, together with topsoil, she gradually improved it. She never has used fertilizers. Instead, twice a year, she top-dresses the beds with several inches of chopped leaves. "The leaves don't last long," she notes. "The earthworms take 'em."

Healthy perennials eventually become crowded and stop blooming. So every four to five years, Liz reworks her borders. "I just lay a tarp on the grass and take out everything but the peonies and roses," she says. She divides the plants that need it, replants everything, and then sells the divisions to pay for someone to help her with periodic maintenance. Some of Liz's helpers take their pay in plants.

Liz says she needs to redo her borders again this year. But she's holding off because she's on the Newnan Home and Garden Tour this spring and doesn't want folks to be disappointed. For tickets and information on the Newnan-Coweta Historical Society Home and Garden Tour (April 24), contact the Male Academy Museum at (770) 251-0207. I guarantee you'll tour a garden you won't soon forget.

LESSONS FROM LIZ
Sage advice to beginning gardeners from a master

■ Don't let red clay scare you. You can turn it into pretty good soil by adding organic matter.

■ Go with the flow. If you have wet soil, it's a lot cheaper to choose plants that like it than regrade the area to improve drainage.

■ For the most color, concentrate on perennials that bloom a long time, such as salvias.

■ Choose a size area you can easily maintain; then buy a few choice plants and see how they do. Get a feel for how much time it takes to maintain; then you can decide what size garden works for you.

■ If funds are limited, ask gardening friends for starts, and patiently wait for yours to multiply.

■ The way to have a successful garden without a lot of effort or money is to let the soil dictate what you grow.

■ You can't spend your money any better than on pansies. We get to enjoy them from October to May. ◇

FAR LEFT: *This lavender-pink sweet rocket reseeds year after year, and combines nicely with Pink Meidiland roses, pansies, and other plants.*

LEFT: *Liz designed her garden to be enjoyed from both indoors and out. A bird's-eye view from a third-floor window is of a formal lawn and flower borders with a gazebo as the focal point.*

ABOVE: *The reverse view from the gazebo demonstrates Liz's eye for rhythm and scale. The gazebo and fences echo the color of the house, while the brick landing and edging repeat the color of the chimneys.*

peonies and iris (See pages 116–121.)

May

Checklist for May

EDITORS' NOTEBOOK

Every plant-lover knows the feeling. You order a rare flower from Tibet, coax it into bloom for the first time, invite your garden club to admire it, then discover some pest has turned it into goop that resembles strained bananas. Two questions immediately pop to mind: "What fiend did this?" and "How do I get even?"

The *Southern Living Garden Problem Solver* has the answers. A companion to *The Southern Living Garden Book,* it describes more than 300 of the worst pests in the South, including insects, mites, fungi, bacteria, viruses, weeds, and folks who routinely go nuts with pruners.

I planned the book with both novice and expert gardeners in mind. For example, say you're a beginner who's noticed azaleas turning yellow and wonder what's wrong. Turn to Chapter 4, "Solving Plant Problems." There you'll find in alphabetical order more than 140 of the South's most popular trees, shrubs, flowers, vegetables, fruits, and vines; color illustrations of their most common problems; and practical solutions.

The cost of this 336-page book is just $29.95 hardback and $24.95 paperback. Look for it in bookstores, or call 1-800-884-3935 to order. *Steve Bender*

◀ **Containers**—For flowers that last a long time in pots, try pentas, blue daze evolvulus, fan flower, Tapien verbena, coleus, and begonias. Pair them with trailing Swedish ivy or English ivy and upright pennisetum or other ornamental grass for a composition that will last from spring through fall.

☐ **Summer color**—For shaded areas choose caladiums, coleus, impatiens, or begonias. Start caladiums from bulbs or plants. If planting bulbs, select large ones at least 2 inches across. For a mass effect, set the bulbs about 12 inches apart and 1 inch deep. ▶

PLANT

☐ **Annuals**—Prepare beds by working in plenty of organic material such as compost, composted manure, or soil conditioner. Also add timed-release fertilizer such as 10-15-10 or one that will encourage flowering, such as 11-40-6. Apply an insulating mulch over the bed, and then set transplants at the appropriate depth and spacing through the mulch.

◀ **Chrysanthemums**—Even the smallest rooted cuttings of garden mums set out now will make picturesque mounds of color in the fall. Although you can buy them budded in late summer, they look more natural when they grow into their place.

☐ **Fall bloomers**—In the Middle, Lower, and Coastal South, these are best set out now for maximum display in four to five months. Space plants 12 to 15 inches apart. Good choices for a long season of fall blooms include mums, Mexican bush sage (*Salvia leucantha*), Mexican mint marigold (*Tagetes lucida*), white rain lily (*Zephyranthes candida*), and aromatic aster (*Aster oblongifolius*).

☐ **Grass**—In the Lower and Coastal South, choose from St. Augustine, centipede, buffalo, Bermuda, Bahia, or Zoysia. Common Bermuda may be started from seed, but the hybirds are best planted as sprigs or sod. St. Augustine grass is the most shade tolerant, and centipede does well in acid soils. Buffalo grass is a Texas native and does well at drier sites.

☐ **Herbs**—Soon last year's parsley will be transformed from a beautiful mound of green to a tall, leggy mess when the weather gets warm. Pull it out and replace it with new transplants or sow seeds in the garden. These plants should last until next spring.

☐ **Vegetables**—Pull out lettuce, mustard, broccoli, and spinach when they start to bolt (flower). Replace them with a variety of summer vegetables such as squash, tomatoes, pepper, Malabar spinach, and beans. Select a sunny site, and till the soil to a depth of 8 to 10 inches. Plant in rows about 3 feet apart. ▶

PRUNE

☐ **Annuals**—Groom summer annuals to keep them shapely and in bloom. Petunias, marigolds, verbena, melampodium, and cosmos can be cut back by about one-third their height if they get leggy. After trimming, fertilize with a liquid food. ▶

☐ **Spring shrubs**—Cut back overgrown spring-flowering shrubs as soon as the blooms have faded. These include azaleas, weigela, quince, and forsythia. Remember to remove entire limbs to reduce the size of the plant without destroying its natural habitat.

CONTROL

☐ **Junipers**—Now is the time to stop mites that feed under and between the needles. Infested branches turn pale green at first. Later they dry up and turn brown as the mites increase. To control, spray the plants with insecticidal soap or SunSpray oil at the first sign of infestation. Continue spraying every week until the pests are gone.

☐ **Lawns**—Fight broadleaf weeds this month by applying a weed control such as 2, 4-D or a weed-and-feed fertilizer before day temperatures reach 85 degrees. Always read the label carefully to be certain the product will not harm your type of grass.

◀ **Rose diseases**—Black spot, powdery mildew, and rust are plagues for those who want vases of perfect long-stemmed roses. If you want to grow hybrid teas for arrangements, you will have to spray them regularly with Funginex (triforine) every 7 to 10 days. For garden roses, look for disease-resistant and disease-tolerant selections that will minimize your need to spray.

FERTILIZE

☐ **Bulbs**—Fertilize amaryllis, crinum, Easter lilies, and other bulbs now to help them produce big blooms for next year. Apply a product especially formulated for bulbs, such as Holland Bulb Booster (9-9-6), at the rate recommended on the label. Remove foliage if it yellows, but never cut off leaves while they are still green.

☐ **Turf grass**—An ideal time to fertilize warm season grasses is after the second or third mowing in spring. Fertilizer with an analysis of about 16-4-8 applied at the rate of 1 to 2 pounds of actual nitrogen per 1,000 square feet of lawn (about 6 to 12 pounds of fertilizer) usually works well, but it is always best to have a soil test done before application. Slow-release fertilizers such as sulfur-coated urea, resin-coated urea, or natural organics such as manure and sewage sludge are less likely to burn.

May notes:

TIP OF THE MONTH

To keep insects off of my tomato plants, I place a dog's flea collar loosely around the base of each plant. (Make sure the collar contains an insecticide, such as permethrin, rather than just a flea growth regulator, such as Vigren.) Last year I found only two insects, which were easy to pick off, at the top of a 6-foot vine. And there are no more cutworms!

ANNE THOMAS
LEEDS, ALABAMA

Remedies *for* Rhodies

BY STEVE BENDER / PHOTOGRAPHY VAN CHAPLIN

Roseum Elegans

Catawbiense Album

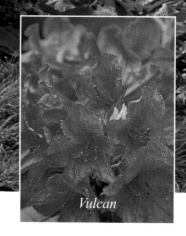

Vulcan

The high, dappled shade of tall tulip poplars provides the perfect light for Scintillation rhododendrons at the Mount Cuba Center in Greenville, Delaware.

Scintillation

If you've ever tried growing rhododendrons in the South, you know the procedure consists of five easy steps.

Buy your rhododendron.
Plant your rhododendron.
Cry over your dead rhododendron.
Throw away your rhododendron.
Surrender. Plant a holly instead.

Why do rhododendrons give us fits? Because they're suited to the more temperate regions of the world, where folks seldom fry catfish on their foreheads in July. Rhodies prefer cool summer nights, regular rainfall, and practically perfect drainage.

That doesn't sound like my garden—and probably not yours either. But don't give up. You can still enjoy beautiful rhododendrons by heeding the following instructions.

Choose the right one. Nurseries sell hundreds of different selections, but relatively few grow well in the South. Stick to the tried-and-true ones (see the chart on page 106). These combine cold hardiness, heat tolerance, and disease resistance.

Buy Southern. Many rhododendrons sold at garden centers come from the Pacific Northwest. Because the heavy soil they're shipped in doesn't allow enough oxygen to reach the roots in the South's more stressful climate, the plants sometimes get diseases and die. One way to prevent disease is to plant rhododendrons correctly (see page 106). But you should also favor plants grown in the South and East over those grown in the West. If you're unsure where rhododendrons in your garden center came from, check the tag or ask the nurseryman. As an alternative, order plants.

Find the right spot. Although some rhodies tolerate full sun, most do best in light, dappled shade. But don't try to plant them beneath maples, beeches, willows, or magnolias

Roseum Elegans lives where other rhododendrons die. These 12-year-old plants decorate the Atlanta garden of Jack and Russell Huber.

because these shallow-rooted trees steal moisture and nutrients. And don't plant them beneath a black walnut, as the roots of this tree release a chemical that is toxic to rhodies. These shrubs will grow much better beneath oaks, pines, tulip poplars, and hickories.

Avoid western exposures. Planting on the western side subjects plants to hot, drying summer sun and cold, drying winter wind. Plant on the north side of your garden instead.

Keep in mind that, with the exception of the Bonneville Salt Flats, the worst spot for a rhododendron may be up against your house. The soil there often reeks of clay and lime and alternates between desert and swamp. Also, snow and ice falling from your roof will snap the shrub's brittle branches. Better locations include shrub borders and the edge of a woodland.

Plant rhododendrons correctly. They need a loose, acidic (pH 4.5 to 5.5), fertile soil containing lots of organic matter. Forget about planting in heavy, red clay.

Jeff Beasley, owner of Transplant Nursery in Lavonia, Georgia, suggests the following regimen for planting a rhododendron: Dig a hole at least 10 inches deep and twice as wide as the root ball. Mix equal amounts of excavated soil and plain pine bark (make sure the bark does not contain lime). Fill the hole with this mixture; do not tamp it when finished. Place the rhododendron atop the filled hole. Then mix one part excavated soil to three parts bark, and mound soil around the sides of the root ball, leaving the top of the ball exposed. Cover the ball with 1 or 2 inches of pine straw.

Go easy on the fertilizer. If the leaves become chlorotic (yellow between the veins), use a product such as Miracid that supplies chelated iron. Otherwise, just sprinkle a half cup of cottonseed meal or 1 tablespoon azalea-camellia food around the dripline of the plant in spring.

"Always water thoroughly," cautions Willis Harden a rhododendron expert in Commerce, Georgia. "Rhododendrons don't respond well to light, daily watering. They need a deep soaking of 1 to 2 inches per week. Water them in the morning, never at night. The leaves need to dry prior to evening or they'll get fungal diseases."

Anna Rose Whitney

That's it—all you need to know to successfully grow a rhododendron. Of course, that leaves you with a new problem. Now where are you going to plant that holly? ◇

(For sources turn to pages 250–251.)

RHODODENDRONS FOR THE SOUTH

NAME	FLOWER COLOR	HEIGHT AFTER 10 YEARS	COMMENTS
A. Bedford	lavender with purple blotch	6'	sun tolerant, handsome leaves
Anah Kruschke	rich purple	5'	glossy foliage, sun tolerant
Anna Rose Whitney	deep rose-pink	8'	fast grower, trouble free
Bibiani	bright bloodred	6'	glossy, deep green leaves; very heat tolerant
Caroline	light pink	6'	fragrant, disease resistant, very heat tolerant
Catawbiense Album	white with chartreuse blotch	6'	vigorous, adaptable, tough
Cynthia	rose-crimson	5'	sun tolerant, extremely durable
Dora Amateis	white with green spots	3'	fragrant flowers; compact; small, shiny leaves
Mrs. Tom H. Lowinsky	white with orange-brown blotch	5'	orchidlike blooms; glossy, dark green leaves
Roseum Elegans	lavender pink	6'	fast grower, dependable, real survivor
Scintillation	light pink with light brown blotch	5'	extremely handsome foliage
Trude Webster	pink	5'	huge flower trusses, easy to grow
Van Ness Sensation	orchid-pink with yellow center	5'	fragrant flowers, heat tolerant
Vulcan	brick red	5'	most popular red for the South

PHOTOGRAPHS: JEAN ALLSOPP / STYLING: HARRIET ADAMS

Just the sight of the screened garden house in the distance is an invitation to wander down the garden path.

Nothing but a Porch

The appeal of a screened porch needs little explanation in the South—the cool evening breeze, the serenade of cicadas, the respite from mosquitoes and their ilk. So imagine taking a porch into the garden where the breeze blows unimpaired by house walls, and tree branches shade the sun. That's exactly what this Tuscaloosa, Alabama, family did; now they have a garden house with the pleasure of a porch all around them.

The spot was a natural. It was at the bend in a path, midway between the house and a creek, a walk just long enough to need a spot to rest. The idea was to have a platform with a place to sit. One thing led to another, and now their little way station has become a destination.

"They really use it a lot," says Harriet Adams of The Potager in Northport, Alabama. She helped put the finishing touches on the house, which is furnished for comfort and decorated with a gardener's favorite things. The little house functions as a casual parlor as well as an intimate retreat.

It's a great place for a simple meal or a cup of coffee. The owner is an artist, and she frequently takes her small easel and paints inside the little shelter.

But beyond the pleasant lifestyle changes it has brought, the house has had a lasting impact on the family's life. What began as a father-and-son building project has culminated in the son's choice of architecture for a college degree and design as his life's work. And this has all come about because his family gardens. In so many ways, gardening can change your life. *Linda C. Askey*

(To order plans, turn to pages 250–251.)

Furnished with a gardener's favorite things, the house provides a respite for reading, painting, or an occasional outdoor meal.

Tangerine Beauty

Stretching for the light, wild crossvine scampers up tall tree trunks. There it blooms with trumpets of red and yellow. Only the hummingbirds can see its blossoms until they fall. That's when we notice them, curious red-and-yellow flowers scattered on the ground.

But this Southern wildflower now comes to us a graduate of North Carolina State University, where several years ago the late J. C. Raulston recognized the potential of this color variant and called it Tangerine Beauty. This year the Raulston Arboretum at NCSU has named it a Raulston Selection, one of a few chosen over the years for their unrealized potential as outstanding garden plants.

Unlike many plants that are the work of university breeders, Tangerine Beauty crossvine was found and given to Dr. Raulston by Texas horticulturist Scott Ogden. "It's a Texas garden heirloom that's been lurking around for a while," Scott explains.

Although fast growing, crossvine *(Bignonia capreolata)* is not a vine to fear. On the contrary, its spring show of orange-red flowers creates a remarkable display. The wild form grows 30 to 50 feet tall, but Tangerine Beauty is easily kept in hand by occasional training and pruning. It is ideal for arbors and trellises, and the evergreen foliage gives it a presence even in winter when the normally green leaves turn reddish purple.

It can be distinguished from other crossvine selections by more than its flower colors. Scott says, "It has no preference or need for the moist, acid soils desired by most crossvines. In fact, the original plants came from gardens with rather dry, alkaline soils." So Tangerine Beauty will grow well in either soil type.

Tangerine Beauty has so many positive traits that Scott says, "In the narrow category of evergreen climbers that bloom, are self-supporting, and won't damage masonry, it's a standout. In fact, it's in a class all by itself." *Linda C. Askey*

(For sources turn to pages 250–251.)

Bright Tangerine Beauty crossvine is a good choice for arbors, trellises, and even the footing of a deck.

PHOTOGRAPHS: LINDA C. ASKEY

TANGERINE BEAUTY CROSSVINE
At a Glance

Light: blooms best in full sun, will take partial shade

Soil: moist, well drained

Growth rate: fast

Hardiness: all but Tropical South

Flowers: reddish orange in spring, repeating several times

Pests: none serious

Expect to pay: $15 to $27

Fun fact: named for the pattern visible in a cut stem

Other selections: Atrosanguinea, Dragon Lady

Variegated Solomon's seal is easy to love. Soft, showy, and hardy, it gives so much more than it gets.

Although they can go unnoticed, charming little white flowers hang gracefully down from the burgundy stem.

Shade Essential

Ask a gardener what to grow in the shade, and the list will begin with hostas or impatiens and continue through ferns, ajuga, and such. Solomon's seal may not make the top 10, but put it in a garden, and then ask the same gardener what plants he or she admires the most. Variegated Solomon's seal is sure to make the top five, if not number one or two.

That's because it is lovely in composition, brightening the abundance of green in a shaded garden. The creamy white edges of the leaves underscore its texture and the graceful sweep of its stalks. Its red stems are subtle but effective.

Each unbranched stalk bears leaves in a flat plane, like a fern. And like a newly unfurled frond, it bows as if it's so fresh and new it can't stand up straight. This lovely habit allows you to see the foliage well and also strategically places the foliage parallel to the ground where it will catch what little light filters into the shaded garden.

Plant Solomon's seal in rich, organic soil that is moist but well drained. The aboveground stalks never branch, but they multiply from year to year by the spreading rhizome below ground. If you want to divide your plant and spread it around the garden, dig it up and divide this rhizome that grows horizontally. Be certain each division has at least one bud. *Linda C. Askey*

(For sources turn to pages 250–251.)

SOLOMON'S SEAL
At a Glance

Light: full to partial shade
Soil: organic, moist, well drained
Pests: voles
Uses: combine with ferns and hostas
Expect to pay: $6 to $12

PHOTOGRAPHS: VAN CHAPLIN / OWNER: SHARON ABROMS-MCHALE, ATLANTA

A Reawakened Rose

NEW DAWN
At a Glance

Size: 15 to 20 feet
Light: full to partial sun
Soil: tolerates a wide range of growing conditions
Growth rate: vigorous, lots of thorns
Pests: none serious
Range: Upper to Coastal South

Fragrant flowers that are the delicate pale pink hue of clouds blushed by the early morning light on a plant you couldn't kill with a highway department roadside mower—that's a combination that makes a good garden rose. And the modern climber New Dawn has been one of the best ever since its introduction in 1930.

An exquisitely beautiful rose, New Dawn climbed the plant popularity charts as the everblooming offshoot of the existing favorite Dr W VanFleet. The original rose had an outrageous spring display, then shut down while its off-spring produced the same lovely flowers throughout the growing season.

New Dawn received the first plant patent ever granted, and this bit of historical trivia secured the rose a place in the horticultural record books, but its performance as a climbing rose secured its place in the hearts of gardeners. Because both New Dawn and Dr W Van-Fleet are still grown and can sometimes be confused, it's a good idea to buy from a reliable nursery or purchase the blooming rose in the fall to ensure that the desired variety is chosen.

A full-size climber, New Dawn throws out long canes that can eventually reach 15 to 20 feet in any direction. The dark green, semiglossy foliage is rarely troubled by pests or diseases. The prickles are healthy too. But scratches aside, New Dawn is an easy rose to train if you start with a young plant. The flexible canes can be arranged in attractive patterns before they stiffen with maturity.

As with any climbing rose, training the canes to the side (or letting their own weight arch them over) helps produce greater quantities of bloom, with flowers at every leaf axil. And climbing roses never need to be pruned back, just cleaned of dead canes and unattractive branches. If you decide to plant New Dawn in a natural area where it will mound over meadow fences or clamber into the trees, you don't have to do any grooming at all.

If New Dawn has a flaw, it's the tendency of the pale pink flowers to fade white under strong summer sun. Otherwise, this fragrant, vigorous rose tolerates most soils, blooms often, requires little feeding or watering once established, propagates easily from cuttings, and is at home from Upper to Coastal South. *Liz Druitt*

The Volunteer Garden

Sometimes we can't help having a garden. Many flowering plants drop their seeds willy-nilly and come up whether they are welcome or not. Those that are not welcome are called weeds. The rest are volunteers, blessings to be managed wisely.

Managing these reseeders doesn't have to be labor-intensive or time-consuming. You just need to know what to expect, and then intervene at the right time to get the effect you want.

The annual spider flower is a good example. All you have to do is toss a package of seeds onto a prepared bed in spring, and you will have flowering plants the same summer, and every summer thereafter.

But if all seedlings were left to grow to maturity, they would compete and fail to make a good showing. They need to be thinned. A hand weeder or a long-handled scuffle hoe is ideal for cutting through the hundreds of seedlings that may appear per square foot. Leave one

Spider flower is one of the most unsung annuals. All you need is sun, soil, and seeds.

or two of the strongest to develop and supply next year's garden. Transplant any that you want to spread to a new location.

You can also take preventive measures such as mulching. Mulch will keep down spider flowers as well as weeds. A layer of sun-blocking pine needles, bark, or other organic material applied in fall will do the job.

Reseeding is not a characteristic of annuals alone. Many perennials reseed, and for a gardener who longs for borders thick with flowers, these are an affordable choice.

Purple coneflowers are tough, heat-tolerant, and long-lasting. And in addition to being perennial, they multiply. Babies pop up at the base of the mother plant, giving you plenty of opportunities to transplant and share.

Refer to the list at right for more choices. Instead of coddling each flower that blooms, plant a few that you have to beat back with a stick. *Linda C. Askey*

A Southern favorite, purple coneflower blooms during the hottest part of summer. Many seeds drop to the ground and sprout, in spite of migrating birds that enjoy them.

RESEEDING PERENNIALS
blue phlox
(Phlox divaricata)

brown-eyed Susan
(Rudbeckia triloba)

columbine
(Aquilegia sp.*)*

four o'clock
(Mirabilis jalapa)

Lenten rose
(Helleborus orientalis)

purple coneflower
(Echinacea purpurea)

Shasta daisy
(Chrysanthemum x *superbum)*

RESEEDING ANNUALS
cosmos
(Cosmos sulphureus and *C. bipinnatus)*

impatiens
(Impatiens wallerana)

melampodium
(Melampodium paludosum)

petunia
(Petunia x *hybrida)*

spider flower
(Cleome hasslerana)

sunflower
(Helianthus annuus)

tithonia
(Tithonia rotundifolia)

Brown-eyed Susan is a prolific reseeder and a midsummer showstopper.

Timeless Tomatoes

Try your hand at growing a tasty part of history.

A harvest of heirloom tomatoes is a picture of diversity. Their flavor is as extraordinary as their appearance.

Talk to Chip Hope for just a minute and you'll probably end up talking tomatoes. "In the South, everybody just loves tomatoes," Chip says. An instructor at Blue Ridge Community College in Flat Rock, North Carolina, Chip has been growing tomatoes for as long as he can remember. His fascination with heirloom selections has blossomed over the past few years.

"Growing heirloom tomatoes makes sense for so many reasons," he says.

"We're preserving part of our heritage and history. But even more importantly, we're preserving our genetic plant base. Hybrid tomatoes may be pretty, but without heirlooms, the genetics will vanish."

An heirloom tomato is an open-pollinated selection that has been around for at least 50 years. (See "Tomato Terms" on page 113.) Many selections can be purchased through seed catalogs. The catalogs make the old-timey seeds readily available, and the fruit's existence

ZAPOTEC PLEATED

BLACK PRINCE

PRINCIPE BORGHESE

is preserved. "There's also a subsection I call family heirlooms," Chip says. "These have been passed down from generation to generation."

Sharing heirloom seeds is part of the fun. They can be collected from the tomatoes, and the fruit will be the same from year to year. "It's the idea of a sustainable garden," says Chip. "When it comes to sharing, seeds are rarely given without a story. It's just part of gardening with heirlooms."

ODD SHAPES, GREAT TASTE

One of the most appealing things about these tomatoes is their diversity, and fortunately many are now available through mail-order seed catalogs. "Heirlooms are so varied in size, color, and shape. They really are beautiful," Chip says. "But more than appearance, their flavors are unmatched. They're a feast for the eyes and the palate when you serve them."

In taste tests he conducts at the college every summer, Brandywine is a consistent winner. When asked about his own personal preference, Chip replies, "That's like asking a father which child is his favorite. Every year, no every week, I have a favorite in the garden. But it's hard to beat Brandywine. It always has been one of the best for flavor."

Chip finds that many people share the same goal in growing heirlooms. "The bottom line is, we do it for the tomato sandwiches," he confesses. "I love Radiator Charlie's Mortgage Lifter. It is so tasty and huge, one slice covers a piece of bread."

Other favorites demonstrate the range available with heirlooms. Thai Pink was a huge success last summer. With small,

Some heirloom tomatoes are perfect for slicing, others for drying or canning.

plum-shaped fruit that glows iridescent pink, this tomato never quit through the long, hot summer. "It was constantly loaded with tomatoes. The fruit never cracked, and the plants were totally disease resistant. When all the other plants were gone, it was still cranking out tomatoes," Chip says. "They were tasty as can be in a salad."

Principe Borghese is a favorite for drying. "It is *the* Italian drying tomato. There's no better in the world. We dried them in the dehydrator, sliced in half. They're okay fresh, but this way they are magnificent. Our family enjoyed them all winter long," Chip says.

Experiment to find the perfect fruit for your taste and use. When you find it, be sure to save a few seeds at the end of the summer. If you come upon a really special one, send some seeds to Chip. He'll be waiting for your story. "Do I love growing heirlooms? You bet—I'm hooked on it," Chip says. *Ellen Riley*

(For sources turn to pages 250–251.)

TOMATO TERMS

Tomatoes fall into two very broad groups— open-pollinated and hybrid. Jeff McCormack, with Southern Exposure Seed Exchange, explains the difference in simple terms. **Open-pollinated** tomatoes produce seeds that will grow into the same variety next year. You will get exactly what you started with from year to year. **Hybrid** tomatoes have been developed to include very specific characteristics from two different parent plants. "If you save seed from a hybrid tomato, the next year you will have a different fruit. It will revert back to one of its parents, or a different combination of characteristics from the original."

BIG RAINBOW

PEACEVINE CHERRY

YELLOW PERFECTION

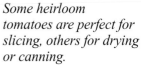

PHOTOGRAPHS: VAN CHAPLIN

Blue Moon's Sharon Lee Smith and Mary Wilhite cultivate a relaxed family atmosphere near Tyler, Texas.

Flowers and a Smile

How do independent garden centers compete with the big boys? It comes down to variety, service, and the personal touch.

Quality plants and highly trained staff are key at Tallahassee Nurseries in Florida, says owner Gene Ellis (in red shirt).

They're the places your dad took you to buy the magnolia that blooms right outside your window. They're the places that introduced you to more azaleas, roses, and bulbs than you ever dreamed existed. They're where your mom went to have someone identify that nasty caterpillar devouring her petunias. They're the South's independent garden centers. The good news is, they still thrive today.

How do these mom-and-pop operations compete with national chains, million-dollar advertising budgets, and low prices? By supplying the things that the big chains can't. For a great example, drive 15 miles west of Tyler, Texas, and visit Blue Moon Gardens near Chandler.

You can almost hear the sun rise in the piney hushed woods where Sharon Lee Smith and Mary Wilhite set up shop in 1984. At first, they specialized in potted herbs. But in 1992, they bought the 85-year-old farmhouse next door and opened a retail garden center. Replete with herbs, vines, perennials, heirloom roses, and Texas native plants, it features an intimate and quirky display garden that feels like your aunt's front yard.

The relaxed atmosphere draws customers from afar. "You have to go out of your way to get to us," admits Mary. "A lot of folks drive here from Dallas or Shreveport just for the country experience. They'll hang around, bring picnic lunches, and walk through the garden. Our display beds are also trial gardens—they show the way plants actually perform."

Birdhouses, pottery, wind chimes, and ornamental iron handmade by Texas artisans decorate the plantings. "We always buy locally if we can," she says. "That way, Sharon and I know the artists and can tell customers stories about them."

In northern Florida, Tallahassee Nurseries has been helping gardeners achieve success since 1938. Gene Ellis, a current owner, took over from his mother and dad in 1964. Over the past quarter-century, his business has grown with the rest of the booming Sunbelt. "We used to be out in the country, and now we're not," he notes. "This whole town just grew up around us."

Key to the nursery's success, he feels, is an unchanging focus on quality plants. "Big chains do a good job with fertilizers and chemicals," he explains. "But what saves us is that we deal in plants that are regional. What grows in Seattle won't grow in Tallahassee."

Are Southern gardeners becoming more sophisticated? "Definitely!" Gene replies. "Thirty years ago, we'd have thousands of redtips, azaleas, and shore junipers on display. Now, the most of anything we'll display may be 20 to 25, but we'll display hundreds of different plants." Answering questions and keeping up with the newest plants demand a staff of trained horticulturists, many of whom have been with Gene more than a decade. "Everybody who works here knows and loves plants," he says.

In Griffin, Georgia, paying a call on

Lynne, Jim, and Rebecca Mock started out with one greenhouse in 1983. Today, The Greenery in Griffin, Georgia, has legions of loyal customers.

An Angel but a Dragon Too

The Greenery seems like dropping in on "The Yard of the Month." Trees, shrubs, grass, and perennials embrace the wide-porched house that serves as a gift shop. A few yards away sits the brick home of Jim and Lynne Mock, who run the nursery with their daughter, Rebecca. They'll forgive you if you overlook the house in favor of the spectacular rose and perennial garden sitting in front of it. The garden is such a hit with customers that many get married there.

Things weren't quite so rosy when the Mocks started with a single plastic greenhouse in 1983. That first winter killed most of their plants. Yet the Mocks persevered. "When you love landscaping, as Jim and I do, you stick with it," explains Lynne. "Jim's motto is, 'As long as you don't quit, you'll never fail.'"

Today, loyal customers celebrate the Mocks' success. Many make the hour's trip south from Atlanta to peruse an outstanding selection of perennials, herbs, trees, shrubs, silk flowers, and garden furniture.

"We cater to our customers," Lynne says proudly. "They can bring in their empty planters and pots, and we'll plant them up and have them ready to go. We'll even make house calls." Being able to help customers choose the right plants and answer their questions is another plus. "We view it as a calling," she says. "If we have the knowledge, it's our duty to share it and help people be successful."

Folks in the central Mississippi town of Kosciusko love plants too. Natchez Trace Gardens has a lot to do with that. Its greenhouse range appears incongruous in a city of about 7,000, but the high quality and variety of homegrown perennials, hanging baskets, poinsettias, and other plants lure customers from as far away as Jackson and Memphis. Many cities 10 times as large don't have a garden center like this.

According to co-owners Mark Terkanian and Lori Hitchcock, growing most of the plants themselves is a big advantage. "If there's a new, hot plant that people want, we can grow it," says Lori. And they'll order plants they don't grow. "If someone's looking for a special tree, I'll order a dozen. When you offer that kind of service, word travels fast."

If there's one drawback to running your own garden center, it's that you're always on call. But owners like Lynne Mock take it in stride. "Sometimes I'm torn because I feel I'm not giving my family enough attention," she concedes. "But if you think about how many people you're making happy, it makes it all worth it." ◇

Steve Bender

(For sources turn to pages 250–251.)

Co-owners Mark Terkanian and Lori Hitchcock run Natchez Trace Gardens in Kosciusko, Mississippi.

Angel wing begonias commonly grace Southern interiors. But now they are moving outdoors. An exceptional angel wing type, known as Dragon Wing, is being introduced into the marketplace this year. I grew this tough, pest-free begonia last year, and it was outstanding.

In early May I planted rooted cuttings of Dragon Wing begonia, and they bloomed until the first hard freeze in the fall. Not only did these plants grow 18 to 24 inches tall, but they also produced a profusion of red flowers that lasted all season.

When planting angel wing–type begonias, be sure your soil is well drained and rich in organic matter. I used a slow-release fertilizer such as 10-15-10 at planting because the plants are rapid growers, and a good fertilization program is important. Keep the plants well watered and apply a liquid fertilizer such as 20-20-20 monthly until the weather cools in the fall. If the edges of the leaves turn reddish bronze, they are not receiving enough fertilizer.

With bright red flowers that grow in partial sun or high-filtered shade, Dragon Wing begonia is a welcome addition to the garden, just as other angel wings have long complemented Southern interiors. *John Floyd*

Close to Heaven

BY CHARLIE THIGPEN
PHOTOGRAPHY
JEAN ALLSOPP

*On a wooded hilltop in Arkansas,
Nancy Porter has gardened for 27 years,
creating a breathtaking garden that
surrounds her New England-style home.*

L ast spring I saw a little bit of New England in Arkansas. Right outside Little Rock, Nancy Gunn Porter built her dream home. The house is a 1730s-style New England saltbox with simple design and classic detailing around the front door. After the house was complete, it was time to create a garden to soften the wooden structure.

Nancy's showy garden connects the house to the land and is encircled by a tidy picket fence. But, the first hole she dug—some 27 years ago—made her wonder if she would need a jackhammer. There was only a thin layer of soil covering the rocky hillside. She had to remove all the rocks from the flowerbeds and replace them with loads of compost, working the soil to make it loose, fertile, and inviting to plants. Pine straw makes cushiony soft pathways leading to the front door and through the garden.

Nancy researched the first plants selected to make sure they were being grown in the 1730s. She tried to match the plants, including old roses, foxglove, larkspur, and hollyhock, with the colonial era. After a few years she found this too limiting so she began to try other plants.

With all the experimenting Nancy has learned what works for her, but each year the garden changes a little because there are always new plants to try. She has a great sense of design, but she also lets Mother Nature assist. Sprinkles of poppies come up here and there and reseed each year. Seedlings sprout wherever seeds fall, making the garden look loose and natural.

The garden has matured nicely over the quarter century. Roses climb and spill over fences and arbors. Peonies have formed thick clumps and produce pink golf

ABOVE: *Nancy tends to her flowers, while her husband, Duncan, finds the vegetable garden more to his liking. Their dog, Sidney, helps keep the squirrels out of both areas.*

NEAR LEFT: *Peek over the picket fence, and you immediately feel the need to walk into this flower-filled garden.*

FAR LEFT: *Poppies reseed each year. They pop up anywhere they please and are a welcome addition to the garden.*

ABOVE, TOP: *Heavenly Glow Louisiana iris sports radiant orange-red petals with green-and-yellow centers.*

ABOVE, BELOW: *Stately spikes of foxglove stand proud. These easy-to-grow, yet elegant, plants are one of Nancy's favorites.*

NEAR RIGHT: *These peonies and iris were dug from Nancy's mother's yard. They fill the garden with both flowers and memories.*

FAR RIGHT: *French hollyhocks stand out against the dark weathered wood.*

ball-size buds that unfurl and transform into bowl-size blooms. Nancy carefully stakes each clump with round metal plant supports to help hold the hefty flowers up during spring rains.

The peonies were dug from her mother's yard and are more than 50 years old. Siberian iris have colonized and their blue blooms are surrounded by masses of sword-like foliage. Dianthus and verbena grow close to the ground and make a floral carpet by the front door.

The spring garden is a welcome sight after a cold winter, but each season is special. In the summer, towering hollyhocks frame the front door. Butterflies flock to buddleia, white phlox, cosmos, and *Verbena bonariensis.* In the fall, sugar maples Nancy planted years ago rain golden leaves on the garden. Purple asters and Mexican bush sage supply late-season flowers. The winter garden isn't showy, but it allows you to see its framework. Winter is also a great time for Nancy to regroup and select new plants for the upcoming year. Fallen leaves are collected, ground up, and used to mulch the beds.

On top of this rocky ridge in Arkansas, a dream home was built and around it a dream garden was created. Not many people fulfill their dreams, but Nancy is living hers. This garden is very much a part of her—and part of her mother, for plants that her mother grew have been passed down and enhance the garden with beauty and memories. Nancy regrets that her mother isn't alive to see the garden. But I think she has seen it, because anything this beautiful is close to heaven. ◇

Nikko Blue mophead hydrangea (See pages 144–147.)

June

Checklist for June

EDITORS' NOTEBOOK

As much as I love gardening, I hate watering. In my view, standing for an hour at the end of a garden hose is only slightly more exciting than watching Old English sheepdog trials on TV. Which is why I question my sanity when I go to the store intent upon buying no plant thirstier than common asphalt and arrive home instead with water-guzzling gerberas. These tender perennials demand lots of sun, can't stand clay, scream for fertilizer, and throw a fit if they ever dry out. So why torture myself? Because their red, orange, pink, yellow, and white blossoms look too fantastic to be real. When cut, these beauties last nearly a week in water. So here I go again, watering and watering my gerberas. "Beauty and folly are old companions," said Benjamin Franklin. Don't I know it.

Steve Bender

☐ **Daylilies**—Plants are coming into full bloom, so now is the best time to buy new ones. Choose color, flower form, and size to best fit your garden. They prefer well-drained soil and four to six hours of direct sun or filtered shade from tall trees during most of the day. ▶

☐ **Houseplants**—Rejuvenate houseplants by moving them to a shady, protected area of the garden for several months. Sink the pots to prevent them from drying out and blowing over. Water as often as needed, and apply water-soluble fertilizer (20-20-20) monthly to encourage continued growth.

☐ **Lawns**—Arrange to have your lawn mowed while you are away on vacation. Allowing it to get too tall and then cutting it severely will open the lawn to drought and weeds. On the other hand, if the summer is dry in your area and your grass is not growing very fast, don't mow at all, or raise the blade on your mower slightly.

☐ **Mail order**—In the Coastal South, now is a good time to order flower and vegetable seeds for the fall garden. If you plan to start your own transplants, allow four to six weeks for the plants to grow 2 to 4 inches tall; then set them in the ground in September.

☐ **Mulch**—Apply several inches of mulch to planting areas and at the base of newly planted trees to conserve moisture and reduce heat stress. Mulching between the rows in vegetable gardens helps control weeds while keeping the soil moist and cool.

☐ **Soaker hoses**—When you need to water newly planted trees and shrubs, try a soaker hose for an easy way to provide water. You can hide the soaker hose under a layer of mulch.

☐ **Tomatoes**—If your ripening tomatoes have rotten spots on the bottom, the problem is variation in soil moisture. Mulch to help conserve moisture, and water each week that it does not rain. Avoid using high-nitrogen fertilizers. In the future, have a soil test, and lime your soil before planting if the pH is below 6.

☐ **Vacation watering**—Before you leave, water flowers and shrubs well and be sure they have a good layer of mulch. For large, potted plants, consider a drip irrigation system on a timer. Small potted plants can be clustered under an overhead sprinkler on a timer.

◀ **Annuals**—In the Upper South, plant heat-tolerant annuals, such as cosmos, zinnias, cleome, marigolds, celosia, purslane, and portulaca now. Work in several inches of organic material such as sphagnum peat moss, composted pine bark, or compost into the soil. Then spade or till to a depth of 6 to 8 inches prior to planting.

☐ **Flowers from seed**—In the Tropical South, it's time to start flowers for fall. Plant zinnias, cosmos, blanket flower, marigolds, spider flower, and sunflowers from seeds, and they will bloom in two to three months.

☐ **Salad garden**—You can still plant tomatoes, peppers, and Swiss chard now for an early fall harvest. If transplants are not available, you can sow seeds directly in the garden or in small pots.

☐ **Seeds**—Start your child with seed packets full of fun. Try four o'clocks that open every afternoon, zinnias they can cut, or a tepee pot of pole beans they can sit inside and pick and eat.

☐ **Summer bulbs**—Cannas, caladiums, gladioli, dahlias, montbretia, acidanthera, and tuberoses are all in the garden center, offering excellent opportunity for summer flowers. Set them in a sunny, well-drained spot. ▶

◀ **Sunflowers**—Plant seeds directly in prepared garden soil and keep them moist. For hardy flowers you can cut, choose branched selections such as Lemon Queen, Sonja, Sun Goddess, Valentine, and Park's Velvet Tapestry.

☐ **Vegetables**—Upper South gardeners can plant warm-weather vegetables now, including tomatoes, squash, beans, peppers, and okra. In the Middle South, remember to keep vegetables harvested to ensure your plants keep producing. In the Lower South, remember that you can replant as soon as the first planting starts to decline.

PRUNE

☐ **Leafy annuals**—Snip back the tips of coleus, copperleaf, and Joseph's coat to keep plants full through summer and fall. Water during dry weather. Apply a slow-release fertilizer or liquid feed monthly. ▶

CONTROL

☐ **Roses**—Continue spraying susceptible plants with Funginex to combat black spot and powdery mildew. Apply early in the morning so that the spray can dry before the day gets hot. Spraying in sunny weather when the temperature is above 85 degrees can cause the leaves to burn.

The fungicide will help protect new foliage from disease, but spots already present on older leaves will not go away. Spray every 7 to 10 days through the fall.

☐ **Weeds**—The best cure for future weeds is to get rid of the ones you have before they can drop seeds all over your garden. Pull them if they are tall enough, or use a scuffle hoe or hand hoe to uproot them. Gather weeds, and put them in the trash. You don't want to unintentionally spread weeds in your garden by putting ones that bear seeds in your compost pile.

FERTILIZE

☐ **Roses**—Small amounts of fertilizer should be applied to roses every four to six weeks during the growing season. Cottonseed meal, timed-release chemical fertilizers such as 7-11-9, and composted manure work well. Be sure to water thoroughly after fertilizer is applied.

June notes:

TIP OF THE MONTH

Insects are attracted to the color yellow. So I cut those yellow, plastic detergent bottles into strips, tack them onto wooden stakes, place the stakes throughout the garden, and coat the strips with Tangle-Trap. These sticky traps do a good job of eliminating aphids, whiteflies, and leafhoppers.

BETTE THOMSEN
CLARENDON HILLS, ILLINOIS

Makeover Magic

A little landscaping and an updated porch give this small house a big face-lift.

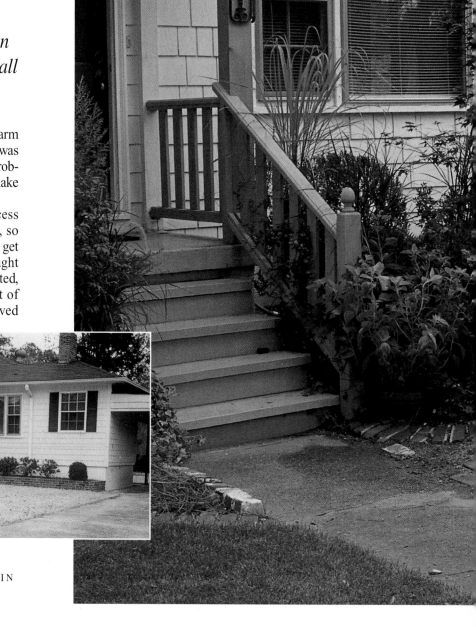

BEFORE

This tidy little house lacked charm and curb appeal but otherwise was in pretty good shape. A few problem areas needed to be addressed to make it more functional and attractive.

To begin with, there was no access from the driveway to the sidewalk, so you had to traipse through the yard to get to the front door. The spindly wrought iron railing on the porch looked dated, and the angular brick wall in front of the house was unattractive and served

BY CHARLIE THIGPEN
PHOTOGRAPHY VAN CHAPLIN

no purpose. Also, the downspout on the right side visually cut the house in two.

The landscape lacked personality as well. Sparse shrubs on the right side of the entry left the gas meter exposed. And without flowers, the front of the house was devoid of color.

Several small projects proved to be just what this house needed to spruce it up. The first order of business was to tear out the angular brick wall and then use the bricks to build a new, curving walk from the driveway to the front door.

The brick wall in front of the house was beginning to fall apart in places, so it was simple to knock down. Leaving some of the mortar on the bricks gives them an aged look.

A row of bricks set on their side creates a sweeping curved edging for the walk. Leftover and broken bricks were inset to form small patches of paving in the walk. Crushed stone fills in around

LEFT: *Built with brick salvaged from the wall, a gently curving path leads from the porch to the driveway.*

BELOW: *New plants, a new walk, and an updated porch make this home more attractive and accessible.*

ABOVE: *Filled with plants, the wrought iron stand brings color right up to the front door and softens a blank wall.*

LEFT: *This arbor topped with a red birdhouse creates a climbing surface for vines and a nice entry for guests.*

the bricks and provides a hard-packed walking surface.

Next, the downspout on the right side of the large window was moved about 12 feet to the end of the house. But that left a hole in the gutter. A piece of tin sealed with silicon patches the hole nicely. This only took around 30 minutes to do. A large columnar growing Will Flemming yaupon holly (*Ilex vomitoria* Will Flemming) camouflages the relocated downspout.

Replacing the wrought iron railing with a wooden railing and column updates the entry. The column, fashioned from a 6 x 6 with a little trim, makes a substantial support for the front porch. And 2 x 4s routed on the edges provide sturdy handrails. Pickets secure the steps and landing. Staining the new wood gray gives a fresh, clean look.

An iron crest added over the porch and iron pieces on the column lend character. Lots of garden shops sell old ironwork, and it looks great in the garden. Little touches like this give a house personality.

After the house and walk started taking shape, it was time to concentrate on the yard. A few new shrubs was all it took to hide the gas meter. Annuals and perennials planted along the walk add color to the front of the house.

The simple arbor is the finishing touch. It makes you feel as if you're entering a garden instead of a yard. The rapidly growing, tropical bleeding-heart vine (*Clerodendrumn thomsoniae*) planted at the base of the arbor creates a colorful entry. Small climbing roses will eventually cover the structure.

It takes a little time and money to dress up a front yard, but improvements will make you feel proud every time that you pull into the driveway. It's also fun watching your neighbors strain their necks as they drive by trying to figure out what you're going to do next. ◇

Crepe Myrtle Pruning Tips

Like many of us, crepe myrtles need to be trained to be their best. Although most pruning is done in late winter before the leaves emerge, a little guidance during the growing season can eliminate big pruning jobs in the future. But if you've let your trees get untidy, don't worry. It's not too late to clean them up. Follow these tips for well-groomed crepes. ◇

RIGHT: *To prune new sprouts that are poorly placed, just rub them off with your thumb.*

ABOVE: *If you didn't remove a limb by cutting close to the trunk, you'll get several shoots in its place. Go ahead and cut off the stub.*

RIGHT: *Crepe myrtles send up suckers from the base of the tree. Remove them any time of year. Cut suckers off as close to the soil level as possible.*

Narrowleaf zinnia blooms all summer in a cascade that fills an entire bed or the front of a border. Practically carefree, it's a busy gardener's choice for a sunny spot.

Although the plant usually has golden orange flowers, you can find selections with gold or white blooms.

Zinnia's New Look

If you expect a bed of zinnias to have the primary colors found in a fistful of helium-filled balloons, look again. Unlike the stand-up habit of their bright cousins, narrowleaf zinnias lie down in their bed, making a carpet of color that lasts all summer. And the golden orange blooms among blue-gray leaves appear like a meadow in full flower.

Narrowleaf zinnias (*Zinnia angustifolia* or *Z. linearis*) are long lasting and tough. Plant them in full sun atop a raised bed, and give them good drainage and adequate moisture; they will hardly droop a leaf on the hottest summer day. In fact, narrowleaf zinnia will bloom steadily from the time it is planted in spring until frost nips it in fall. You don't even need to snip off the faded flowers.

While other zinnias succumb to summer's mildews, narrowleaf zinnias take no notice and grow on with scarcely a blotch on a leaf. The naturally bluish tint to the abundant foliage sets the flowers apart, creating a harmony rarely enjoyed between blossom and leaf.

Narrowleaf zinnia is readily available from garden centers among the spring and summer bedding plants. Look for orange (Golden Orange), golden (Star Gold), and white (Crystal White) forms.

Choose a location where it can trail over a wall, or place it along the front of a border. Plants will grow about 12 to 15 inches tall, but little more. They won't be seen behind taller annuals and perennials, so put them out front. Set transplants 12 to 15 inches apart, and any gaps will be filled in only a few weeks.

Narrowleaf zinnia is also an ideal choice for a plant to trail over the edge of a container. Plant it in large pots that contain upright shrubs or small trees, and it will soften that hard edge with a drape of summer flowers.

Before setting plants out, amend garden beds with organic matter to improve the drainage in clay soil and help sandy soil retain moisture. Incorporate a slow-release fertilizer into the bed at planting time to ensure vigor through the long growing season. *Linda C. Askey*

NARROWLEAF ZINNIA
At a Glance

Light: full sun to light afternoon shade
Soil: amended, well-drained garden soil
Moisture: Irrigate when dry.
Pests: mildew resistant, some spider mites in hot, dry weather
Expect to pay: $12 to $15 for a tray of 36

Enchanting Enclosure

BEFORE

We owners of narrow lots know we're supposed to do something with the front yard and back-yard. It's those narrow walk-through spaces on the side that stymie us; but they offer potential for an intimate and favorite garden retreat. It's all in the planning—as this charming Columbia, South Carolina, courtyard shows.

Duplex owners Billisue Hayes and Warren Light garden the area around the house. They had already developed the rest of the site. Only this narrow side yard remained. "I called it the last frontier because it

The owners' favorite retreat is enclosed by brick walls and planted with several types of hydrangeas. Creeping fig cloaks the house, and lush ferns frame the entrance where a bronze frog stands sentinel. An antique jar-turned-fountain serves as a focal point.

was the last part of the garden we did, and it was so barren," recalls Billisue.

They put a lot of thought into what they wanted. They had measured it, made several conceptual drawings, and bought an old olive jar to use as a fountain, but many questions remained. It was time to call in a professional to help site the patio and fountain, to define the boundary between side garden and back garden, and to handle the level change between the front and back.

Landscape architect George Betsill came to the rescue, helping with the siting and the sizing of the 12-foot-square patio and the fountain pool, which measures 3½ feet square. He accommodated the change of level from front to back by placing a step just outside the gated entrance and used a knee-high brick wall with a 4-foot opening to separate the courtyard garden from the one in back. By extending the low brick wall around the back garden in the form of raised planting beds, he provided plenty of seating and at the same time added an extra dimension to an almost flat lot.

With the hardscape in place, Billisue and Warren selected plantings to suit their lifestyles. Early mornings, nights, and weekends are the primary times they use this garden. The cool color scheme of white, blue, and yellow glows at night. Variegated plants and mixed textures work well in the most shaded area.

"We call this the hydrangea room," says Billisue, referring to the dominant plants here, including oakleaf, Nikko Blue, Sister Theresa, and variegated lace cap hydrangeas that contribute a long season of blue and white. The large foliage of elephant's-ears and yellow cannas add

Antique wrought iron gates create an irresistible invitation into this courtyard. Aspidistra frames the entrance, while the foliage of elephant's-ears gives a tropical feel.

to the color theme and create a tropical feeling.

Layers of vines provide texture in narrow planting beds. In front of the wall covered in creeping fig, they planted fatshedera in one place and English ivy in another, adding a rich evergreen effect. In summer, annual or deciduous vines such as moon vine, potato vine, and hybrid clematis add flowers and more layers of color and texture. White wax begonias are used

as fillers among perennials. A Japanese maple holds down one corner of the courtyard garden.

The fountain, designed by local water and lighting expert Glenn Clonts, is the undisputed feature of the garden. The lovely antique olive jar rests in its quiet pool as smooth sheets of water spill over the sides, mimicking the sound of a murmuring brook (see illustration below). Lighting makes the fountain even more enchanting.

Warren enjoys the garden early in the morning while it's cool. Billisue loves to bring her dinner out because it's so peaceful. "I also love to read the paper here early on Sundays," she says.

Careful planning and the gardeners' personal choices are keys to the success of this hideaway. The beautiful antique wrought iron gates, found at an auction and adapted for the opening, are the first hint that this is a special place. Walking by on the street, you are lured by the fragrance of a tea olive hedge along the side property line. Now step up to the gates and, with the sound of the fountain beckoning, look down the lushly planted walk. If the gate is ajar, who can resist going in for a peek? *Orene Stroud Horton*

Ferns, hostas, hardy orchids, violets, and Lenten roses mix with variegated plants such as coleus.

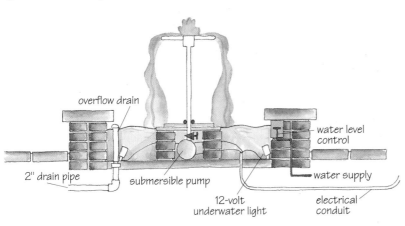

overflow drain

water level control

2" drain pipe

submersible pump

water supply

12-volt underwater light

electrical conduit

Hillside Paradise

Gardening an unforgiving patch of mountainside yields unforgettable results for this West Virginian.

BY JULIE MARTENS / PHOTOGRAPHY JEAN ALLSOPP

To say that gardening among the peaks and along the ridges in Charleston, West Virginia, is a challenge is incorrect. More accurately, gardening becomes akin to an Olympic sport—even the most modest garden project requires terracing, taming the wild brush that scrambles up and down the hills, and battling the extremes of Appalachian weather.

The successful gardeners are the ones who possess a pioneer spirit of can-do-it and determination. Carter Giltinan fills that bill. She's been gardening in West Virginia for 44 years, and she knows the grit it takes to carve a garden out of a mountainside. Her little bit of paradise thrives on a 40-degree slope, where she has tucked perennial beds and hewn winding trails among towering trunks of 87-year-old beech and hemlock trees.

"I reclaimed this garden from woodland brush and a sea of English ivy," Carter says. "A big beech tree tumbled down in a storm, and that gave me a toehold on the hillside wilderness." About the same time, the back porch of the house rotted away, and workmen uncovered a treasure trove of native stone buried underneath it.

As a woman who recognizes opportunity when she sees it, Carter quickly commandeered the stone, laid out hoses to define bed edges, and hired workmen to build retaining walls. "While they laid stone, I

ABOVE: *Carter Giltinan and Scrap*

RIGHT: *Perennial borders wrap the house from front to back in sweeps of constantly changing colors. Compost is the secret ingredient to rich soil on a rocky hillside.*

grubbed brush," she remembers. Several weeks and truckloads of fill dirt later, her beds were ready for planting.

Over the years, those first hillside plantings have grown from modest borders—maybe 3 feet deep—to lush, 5-foot-wide sweeps of perennial textures and hues that clamber up the slope and cling along the ridges of the yard. Carter happily sacrificed expanses of lawn for grass paths, so the perennial areas could sprout within a network of green walkways that turn and curve much like the roads of Charleston.

The perennial plantings grow and flower in a rich symphony. While Carter is quick to admit that she loves the "colors and textures of the garden in winter," she also thrills to the discovery of small springtime treasures, such as the bloodroot, trillium, and dog-tooth violet. "Those

tiny flowers poke through the ground and hold their own on days when the big plant material is still asleep," she says.

If spring offers jewels of tiny, tender beauty, summer tears through the garden in grandiose swaths of greens and blue-greens, punctuated by splashes of strong colors—orange, yellow, red, white. Carter created the garden from foliage to flowers, concentrating on the subtleties of shades and textures in green before filling in with perennial bloomers.

"Green is a great teacher. It teaches you to consider plant form and foliage texture," she says emphatically. "I look out and see 35 shades of green in my hosta bed." Add in texture, and there's green in tall, fine-leaved foliage, short, broad-leaved foliage, feathery foliage—it runs the gamut. "Once you get green under your belt, you can master flowers."

Summer bloomers include bee balm, Queen Anne's lace, astilbe, daylilies, and primroses, which thrive with untamed

ABOVE, TOP: *Bee balm is a favorite among the hummingbirds, butterflies, and bees.*

ABOVE, BELOW: *Plumes of deep pink Granat astilbe paint a textural tapestry tucked between clumps of larkspur.*

Silver-leaved lungwort and Japanese painted fern make an exquisite combination.

abandon in native-looking drifts of color. Carter attributes the natural look to Mother Nature. "A reseeding garden takes over and literally does its own thing," she laughs, pointing to ox-eye daisies sprouting between stone steps.

The secret behind this lush perennial paradise lies in the compost-enriched soil. The hillside offers only a 2-foot-thick layer of rocky soil over shale and/or a subsoil of clay. Couple the skimpy soil layer with the number of trees, and it's easy to see that this corner of West Virginia is not an easy place to garden. "There are tree roots everywhere competing for moisture and nutrients," Carter says. "The shale is a saving grace, as it provides good drainage at depth. But the compost is the real savior. Over the years, I have replaced most of the original soil with compost."

One of the advantages to gardening in a woodland is having access to large amounts of organic material. Carter composts religiously,

adding a truckload of manure to the compost pile once a year. In return for her efforts, she harvests no less than four or five dump truck loads of black gold annually. She top-dresses the perennial gardens twice a year, every spring after weeding and again in late fall, after cleaning up the garden.

Harvesting wheelbarrow loads of compostable material from the surrounding woodland isn't the only benefit to gardening in a tamed bit of West Virginia. Carter also plays host to an array of wildlife, from owls to frogs to raccoons to insects. That's why you're most likely to find her prowling through the garden early in the morning, decked out in her nightgown and clogs, clippers in hand.

"It's in the quiet of the morning that I can observe those things I like so much. I see what's going to happen that day and watch my wild friends busy about their lives. The garden is full of hope in the morning—and so am I." ◇

Shade-loving plants—ferns, astilbe, smooth hydrangea, and hostas—thrive at the foot of an 87-year-old beech tree.

The leathery leaves of red yucca form a nondescript clump, but when the 5-foot flower stalks emerge, the plant makes a statement.

Red Hot Shrub

If you've been looking for a plant that is tough, that produces attractive flowers for many months, and that can go weeks without irrigation in the summer, consider red yucca.

The name is a bit deceiving, because botanically it is not a yucca at all; it's a hesperaloe *(Hesperaloe parviflora)*. And although the foliage is slender and spiky, it is not dangerously sharp like some of the true yuccas. This shrub is one of the most attractive plants for gardeners in Texas or anywhere heat and drought are a challenge. Cold hardiness is not a problem because it will endure in all but the coldest areas of the Upper South.

The long, slender leaves are stiff and gray-green in color, and they form stemless clumps. The leaves sprout fine, white threads from their edges, but the real drama comes with the flowers. Gracefully leaning stalks reach 5 to 7 feet tall and bear coral-pink flowers from May through early fall. The individual flowers are about 1½ inches long and continue opening for many weeks. It is not unusual for mature clumps to have six or eight flower spikes during the season.

Red yucca is not particular about soil; it flourishes in alkaline or slightly acid conditions. It also tolerates fairly moist sites and thrives as a low-maintenance container plant. This shrub revels in full sun and reflected heat. When given a half-day of shade it may bloom less. About the only maintenance necessary is to remove the old flower stalks at the end of the bloom season.

Another appealing quality is its attractiveness to butterflies and hummingbirds. The long flowering season allows plenty of time to lure these colorful creatures into your garden.

This shrub is readily available at garden centers. One-gallon container plants usually bloom the first year they are planted, although growth is rather slow. For the best effect, use it in drifts of three or more. Water well at planting and every few weeks the first growing season if rains are infrequent. After that, just sit back and enjoy the colorful flowers and interesting texture, as well as the butterflies and hummingbirds that—like you—will find the flowers irresistible.

Bill Welch

RED YUCCA
At a Glance

Light: full sun to partial shade
Soil: not particular
Moisture: drought tolerant
Problems: Deer love the flowers.
Expect to pay: $6 per gallon can

Enhancing this garden path, colorful flowers and foliage pour out of the tops of salvaged pipes that rise from the ground.

Pipe Dreams

Last spring, I had a dream—a dream that turned into my wife's worst nightmare. When trying to figure out how I could make a garden path a little more interesting, I came up with the idea of placing pipes along its sides. I thought this might look neat, but my wife thought differently.

I began collecting old terra-cotta, cast-iron, and even metal pipes. Then I set them upright in the garden, burying one end of the pipe in the ground just deep enough for it to be firm and secure.

Some I filled with soil and topped with annuals, succulents, and herbs. Others I used as pedestals to hold hanging baskets off the ground. My pipe path was starting to take shape.

One day, a friend gave me a large concrete pipe with a flared end. The pipe was old and aged looking and seemed perfect for my garden. I drove home, proud of my new find. I parked on the side of the house and slowly and carefully began to unload the heavy pipe. Just as I got it off the truck I heard my wife, Cindy, yell "What's that?" in a stern voice. I turned to find her on the front porch with her hands on her hips, and I knew I was in trouble. In a meek voice I told her, "It's a beautiful concrete pipe." "That's it—no more pipes," she said as she turned and walked back in the house. I guess I was pretty lucky to have set up 14 of them before she stopped me.

The pipes might look a little unusual, but really they are simply tall containers. Plants that require well-drained soil, such as herbs and succulents, work great in them. The pipes also keep invasive plants contained and in bounds. You can use potting soil or any type of soil that the plants require. The pipes are also excellent for holding hanging bas-

ABOVE: *Set in a broken pot, this metal pipe holds plants growing from holes punched in its side. An obelisk dresses up the two pieces.*

kets high above the ground and making them stand out.

By the middle of the summer, the planting began to fill out and Cindy told me that the path looked nice. I asked if I could get some more pipes, but the answer was still no. Oh well, I guess I should be satisfied with 14. These pipes really did frame the path nicely, and they gave it a unique look. I know pipes in the garden aren't for everyone, but they show you how a little imagination can give you a different look.

So be open-minded, have fun in your yard, and don't be afraid to try things a little out of the ordinary. There are no rules in gardening. Everyone's taste is different. If you think it looks good, that's all that counts. *Charlie Thigpen*

A collection of cast-iron pipes holds flowering chives and succulents and makes a setting all its own.

ABOVE: *Calla lilies and yarrow nestle together for a pretty-in-pink bouquet.*

RIGHT: *The Black-eyed Susan family is well represented in this sunny arrangement. Stems are placed in a pint mason jar inside the tin.*

Summer Bouquets

You don't need a special occasion to cut a bouquet of flowers. A few blossoms are all it takes to bring a small piece of the garden indoors.

Loosely gathered, summer flowers seem to find their own place in a vase and require little arranging. What they do need is tender loving care from the moment they are cut. We asked floral industry consultant Libbey Oliver of Williamsburg, Virginia, for tips on cutting and conditioning blossoms to give bouquets a long life. Plus, we have a few hints for simple fresh arrangements.

"Our days become hot and humid so quickly—early morning is really the only time to cut garden flowers," says Libbey. "Evenings don't cool down enough before darkness moves in."

Bring along sharp clippers and a container of water. A clean cut made with a sharp tool lets water to travel up the stem into the flower head, prolonging the life of the bloom. Dull clippers crush the stem. Choose blossoms that are newly opened and buds just beginning to unfurl. Cut flowers one at a time, and immediately place each stem in the water.

CONDITIONING

Before arranging, remove excess foliage. A few leaves give flowers a natural appearance, but too many will detract from your bouquet. Remove all leaves that will be underwater in the container. Left on, they will breed bacteria in the vase and shorten the life of the arrangement.

Cut the stem again, underwater. This enables water instead of air to travel up the stem. "I never realized what a difference this makes until I tried it," Libbey says. "It especially perks up flowers that have wilted slightly between the garden and indoors." If you've only cut a few flowers, recut the stems under a running faucet. For a larger bouquet, Libbey puts several inches of water in the sink or a wide container. "Cut the stem below the water's surface, watching out for your fingers," she says. Place freshly cut flowers in water, and place in a cool, dark spot for several hours before arranging.

FOOD FOR THOUGHT
Garden flowers make the freshest bouquets. Taken from yard to vase in a short length of time, few precious nutrients are lost. "There are many old wives' tale recipes for flower food," Libbey says. "Flowers fresh from the garden really don't need extra nutrients. Instead, every few days recut the stems and change the water in the vase. This will prolong their life more than anything added to the water," she says.

If you're giving the bouquet as a gift and feel the need to add a nutrient to the vase, manufactured flower food is available through florists. It has been developed to provide both nutrients and antibacterial agents to keep water clean. It can be purchased in sachet-size packets or large containers. Libbey says, "A small packet is usually sufficient for only 1 quart of water. If you use a flower food, be certain you have enough for the amount of water in the container."

ARRANGING TIPS
Choose a vase that complements the bouquet in size and style. Browse through cabinets and closets for an out-of-the-ordinary container. If it will not hold water or is very large, place a jar or cup inside to hold the flowers.

Simple bouquets are the most appealing. Interest comes from varying flower shapes and colors. Bouquets need not be large, but cut flowers should be of similar size.

Before placing flowers in the vase, gather them in your hand. Start with a few stems, and add more, one at a time. Hold the bouquet at arm's length and see how they fit together. If a flower is out of place, gently pull it out from the top. Once you have a pleasing bouquet, use your free hand to cut the stems the same length. Then place them into the vase. Loosen the cluster to fill the container; place more flowers as needed. *Ellen Riley*
(For sources turn to pages 250–251.)

Zinnias, crocosmias, and dill flower heads stand tall in a rusted container. Strawberry Fields gomphrena carries the color down to the glass vase below.

Built around pink and purple, this arrangement is plentiful with only a few stems of each type of flower from your garden.

A bed of pineapple sage brings bright color to the garden of Caroline Benson in Easton, Maryland. Here in the Middle South, this tender perennial behaves as an annual.

No Mystery to Pineapple Sage

It's hard to figure out how certain plants got their names. For instance, no one seems to know how jackson vine *(Smilax smallii)* came to be called that (if you're privy to the secret, please clue me in). But there's no such mystery regarding an herb named pineapple sage *(Salvia elegans)*. Just tear a leaf in two and hold the pieces to your nose. Smells like pineapple, doesn't it?

But a heavenly scent is just half the story. Scores of scarlet-red blossoms, favorites of hummingbirds and butterflies, festoon the branches for months on end. In the Upper and Middle South, the plant begins blooming in early September, while from the Lower South on down, blooms may first appear in July. This Mexican native also grows quickly. Set out in spring, a nondescript plant in a 4-inch pot becomes a 3-foot showstopper by late summer.

Cold hardy to about 20 degrees, pineapple sage is what's termed a "tender perennial." The first hard freeze kills it to the ground. Whether it comes back depends on where you live. In the Upper and Middle South, forget it. In the Lower South, it's hit-and-miss. In the Coastal

PINEAPPLE SAGE
At a Glance

Size: 2 to 3 feet tall and wide where tender; 4 to 5 feet where hardy
Light: full sun
Soil: well drained, acid or alkaline
Growth rate: fast
Pests: whiteflies, aphids, spider mites; not usually serious
Expect to pay: $2 to $5

and Tropical South, count on it.

"Most years, it comes back for us," says Madalene Hill, who gardens just southeast of Austin. "It all depends on how warm it is in fall when the first real cold hits." Mild temperatures combined with substantial autumn rains often spell doom because the plant doesn't harden off in time. Cutting it back before late January may also speed its demise.

Fortunately, it's easy to save pineapple sage over the winter by taking cuttings in the fall and growing them indoors. Cuttings root quickly in water. But successfully rooting them in soil means taking them at the right time. "I found out years ago that you waste your time if you take cuttings before the night temperature falls below 60 degrees," says Madalene. "Night temperatures between 50 and 55 degrees are ideal." Rooting powder isn't necessary.

Madalene notes that while some new selections of pineapple sage have recently appeared, the old-fashioned species can't be beat for color, fragrance, and vigor. "Who could do better?" she asks rhetorically. Who indeed? *Steve Bender*

(For sources turn to pages 250–251.)

Hydrangea Blues

PHOTOGRAPH: VAN CHAPLIN

Hydrangea blooms cover a wide spectrum of color. While predisposed to be light or dark hued, they may change color from year to year, depending on soil and climate conditions.

It's the curly hair-straight hair problem," Elizabeth Dean says. "People always want the opposite of what they have." Experience as a retail grower gives her ample reason to express this point of view. The hydrangea Elizabeth refers to is the large mophead type, *Hydrangea macrophylla.* Its flower color seems to change as often as the season. "If you have great acid soil and grow fabulous blue hydrangeas, you probably would rather have pink. And if your soil is base and sweet, you want blue ones. This is just the way we are," she says.

"Hydrangeas seem to be more visibly affected by cultural and climatic aspects than any other shrub or flower I can think of," she says. "One year they might bloom a good deep blue, and the next year, due to many uncontrollable elements, they might look really washed out. To me, this is part of the fun and intrigue about hydrangeas."

But the truth of the matter remains, that hydrangea color can be controlled to a certain extent by soil acidity, or pH. Simply put, a pH of 6.5 is considered neutral. Any reading below this number indicates acid soil. A mophead hydrangea will produce blue-hued flowers in acid soil. To encourage blue flowers, Elizabeth recommends a treatment of ¼ ounce aluminum sulphate and ¼ ounce sulphate of iron mixed into 1 gallon of water. Water the hydrangea, using no more than 2 gallons per plant. This may be done once in spring and fall.

Alkaline soil, with pH above 6.5, will encourage pink and red hydrangea blossoms. Lime will turn a neutral or acid soil more alkaline, or sweet. Lime may be applied to the soil in spring and fall; spread it around the base of the shrub.

Dramatic color change in hydrangeas is slow. It may take several years to see a discernable difference. Elizabeth says most hydrangeas are grown for sale in neutral potting mix. "If you're purchasing a hydrangea based on the color in the nursery, remember that it will probably change when planted in your garden." By purchasing a named selection, you can predict the plant's disposition toward a certain color and density of that hue. But the color will be determined by the nature of the soil.

Hydrangea color can also be affected by the plant's location. In a bed bordered beside a concrete walk, the lime from the cement will slowly permeate the soil and change hydrangea flowers to pink tones. If planted under a stand of pine trees, the soil will be decidedly more acidic. Blue hydrangeas will be prevalent.

If you suffer from the curly hair-straight hair syndrome, there's plenty of room to experiment with hydrangeas. Left alone, they change a bit from year to year without assistance. But as Elizabeth says, "I just like them whatever color they are." For more on this flowering shrub, see "Fashionable Hydrangeas" on pages 144–147. *Ellen Riley*

(For sources turn to pages 250–251.)

No matter what color—blue, pink, or somewhere in between—the beautiful blooms of this flowering shrub will keep you guessing and grateful.

FASHIONABLE
Hydrangeas

This flowering family offers
endless variety.

BY ELLEN RILEY
PHOTOGRAPHY VAN CHAPLIN

*Each branch of
Nikko Blue mophead
hydrangea bears a
bouquet of blooms.*
OWNER: BARBARA ASHFORD, BIRMINGHAM

With a look as old-fashioned as grandmother's garden, or as stylish as the latest summer fashions, hydrangeas have become a renaissance flower in our landscape. As Elizabeth Dean, of Wilkerson Mill Gardens in Palmetto, Georgia, says, "There's a newfound madness about hydrangeas."

The well-known mophead selections are only the beginning of what this family of flowering shrubs has to offer. "When people come in to buy a hydrangea, they want one of two things," she says. "They either want a hydrangea just like their grandmother grew, or they want anything but what their grandmother grew." Either way, they have plenty of choices.

ABOVE, LEFT: *Générale Vicomtesse de Vibraye, with its electric blue mopheads, is less susceptible to cold damage because it remains dormant throughout winter.* ABOVE, RIGHT: *Given the right growing conditions, hydrangeas bloom pink rather than blue. For more on color, turn to page 143.*

French hydrangeas *(Hydrangea macrophylla)* have luscious, round, globelike flowers also known as mopheads. These are our grandmother's hydrangeas. Ranging from deep lavender-blue to pure white with a healthy assortment of pinks and reds in between, these dense flowers make a colorful splash in the garden. (For more on color, see "Hydrangea Blues" on page 143).

Lace caps are a prissy sister of mopheads. These lesser known hydrangeas have flowers that seem to float in flat, delicate-looking clusters above the foliage. Their appearance is light and airy, with gentler colors than the voluptuous mopheads.

WINTER WOES

If these hydrangeas suffer a down side, it's their eagerness to break dormancy and leaf out in late winter. This is especially true in the Lower and Middle South where warm days in late January and February are not uncommon. Then, along comes a cold snap, and tender new leaves are burned or destroyed. "A lot of hydrangeas have been developed for the florist trade," says Elizabeth. "They are grown quickly in a greenhouse and put in a pretty container to be sold for Mother's Day. They grow in controlled conditions and have beautiful flowers. But they may not necessarily be garden-hardy selections and may not know how to go dormant. You will find these hydrangeas available in nurseries even though their cold hardiness is questionable."

Through years of experience, Elizabeth and husband Gene Griffith have identified several selections that are more inclined to stay dormant

RIGHT: *Lilacina sports lovely lace cap blooms. It is also an excellent choice for Lower South gardens where winter days occasionally warm up.*

BELOW AND FAR RIGHT: *This Blue Billow has reached mature size and is an excellent choice for a small garden.*

The mophead flowers of Preziosa deepen in color as they mature.

until spring. "We've found Générale Vicomtesse de Vibraye to be slow to produce its foliage and begin spring growth. It is a large mophead with electric blue flowers. Lilacina is a lace cap that also waits until spring to leaf out," Elizabeth says.

EXTENDED FAMILY

H. serrata is an excellent choice for gardens in the Middle and Lower South where variable late-winter temperatures lure hydrangeas out of dormancy. "They seem to be more able to go dormant and stay there," Elizabeth says. They also flourish in the Upper South where temperatures are more constant throughout winter.

Their overall size is more petite than their *macrophylla* cousins, making them a good fit for small gardens. They are even happy in pots.

You will find both mophead and lace cap flowers in this family. Preziosa has demure, mottled-color mophead blooms, while Blue Billow produces lace cap flowers.

Elizabeth and Gene recommend that you, "Look for the best size plant for your garden. Then choose the bloom type you prefer. Whether you do a mixed bed of all sorts of hydrangeas or just one kind, enjoy them for their flexibility, versatility, and great summer color." ◇

(For sources turn to pages 250–251.)

Cape Plumbago (See page 163.)

July

Checklist for July

EDITORS' NOTEBOOK

"I just don't get it," my neighbor fumed. "I've been staring at those bright green flowerbuds on my crepe myrtle all summer and they absolutely refuse to open." Well, mercy me, there's a good reason. The offending "flowerbuds" aren't flowerbuds at all, but seedpods that formed after the early flowers dropped. No amount of staring will force out another flower, but you can make your plant bloom again in the summer. This month, cut off all of the seedpods you can reach without killing yourself. Your crepe myrtle, desperate to reproduce before winter, will immediately send out a second flush of blooms. In this way, most Southerners can enjoy bounteous blooms from June all the way to October. Of course, now you'll need something else to stare at all summer. Try your neighbor's new hairdo.

Steve Bender

☐ **Basil**—You grow it for the flavorful foliage, so cut it and enjoy. When basil begins to bloom, don't pinch out the flowers. Cut the plant back several inches, and take the trimmings to the kitchen. Then spread a little composted manure on top of the soil beneath the plant. ▶

☐ **Cuttings**—This is a good time to root cuttings of roses, hydrangeas, viburnums, azaleas, and other woody trees and shrubs. Cut stems that grew this year and that have at least two pairs of leaves. Remove the lower leaves, dip each stem in rooting hormone, and stick 2 or 3 stems into each pot of sterile potting mix recommended for starting seeds. Cover with a glass jar or plastic bag, and wait for signs of new growth to tell you roots have formed.

☐ **Grass clippings**—If lawns are mowed every 6 to 8 days, the clippings can be left to decompose into the soil as fertilizer and mulch. However, if heavy drifts of clippings are apparent, remove them and put them in the compost pile.

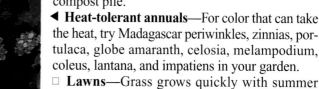

◀ **Heat-tolerant annuals**—For color that can take the heat, try Madagascar periwinkles, zinnias, portulaca, globe amaranth, celosia, melampodium, coleus, lantana, and impatiens in your garden.

☐ **Lawns**—Grass grows quickly with summer rains and warm weather, so this is a good time to renovate a lawn or plant anew. When planting plugs, be sure to keep the spaces between them faithfully weeded or your new lawn will have problems from the start.

☐ **Mulch**—Check the thickness of mulch in planting beds. It decomposes quickly in warm, humid weather and may be too thin to discourage weeds. Add enough to make it about 2 inches thick.

☐ **Photographs**—Take pictures of your garden several times during the growing season. This will help you remember what plants are needed when ordering from catalogs next winter.

☐ **Tomatoes**—Although flowers frequently fall off while night temperatures are above 75 degrees, you can minimize the problem by watering often enough to keep the soil evenly moist and by mulching. Fruit set should improve as temperatures cool. ▶

☐ **Trees and shrubs**—Although most plants are easiest to transplant during dormant periods, many will do just fine during the growing season if properly handled. They will need careful digging and transplanting, as well as some extra watering, but you don't have to stop gardening because it's hot.

☐ **Vegetables**—Don't let your vegetables stay on the plant too long. If in doubt, it's better to pick them young and tender than old and seedy. Cucumbers should be green with small seeds. Yellow squash and zucchini only take a few days from the time they bloom until they are ready to pick. ▶

□ **Water**—Provide extra moisture for large-leaved plants such as hydrangeas, coleus, and caladiums. Even in shade, water is used quickly at this time of year, and usually there are tree roots competing for available moisture. Soak the soil at least 3 to 4 inches deep every five to seven days when rains are inadequate.

PLANT

□ **Annuals**—Sow seeds of cosmos, sunflowers, and cleome into prepared beds. After seedlings are about 2 inches tall, thin them out in areas where they are too crowded. You can transplant extra seedlings to other parts of the garden.

□ **Plant again**—You still have time to set out a second planting of many summer vegetables that will extend your harvest into fall. Remove any tomatoes, peppers, squash, and beans that are tired or diseased; then set out new plants or sow seeds.

□ **Pumpkins**—If you're going to grow your own jack-o'-lantern, it's time to plant. Choose a sunny spot with plenty of room for the vine. Plant 3 seeds on a small mound of enriched soil.

◀ **Zinnias**—For bright splashes of color in your garden, plant zinnias. They can be started from seed or transplants now for late-summer and fall flowers. Cut the blossoms often to encourage continuous flowering until fall.

PRUNE

□ **Perennials**—Cut back tired foliage and spent blooms on plants such as hostas and phlox. Fertilize with timed-release granules to encourage the foliage to grow. You may be surprised by another crop of flowers on many perennials. ▶

CONTROL

□ **Roses**—Continue spraying susceptible plants with Funginex to combat black spot and powdery mildew. Apply early in the morning so that the spray can dry before the day gets hot. Spraying in sunny weather when the temperature is above 85 degrees can cause the leaves to burn. The fungicide will help protect new foliage from disease, but spots already present on older leaves will not go away. Spray every 7 to 10 days through the fall.

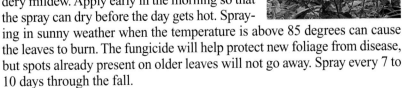

FERTILIZE

□ **Blueberries**—Yellow foliage may signal an iron deficiency. Apply a granular iron soil supplement such as Ironite as directed on the label.

July notes:

TIP OF THE MONTH

Here's a good way to put a dent in your garden's snail, slug, earwig, and pill bug population. Mix together 1 tablespoon each of nondairy creamer, sugar, and jelly. Add water; stir until all is dissolved. Pour into a smooth-sided bowl with no lip. Place the bowl in the garden so that the edge is level with the soil surface. Cover with a small piece of corrugated roofing to keep debris out but let bugs in. Then stand back and watch the fatal stampede.   NORMAN DAVIS
KERRVILLE, TEXAS

SUMMER'S AZALEA

*As surprising as it is welcome, plumleaf azalea
wears hot colors in the heat of the season.*

If you had to choose one plant to grow outside your window, what would it be? That was the question Dick Bir asked himself a few years ago. Consider that Dick is an Extension horticultural specialist at North Carolina State University, and he knows more plants by name than most of us will ever see in our lifetimes. His dilemma was huge, but his answer was simple: plumleaf azalea *(Azalea prunifolium).*

"It is wonderful," Dick says. "It blooms when you've got nothing else. It is so startling to see an azalea in bloom this late, never mind one that is so attractive. I've seen them start blooming in late June and continue until the end of August, and one cool year into early September. The color can range from red-orange to brick red, but not scarlet."

While most of our native plants were discovered and named in previous centuries, plumleaf azaleas bloomed unnoticed in shaded ravines and along streams in southwest Georgia and nearby Alabama until 1913. Cason and Virginia Callaway of LaGrange, Georgia, were so taken with the plant, it spurred them

toward the creation of Callaway Gardens. It remains the signature plant of the gardens, and that is where you can see some of the finest specimens anywhere, blooming every summer along their Five Mile Scenic Drive.

Reaching heights of up to 15 feet at maturity, plumleaf azalea loses its leaves in winter like most native azaleas. But unlike the rest, it holds its blooms against a background of green foliage. The clusters of red are like little bouquets, and the branches create layers like clouds settling into a mountain valley. The effect is both airy and dramatic.

They are also wonderful hummingbird plants. "Imagine a male ruby-throat feasting on those red blossoms," Dick says with a smile, the image vivid in his memory.

Because they originated so far South, plumleaf azaleas are extremely heat tolerant, but like every other azalea, they prefer a lightly shaded spot with well-drained, acid, organic soil that holds moisture. Dick reports seeing plants growing happily in Connecticut, so they will certainly prosper in the Lower, Middle, and Upper South. ◇

PLUMLEAF AZALEA
At a Glance

Light: partial shade

Soil: well drained, organic, acid

Moisture: moist but not wet

Bloom season: midsummer

Expect to pay: $15

BY LINDA C. ASKEY / PHOTOGRAPHY TINA CORNETT

Plumleaf azalea grows tall, but its airy drifts give it a delicacy that belies its tough summer-flowering niche.

Cars park where there was once a lawn. A new parking court didn't ruin the looks of this house.

ORDER
IN THE
COURT

BY CHARLIE THIGPEN
PHOTOGRAPHY VAN CHAPLIN

Dick and Donna Gardner have worked hard to maintain a handsome landscape. They plant annuals for color and are constantly making little improvements around the yard. Their grass is always manicured like a golf green. Little did they know that when their son, Will, turned 16, the shape of their lawn would change.

When Will got his driver's license and a car, where to park became a problem. They needed a parking court to keep his vehicle off the road and to prevent traffic jams in the driveway.

The parking court would eliminate some of the grass in the front yard and reshape the lawn. It had to be large enough to accommodate

Flowering crepe myrtles soften the flat facade of the house.

two cars, yet not look like a used car lot. When vehicles weren't parked in front of the house, the Gardners didn't want to have to see a big concrete slab. They wanted an attractive parking pad that would not cost a bundle.

After weighing all their options, they decided to recess the parking area slightly and edge it with stone. Because the parking pad is on grade with the existing sidewalk, there's no need for steps, and there is a smooth transition from parking to the front walk. The stone and mortar edging the parking pad match the sandstone sidewalk.

The Gardners used a gridlike pattern of stone set in concrete to break up the large parking area. Nine large

squares form the parking pad. These grids help contain the crushed stone spread in each square.

They chose crushed stone instead of concrete or asphalt to save money. The fine gravel packs firm and forms a hard base. On a level surface, the gravel won't wash away during heavy rains. (Gravel is not recommended for sloping surfaces.) After the gravel was poured in the squares, it was watered and packed.

A new copper awning over the front door improves the house's flat facade and helps keep rain from soaking the family when they unlock the door.

ABOVE: *The gridlike pattern breaks up the large parking pad and helps hold the gravel in place.*

After the construction was complete, the Gardners went back to tending their yard. White caladiums flank the front door, and impatiens cover the ground under the two large crepe myrtles. Terra-cotta planters on the front steps hold hefty ferns for a splash of green.

Good design provided an inexpensive, attractive solution to the Gardners' parking dilemma. Now Will has a place to park, and the yard still looks great. ◇

BEFORE

PHOTOGRAPH: JEAN ALLSOPP / OWNER: EMILY MAJOR, MOUNTAIN BROOK, ALABAMA

PHOTOGRAPH: TINA CORNETT / OWNER: LIZ TEDDER, NEWNAN, GEORGIA

ABOVE: *Clip seedheads to keep plants from spreading. Saved seeds can be passed along to friends.*

LEFT: *Lacy white flowers of garlic chives add freshness to hot August gardens.*

Dog Day Blossoms

GARLIC CHIVES
At a Glance

Size: 18 inches high
Light: full sun to partial shade
Soil: any well drained
Range: all South
Comments: Deadhead spent blooms to avoid prolific reseeding.
Expect to pay: $5 to $6 for a 1-gallon container

You gotta love a plant that's determined to bloom in the heat of summer. When the rest of the garden is wilted and tired, garlic chives sprout tall, graceful stalks topped with lacy topknots of star-shaped flowers. The white blooms add elusive freshness to borders beaten by the heat.

Garlic chives *(Allium tuberosum)* are tough little perennials you can stick in the garden and forget. Neglect, lack of water, and broiling sun are not problems for this late bloomer. Start garlic chives from seeds or transplants in spring or fall. Clusters of gray-green narrow leaves will grow throughout the warm months. Overgrown clumps may be lifted and divided in fall. Garlic chives are evergreen in mild winters.

Perhaps the biggest challenge in growing this perennial is keeping it from taking over the planet. In autumn, each flower cluster yields dozens of black seeds, each seed a potential plant. To control the spread, diligently snip flower stalks at their base before seeds are released. And you can dry the seedheads for winter arrangements. Share collected seeds and seedlings with a friend if you like, but be sure to pass along clipping instructions. Poor, dry soil with a heavy clay content may also discourage plants from spreading.

The garlicky aroma of cut foliage earned this plant its name, though the smell reminds some of onions. Chopped leaves are edible and may be used as a substitute for chives. If you prefer to pick the blossoms, you'll notice a violet-like fragrance. Cut flowers are pleasing additions to fresh arrangements. Or simply enjoy stalwart blossoms as they decorate your garden right through the hottest days of summer. *Jo Kellum*

A cool, grassy path takes you down to the pool. Thick border plantings blocking views of nearby neighbors make you feel as if you're alone in the country.

A Capital City Surprise

Imagine walking from your car on a busy D.C. street as horns blare and tires screech. You approach the front of an unassuming house, step around to the back, and in the space of 30 seconds find yourself smack-dab in the middle of the quiet English countryside.

No, your name isn't Alice, and you didn't fall down the rabbit hole. Instead, you're a visitor receiving a guided tour by garden designer Jane MacLeish.

This expansive backyard, she explains, consists of adjoining lots owned by a sister and brother. When Jane embarked upon the project, nothing much existed here beyond a few trees and a chain-link fence. Busy streets and nearby neighbors bordered the yard on three sides. So one of her first tasks was cloaking the property's periphery with a dense border of trees and shrubs. Today, you'd never know neighbors were there.

The bowl-shaped site falls away from the house. A winding network of grass and stone paths leads you through a complex tapestry of shrubs and perennials to the garden's centerpiece, a beautiful pool.

The best-kept secret in Washington, D.C., isn't part of a Pentagon file. It's a backyard hideaway.

A stroll along the shady paths reveals a pretty combination of hostas, impatiens, and violets.

An extensive underground drainage system keeps runoff from heavy rains from dirtying the water.

With grass nearly up to its edge and water darkened by black dye mixed into the concrete, the pool looks more like a bucolic pond. "One of [the owners'] friends came over," Jane recalls with satisfaction, "walked all around the garden, came back into the house, and said, 'So where's the swimming pool?'"

Grass terraces stairstepping down an 8-foot slope at one end of the pool function as both steps and living lounge chairs. "I really love to sculpt the earth," says Jane, "so this was a wonderful opportunity to make grass steps that people could sun on. It was a soft way of getting people down the 8 feet without them really knowing it."

Your one-of-a-kind visit concludes back at the house. Looking out at the peaceful landscape below, you marvel how the city seems so far away. "I like people to walk into my gardens and go, 'Wow!'" comments Jane.

Wow. *Steve Bender*

F R E S H
HERBS
FOR A KITCHEN

Culinary gardens can be both

functional and attractive. This one

provides ingredients for many

Southern Living *recipes.*

The *Southern Living* kitchens test more than 5,000 recipes each year. In order to make these recipes taste their very best, we often use fresh herbs. Sometimes herbs aren't available at the local grocery store, so we wanted to grow our own. That's why three years ago we started a small garden.

It began as a circular bed with a few herbs. Each year we expanded it. Now the garden is really more of a kitchen garden than an herb bed because we also grow a few vegetables and berries. Flowers and ornamental plants are tucked in to make it a delightful place to clip flavorful foliage.

The site chosen receives eight hours of full sun. Most herbs need at least six to eight hours of sun. The area was flat as a pancake and the soil was mostly hard, red clay. After heavy rains the ground would become saturated and stay wet for extended periods. Most herbs prefer well-drained soil; therefore, we had to till in lots of sand and a clay soil conditioner such as Perma Till or Profile to make

ABOVE: *A vine-covered arbor creates an entrance into the garden.* LEFT: *Lemongrass looks great in a pot surrounded by Blackie sweet potato vine.*

the site drain better. (These products, available at local garden shops, improve drainage and reduce compaction.) We also amended the soil with leaf mold. For better

BY CHARLIE THIGPEN / PHOTOGRAPHY VAN CHAPLIN

BEFORE

drainage, we built up the area and crowned it to allow surface water to run off the sides.

Metal and wooden edging form the boundaries. Small concrete pavers were set out to allow visitors to easily walk around the garden. As you stroll through the herbs you can harvest on both sides of the pavers without stepping on tender plants. The stepping pads also keep foot traffic from compacting the loose soil.

A view of the garden three years ago shows its circular shape. Each year we expanded it to test a variety of different herbs and vegetables.

ABOVE: *Stepping-stones, interplanted with thyme, ring the garden.*

BELOW: *Herbs grow in creative containers such as this old boot.*

and thyme. The kitchen staff also requested mint. We were reluctant to plant mint since it can quickly take over a garden, but we set out a few plants in large pots to keep them contained.

Don't be confused when trying to select herbs. I was shocked the first time I went to buy basil and saw 10 different types. When in doubt, I just buy a couple of each and try them, noting what tastes good and what works in the garden.

Most herbs perform better when clipped periodically during the growing season. Plants such as lemon basil need to be tipped regularly to remove flowers and prevent them from going to seed. Harvest herbs freely, but don't overharvest. Plants shouldn't be stripped of all their leaves. The best time to clip herbs is in the morning before the hot sun dissipates the strong oils, but any time will do. I usually harvest in the evening when I'm cooking dinner. Always use sharp pruners or scissors to cut herbs. Never try to snap or break them off.

Two trained Will Flemming yaupons planted on the front side of the simple entry arbor form a green arch. Vines are encouraged to climb over the structure, creating a tunnel effect. Last summer cherry tomatoes and Blackie sweet potato vine covered the arch. The clusters of red tomatoes and Blackie's dark foliage made a striking combination.

We used pots of herbs and ornamental plants in and around the garden to add color and interest. Small pots top the four posts on the arbor, making grassy finials. These containers are threaded onto wooden dowels screwed into the top of the posts for stability. Most herbs do well in containers, so if you don't have much space you can grow all your herbs in pots.

We filled the garden with the basic and most used herbs—basil, chives, dill, marjoram, oregano, parsley, rosemary, sage,

Our garden thrives in the spring and summer, and it peaks in the early fall. Fall is also a great time to seed greens and lettuce around the garden. Frost usually kills tender plants, but during the winter the garden does retain a few herbs to hold us through the cool season. Plants such as thyme, parsley, chives, winter savory, marjoram, oregano, and some selections of rosemary tolerate the cold in the South.

Plant a little garden for herbs and see what works for you. If you want to start small, grow a few in pots. You don't have to be a purist; you can mix ornamental plants and a few vegetables with herbs. There's nothing like walking through herbs that have been bathed in the morning dew and rubbing your hand across these aromatic plants. Their smell will make you happy even before you get them to your kitchen. ◇

Anything but Common

Vibrant color adds impact to a summer garden. Common Purple phlox blooms from July into the fall with flowers that butterflies find irresistible.

While the name might lead you to believe this plant is a ho-hum perennial, Common Purple phlox (*Phlox paniculata* Common Purple) is quite above average. "It is gorgeous up close and from a distance too. It blooms for such a long time during the hottest part of the summer and continues into fall," says Lella Bromberg, who grows it in her Birmingham garden.

Rick Berry and Marc Richardson, owners of Goodness Grows Nursery in Lexington, Georgia, discovered this phlox many years ago. "We were in Greensboro, Georgia, and found an old abandoned homesite. Growing against the foundation was this vivid purple phlox. It had obviously been there a long time and neglected for years. In the middle of the hot summer it was in full bloom, happy as you please," Rick says.

Plant this tenacious perennial in a location that receives at least a half day of full sun. In bloom, heavy flower heads require support. A round, plastic-coated metal grid on tall legs works well. Place the support over the plant in spring, and foliage will grow through the windows of the grid. (Look for these supports at garden centers.)

A common complaint among gardeners is the propensity of phlox to become covered with powdery mildew. Common Purple phlox rarely has a problem with this fungus. Its leaves remain clean and healthy in most situations. Good air circulation helps keep this disease at bay, so plant phlox with some surrounding space.

Another way to control mildew is with deep, thorough watering. Rick's experience has shown that high humidity and dry soil are perfect conditions for mildew. "Phlox love evenly moist soil. Water the roots deeply at least once a week. If you use an overhead sprinkler, water early in the day so the foliage will dry before the plant becomes shaded."

Long-lasting flowers begin to appear in July. With proper pruning after the initial bloom, phlox can be coerced to bud several more times, adding rich color to late-summer and fall gardens. After the first flowers fade, cut the stem above a set of leaves one-third of the way down from the spent bloom. Within several weeks it will be budded again.

If there is a perfect summer perennial, this old-fashioned phlox is a strong and vibrant contender. *Ellen Riley*

(For sources turn to pages 250–251.)

PHOTOGRAPH: SYLVIA MARTIN

COMMON PURPLE PHLOX
At a Glance

Light: full to half-day of direct sun

Fertilizer: spring: well-balanced timed-release fertilizer; midsummer: liquid all-purpose fertilizer; late summer: liquid all purpose

Water: thoroughly, once a week

Bloom time: July through fall; cut back spent blooms to encourage new flowers.

Give Beach Plants A Chance

Leathery evergreen leaves and picturesque trunks make sea grape a striking waterfront accent in this Tropical South garden.

For plants that endure seaside conditions, life is no walk on the beach. Given the hurdles they must overcome, it's tough enough just to survive.

Bob Hartwig, a landscape architect in Jacksonville, Florida, knows the challenges of oceanfront gardening. The main obstacle, he says, is the nearly constant, salt-laden wind that robs moisture from plants and fries their foliage. This desiccating effect is magnified in winter, when plants grow slowly, if at all, and have a hard time dealing with stress.

A beach's front-line dunes are truly a "no-plant's land." Very few plants survive the unbuffered wind (ones that do are marked by an asterisk below). But when certain trees and shrubs are clustered together, they provide each other with enough shelter to become established. "Live oak, holly, oleander, magnolia, yaupon, wax myrtle—none of them will make it if they are stuck out there alone," states Bob. "But cluster five or six together, and they will."

Cabbage palmettos are the classic trees for the beach.

Another way to buffer the wind is by planting behind dunes, berms, or walls that deflect wind over or around the planting. For example, a retaining wall that's 2 feet tall can shield many low-growing plants whose foliage doesn't reach the top of the wall.

The leeward side of a house provides shelter as well. Bob says you can grow almost anything there, including azaleas, camellias, roses, and tender perennials. Just remember that wind acts like a wave rolling over a barrier.

Wind and salt are not the only problems on the coast. Sandy soil drains quickly, retaining little moisture. To improve the situation, amend the soil with copious amounts of organic matter, such as sphagnum peat moss, compost, pine straw, and ground bark, before you plant. Still, you'll likely have to water more often than you would elsewhere. If that isn't your style, choose drought-tolerant plants, such as century plant, yucca, prickly-pear cactus, oleander, juniper, Eastern red cedar, lantana, and Indian blanket.

And don't forget to stake large trees for the first year after you plant them. Trees growing in sandy soil need this to anchor themselves against the wind. *Steve Bender*

SURE THINGS FOR THE SHORE

Annuals and Perennials
century plant (*Agave americana*)—CS, TS*
daylily (*Hemerocallis* sp.)—US, MS, LS, CS, TS
Indian blanket (*Gaillardia pulchella*)—US, MS, LS, CS, TS*
lantana (*Lantana* sp.)—US, MS, LS, CS, TS
liriope (*Liriope* sp.)—US, MS, LS, CS, TS
prickly-pear cactus (*Opuntia humifusa*)—MS, LS, CS, TS*
yucca (*Yucca* sp.)—US, MS, LS, CS, TS*

Shrubs
coontie (*Zamia floridana*)—CS, TS*
Indian hawthorn (*Raphiolepis indica*)—LS, CS, TS*
inkberry (*Ilex glabra*)—US, MS, LS, CS
Japanese pittosporum (*Pittosporum tobira*)—CS, TS*
Natal plum (*Carissa grandiflora*)—CS, TS
oleander (*Nerium oleander*)—LS, CS, TS
shore juniper (*Juniperus conferta*)—US, MS, LS, CS
thorny elaeagnus (*Elaeagnus pungens*)—US, MS, LS, CS*
wax myrtle (*Myrica cerifera*)—MS, LS, CS

Trees
American holly (*Ilex opaca*)—US, MS, LS, CS
cabbage palm (*Sabal palmetto*)—LS, CS, TS*
coconut palm (*Cocos nucifera*)—TS*
Eastern red cedar (*Juniperus virginiana*)—US, MS, LS
Japanese black pine (*Pinus thunbergiana*)—US, MS, LS, CS
live oak (*Quercus virginiana*)—LS, CS, TS
sea grape (*Coccoloba uvifera*)—TS*
Southern magnolia (*Magnolia grandiflora*)—US, MS, LS, CS
Southern red cedar (*Juniperus silicicola*)—CS, TS
yaupon (*Ilex vomitoria*)—MS, LS, CS

Vines
beach morning glory (*Ipomoea pes-caprae*)—CS, TS*
bougainvillea (*Bougainvillea* sp.)—CS, TS
cape honeysuckle (*Tecomaria capensis*)—CS, TS
common allamanda (*Allamanda cathartica*)—TS

CS=Coastal South, LS=Lower South, MS=Middle South, TS=Tropical South, US=Upper South. *Will grow unshielded from wind on front-line dunes.

*Graceful branches and showstopping blue flowers make
Cape plumbago a valuable accent plant for containers and landscape.*

*With occasional light pruning,
blooms will keep coming into fall.*

Cool Plumbago

Cape plumbago's soft blue flowers cluster in cool color during the hottest days of summer. In Coastal and Tropical South gardens, this woody shrub may grow 6 feet tall and wide, blooming all year long. For the rest of us, it's a handsome annual that blooms until first frost.

Dottie Myers, of Dottie Myers & Associates, a landscape architecture firm in Atlanta, frequently uses plumbago in containers for her clients. "This plant adds a flower color that is almost nonexistent," she says. "I find that plumbago is most effective when planted in containers that are viewed up close. The icy blue color is difficult for the eye to detect at a distance."

Cape plumbago is versatile in light preference. It blooms beautifully with three and a half hours of direct midday sun, but it is also tough enough to withstand all-day exposure. Diligent watering is a must as the amount of sun increases.

Sprinkle a small amount of timed-release all-purpose shrub fertilizer (12-6-6) on top of the soil when you plant. "We also recommend containers be watered with a liquid food every two to three weeks," Dottie says. *Tip:* Never fertilize a plant when the soil is dry. Water prior to feeding so the food will not burn the roots.

CAPE PLUMBAGO
At a Glance

Light: half day to full day sun
Water: Keep evenly moist.
Fertilizer: Feed every two to three weeks with liquid blossom booster or fish emulsion.
Nice To Know: There is also a white selection of plumbago, equally as lovely as the blue one.

Mike Shoup, owner of the Antique Rose Emporium in Brenham, Texas, recommends an organic approach. "Amend the soil well with organic matter prior to planting. If necessary, supplement with an occasional watering with fish emulsion to keep the plant blooming," he says.

Plumbago can be considered maintenance-free, but a little attention goes a long way. "This plant is forgiving and will flower without any extra care," Mike says. "It blooms on new growth and always has a sporadic cover of flowers. When it is pruned back, it will bloom with intensity."

One way to prune is to cut back the branches severely into a controlled shrub. This produces a tight mass of foliage and blue flowers. Or cut only the spent blooms from the tips of branches. This encourages new growth and flowers while maintaining the plant's flowing appearance in the garden. Always cut plumbago back directly above a set of leaves. If you choose not to trim it, plumbago will acquire a natural grace with arching branches.

Before first frost in autumn, cut your container plant back and bring it indoors. It will happily reside in a sunroom or frost-free garage until spring. Blooms are minimal during winter months, returning when the weather becomes consistently warm in late spring. *Ellen Riley*

Votive candles perch like fireflies above this window box dressed for a party.

WINDOW DRESSINGS

Let your garden style shine in a well-planted window box.

BY ELLEN RILEY / PHOTOGRAPHY TINA CORNETT

Window boxes make an entrance welcoming, dress up the facade of a home, and give you the chance to show off a little," says Janie Singletary. She should know. In Greenville, South Carolina, her business, Gardenhaven, has flourished with good ideas.

"A window box should reflect the owner's personality," she says. "I try to choose plants with that in mind." Besides having personality, the planter should also suit the home. But within that framework, your imagination can grow. "It's a chance to do the unexpected," she says.

With Janie's ideas in hand, we went to work.

PARTY LIGHTS
The collection of white flowers and foliage (above) is simple and elegant. It brightens the shady entrance to

Marsha Twiford's brick home.

The base of the window box is a metal frame called a hayrack. It's lined with sheet moss and filled with soil. Impatiens and caladiums fill the top, while variegated vinca and asparagus fern trail over the side. The result is a window box so fat and full that the metal form is invisible.

"Impatiens are great plants to use as water indicators," Janie says. "If you're not sure it's time to water, take a look at the impatiens. They will wilt before anything else and let you know the box is dry," she says. "In a sunny box, add water-retaining polymers to the soil to hold moisture longer," she says.

With company coming, we spruced up using a Gardenhaven idea: Wire glass votive candle holders to plant stakes. Cut the stakes different lengths and carefully push them into

the window box. The candles should sit above the flowers and foliage. Light the candles as company arrives. "This is also a great look on a patio near an outdoor dining area. But don't leave the candles unattended," Janie says.

ARCHITECTURAL ADDITION
Peter Allsopp wanted a project. His wife, Jean, wanted to dress up the front of their house. So Peter built a box that matched the trim on their home (top, right). Then he had a tin insert made to slip inside the planter for moisture protection. We used Janie's idea of planting small shrubs in the box to give it a formal look. "Manicured shrubs are terrific in window boxes," she says. "They will last for several years and then can be moved into the garden."

An ivy garland softens the edge of the box without hiding the trim.

LEFT: *Complement the architecture with your window box.*

CENTER: *Painted sap buckets filled with basil, petunias, and Blackie sweet potato vine add character to a garage window.*

BELOW: *Clarke the cat peers over the silvery foliage and cool-colored flowers of this vine window box. Artemisia, blue and white tropical plumbago, rex begonia, variegated vinca, and creeping jenny fill the planter with soft colors and texture.*

"Purchase ivy hanging baskets with long runners," Janie says. Her instructions: Gently break each plant into two or three pieces. Place them along the front edge of the box at each loop's anchor point. Tie a piece of twine to a short stick. Push the stick into the soil at one corner of the box. Make a loop and fasten it into the soil with another stick. Repeat this process for all loops, ending at the opposite corner of the planter. Wind the ivy tendrils around the twine. Within a week or so, the leaves will turn in the same direction.

"With a year's growth, the garland will become 5 to 6 inches thick. Keep winding and trimming runners to keep the garland neat," says Janie.

WOODSY AND COOL

Window boxes are not restricted to the front of a home. Catherine and Jon Thompson use their backyard patio regularly during warm months. Their window box adds warmth to this well-used area (right, below). We began with a metal hayrack and turned it into a woodland planter.

We dismantled and soaked a grapevine wreath, and while the vine was wet and pliable, we wired it to the metal form. A purchased liner and soil readied the box for planting.

The Thompsons wanted their window box to have a finished look from the day they planted. "Don't be afraid to begin with large plant material,"

says Janie. "Your planter is a focal point of your yard, so plant it to look wonderful from the beginning."

FUN AND FUNCTION

At my home, I wanted some herbs in a convenient place, and the garage window, which is close to the kitchen, needed sprucing up. I was looking for a window box that would exemplify

Janie's rule of personality and the unexpected (left, center).

Sap buckets are available in rainbow colors. I chose a pastel palette, then mounted buckets to a board that matched the garage, and put drainage holes in the bottom of each.

Choosing plants was easy. Sweet basil, lemon basil, and Purple Ruffles were a must. For color, I turned to petunias. A scented lemon geranium added a different leaf texture and the Blackie sweet potato vine gave me a plant to trail and drape over the iron bars. The combination is colorful and compatible. "Water and light compatibility are as essential as color and texture," Janie reminds us.

Whether your window box enhances the landscape or is your only place to garden, be bold. Allow your personality to shine, and don't forget to add the unexpected. ◇

(For sources turn to pages 250–251.)

the colorful flowers of direct sowing seeds (See pages 180–181.)

August

Checklist for August

EDITORS' NOTEBOOK

"Honey, have you been microwaving our tomato plants again?" Tell the truth—isn't that what you were thinking when you came out this morning and saw all the tomato leaves rolled up? Or perhaps you thought this sorry condition was the handiwork of some evil bug or disease. Then rejoice with my happy news. Tomato leaf curl is often a natural response to stress put on fruiting plants by hot weather. Some selections, such as Big Boy, Floramerica, Beefsteak, and Roma, are more prone to it than others. It usually starts at the bottom of the plant and proceeds upward. Even if the curled leaves fall off, this doesn't reduce the yield. If you don't like curled leaves, there are three steps you can take: Don't overwater, don't damage roots by cultivating close to the plant, and don't take the microwave outside.

Steve Bender

☐ **Annuals**—Renew summer annuals one more time before fall. Pinch leggy marigolds and impatiens, cut back or replant zinnias, and pinch browned blooms from scarlet sage. Feed plants with a liquid fertilizer such as 20-20-20 to encourage growth for fall.

☐ **Azaleas and camellias**—These shallow-rooted plants set their flowerbuds in late summer and early fall. To ensure a good crop of flowers, water well between rain showers. Provide enough water with each application to wet the soil to a depth of 6 to 8 inches.

☐ **Bulbs**—Take time now to mail-order spring-flowering bulbs to plant this fall. Order plenty to make a good show; don't stop with a dozen of this and that unless you are growing them in pots.

☐ **Daylilies and iris**—Dig and divide individual plants every two to three years. Replenish the soil by tilling in 4 to 6 inches of organic material and 3 to 5 pounds of balanced fertilizer such as 12-6-6 per hundred square feet of planting area. Set out individual plants about 12 to 16 inches apart in groups of five or more. Water well every two or three days unless rain occurs.

☐ **Dried arrangements**—Start collecting seedpods from iris, sensitive fern, and blackberry lilies now for dried arrangements you'll want to make this fall and winter. You can also dry flowers, such as gomphrena and cockscomb, by hanging cut stems upside down in a dry, ventilated location.

☐ **Lawns**—Raise the cutting height of your lawnmower an inch to help your lawn cope with hot, dry weather.

☐ **Palms**—In the Tropical South, clean up plants by removing dead fronds. If new growth appears yellowish, your plants are probably lacking magnesium. Prepare a solution of magnesium sulfate, and spray it on your plants according to label directions. Add a few drops of dishwashing liquid to the solution to help it stick to the foliage.

☐ **Roses**—Get your plants ready for a big fall bloom. Fertilize them with a granular rose food (7-11-9), liquid fertilizer (20-20-20), fish emulsion, or manure tea (a solution created by placing a shovelful of manure in a bucket of water). Prune shrubs lightly, and train the new growth of climbers onto their support. Water weekly if there is no rain, and mulch to conserve soil moisture. ▶

◀ **Seeds**—This is a good time to mail-order flower and vegetable seeds for fall planting. If you have seed packets that are more than two years old or that have been exposed to heat or moisture, throw them away and order fresh ones. Also take advantage of end of the season sales on seed packets. For transplants ready to set out this fall, sow one type of seed per container of seed starting mix. Label and keep them moist until large enough to transplant into individual pots. Fertilize weekly with half-strength liquid 20-20-20 until planting time.

☐ **Water**—Even a few days without adequate moisture can kill newly planted trees and shrubs. Signs of stress include wilting, dull leaves that should be shiny, and burned leaf tips. A 3- to 5-inch layer of mulch such as pine bark, dried grass clippings, or similar material keeps roots cool and reduces evaporation from sun and wind.

PLANT

☐ **Flowers**—This is the time to sow seeds for biennials such as hollyhocks and fox-gloves, and perennials such as purple cone-flowers and Shasta daisies. The resulting transplants will be ready to set out in fall. ▶

☐ **Grass**—In the Lower South, it's best to plant a new lawn before freezing temperatures in the fall. Select St. Augustine, Bermuda, Zoysia, or centipede for your lawn. St. Augustine is the most shade tolerant. Bermuda covers the quickest. Zoysia is the most drought tolerant. And centipede requires less fertilizer.

◀ **Vegetables**—It will be time for Upper and Middle South gardeners to plant the fall garden later this month, so clean out declining plants and rework soil with compost. Leafy vegetables are heavy feeders and need fertile soil. Count backwards from your expected frost date, and plant accordingly, allowing enough time for your lettuce, broccoli, and such to mature. In the Coastal South, you still have time to plant lima and snap beans, cucumbers, pumpkins, summer and winter squash, peppers, and tomatoes in the first half of the month. In early September, you should begin the fall garden with broccoli, cabbage, carrots, chard, collards, kale, garlic, lettuce, and English peas.

PRUNE

☐ **Pinching**—Break off tips of branches of fall-blooming salvia, copper plants, mums, Mexican mint marigold, and obedient plants to keep them compact for their approaching bloom season in October and November.

☐ **Plants**—In the Tropical South, cut back allamanda, golden dewdrop, hibiscus, bougainvillea, ixora, and tibouchina as needed to keep them in bounds.

☐ **Roses**—Prune moderately about midmonth to stimulate fall flowering. Remove dead or weak canes; then cut back healthy stems about one-third. Apply a slow-release fertilizer such as 15-5-13, or use cottonseed meal at the rate of about one cupful per plant scattered over the root area. Water well.

CONTROL

☐ **Roses**—Continue spraying susceptible plants with Funginex to combat black spot and powdery mildew. Apply early in the morning so that the spray can dry before the day gets hot. Spraying in sunny weather when the temperature is above 85 degrees can cause the leaves to burn. The fungicide will help protect new foliage from disease, but spots already present on older leaves will not go away. Spray every 7 to 10 days through the fall.

☐ **Weeds**—The best cure for future weeds is to get rid of the ones you have before they can drop seeds all over your garden. Pull them if they are tall enough, or use a scuffle hoe or hand hoe to uproot them. Gather weeds, and put them in the trash. You don't want to unintentionally spread weeds in your garden by putting ones that bear seeds in your compost pile.

FERTILIZE

☐ **Roses**—Small amounts of fertilizer should be applied to roses every four to six weeks during the growing season. Cottonseed meal, timed-release chemical fertilizers such as 7-11-9, and composted manure work well. Be sure to water thoroughly after fertilizer is applied.

August notes:

TIP OF THE MONTH

I've found a new use for fabric softener sheets. After they lose their scent, I place them in the bottom of flowerpots to keep the dirt from washing out. The sheets allow excess water to drain and have lasted for 2 years so far.

MARILYN OGLETREE
OKLAHOMA CITY, OKLAHOMA

Gourds are a potent good luck symbol. They represent new life and potential.
—Randy Harelson, owner of The Gourd Garden and Curiosity Shop

Simply Gourdeous

Randy Harelson was headed home. After 18 years in Rhode Island, he was driving south to put his feet back on Southern soil. He was also looking to put down roots in a new business. On his journey, he passed a little white farmhouse with a colony of gourd birdhouses hanging in the side yard. "When I saw that farmhouse the idea came to me—full-blown. The Gourd Garden and Curiosity Shop was born in my mind in that instant," Randy says. After five years it has become everything he envisioned.

Located on a gentle curve of County Road 30-A in the Florida panhandle, The Gourd Garden's circular drive leads you into a garden lush with tropical foliage, flowers, and herbs. Dried gourds hang in raindrop shapes from every porch and eave. This year's new crop dangles from arbors, defying gravity. It is nursery, old-fashioned garden, and roadside attraction rolled into one.

BY ELLEN RILEY / PHOTOGRAPHY SYLVIA MARTIN

The Gourd Garden and Curiosity Shop offers visitors a view of old-time Florida. "I wanted a place that was full of life—lots and lots of life," Randy says.

From smooth to gnarly and large to small, gourd diversity is enormous. You can browse the bins of gourds that are ready to take home, or if growing them is your passion, Randy has an endless seed selection to choose from.

Randy drew upon his training as horticulturist, teacher, and designer to create his multidimensional business. "This is a business about place. I chose Seagrove Beach because it represents old-time Florida. It has the lazy, low-key quality that is rapidly vanishing," he says.

Whimsical charm engulfs this business. "I wanted it to be like an old tourist stop we all remember as children riding through Florida," he says. "It taps our memories of alligator farms and cypress-knee museums. The gourds give this place that quality.

"To me, gardening is about having fun. I resisted doing a traditional nursery because I'm not interested in the kind of garden design that is about pomp and formality. It's interesting plants, vegetables, and unusual things. It's finding the magic in life," he says.

Dried gourds of every size and description fill baskets and bins in the open-air barn. Long-necked dipper gourds remind visitors of days not long gone. "I had a man tell me that water never tasted so good as when he drank from an old dipper gourd," Randy says.

Inside the old Florida-style home nearby, rooms are filled with beautifully crafted gourds. Made into vessels, instruments, and accessories, they are functional art using techniques that have been around for centuries. From tiny animals that fit into the palm of your hand to ornately etched lamps, Randy has fulfilled his goal of offering gourds as art.

"This is a place where people can come to enjoy themselves," he says. With the large assortment of flowers, herbs, and gourds to peruse, a few hours of beach time can quickly vanish. "Several ladies from Fairhope, Alabama, paid me the ultimate compliment a few weeks ago. They drove into The Gourd Garden and told me they'd come just to picnic under our live oaks. It must have taken them several hours to get here, and they just wanted to enjoy the cool shade and fun of this place." At The Gourd Garden and Curiosity Shop, that's easy to do. ◇

(For sources turn to pages 250–251.)

Leaving spaces for ornamental grasses, flowers, and small shrubs gives the terrace a softer, more natural feeling.

Making the Pool a Plus

When Lynn and Doug Parsons moved into their home in Chevy Chase, Maryland, the pool out back wasn't exactly a plus. For one thing, you couldn't get to it from the main floor; the sole access was through a basement door. For another, the pool was surrounded by stark white concrete that was pleasant to sit on only when your feet were dangling in the water.

Off the back of the house, a new deck with steps to the ground solved the first problem. Next, Lynn and Doug replaced the concrete with cooler and less reflective exposed aggregate. But to make their yard realize its full potential required the assistance of Garden Gate Landscaping of Silver Spring, Maryland.

Garden Gate designed a pair of bluestone terraces on opposite sides of the

Set into a slope, the smaller terrace seems like a private getaway. Pines and evergreen shrubs shade both terraces and add welcome privacy.

pool. The larger terrace, nestled among ornamental grasses, perennials, and pots of annuals, is perfect for a group of six to eight people. The smaller terrace, set into a slope and bordered by a stacked-stone wall, offers a private getaway for two. Placing the flagstones atop beds of bluestone dust allows rainwater to percolate through the terraces without running into the pool.

Tall white pines and evergreen shrubs shade both spots during the heat of the day. Folks can relax comfortably without swimming or sunbathing. The evergreens also provide plenty of privacy.

Now the owners love it. Without completely starting anew, they changed a place that was hard to get to into a place where they want to be. *Steve Bender*

(For sources turn to pages 250–251.)

The Art of Watering

PHOTOGRAPH: VAN CHAPLIN, ALLEN ROKACH

This time of year, gardeners are likely to say, "What we need is a good rain."

So what is "a good rain"? It's a shower that is gentle enough to soak in before it runs off and lasts long enough to thoroughly moisten the garden. For gardeners who look to nature as a model to grow by, there is no better example of how to water than a good rain.

If you go out and do a little sprinkling each afternoon, over a few weeks your plants will develop roots in the top inch or two of soil where they find moisture. But when you go away for a week at the beach, the surface of the soil dries out quickly and your plants suffer.

However, if you water enough to moisten your soil 5 to 6 inches deep, and then wait until plants are thirsty before soaking the soil again, your plants will develop deep root systems that will survive your vacation this summer.

You can tell when your plants are thirsty before they wilt. Lawns, annuals, perennials, and shrubs look slightly pale; their green leaves have a grayish cast. Finally their leaves look a little limp before they actually wilt. That's your cue to pour it on. Then sit back until your plants give you the signal again. With luck, you will get a good rain before you have to drag out the hose.

SPRINKLERS VS. SOAKERS

Sprinklers actually simulate rain, and you can buy portable models in a variety of designs. Some are even adjustable in their coverage area. Just as in-ground sprinklers are chosen to fit their niche, select your portable sprinkler to suit your garden. You may need different models to fit different areas. Read packaging to determine how much area a sprinkler is designed to cover.

Tall foliage may block the spray coming from a sprinkler. Buy a tripod for your sprinkler, or simply set yours on a ladder and weight it down with a brick or rock. This will get the spray above nearby foliage so coverage is more even.

Soaker hoses include flattened plastic tubes with lots of little holes that emit short sprays, as well as hoses made of recycled tires that simply ooze water. Both have the advantage of providing moisture economically, delivering it where you need it with minimal loss to evaporation or runoff. These are ideal for long, narrow beds or rows in a vegetable garden, but they are not the best choice for an expanse of lawn.

POTTED PLANTS

Plants growing in containers are especially dependent. Their roots can reach no deeper than the pot in which they are planted. If the container is unglazed clay, it will dry particularly fast, leaving the roots parched.

To water a potted plant, fill the reservoir formed by the inch or so of the container's rim that extends above the level of the soil. Let that soak in. Repeat until water runs out of the drainage holes in the bottom

RULE OF THUMB

How much water you apply and how often you need to water depends on your soil. If you have a clay-based soil, it will hold more moisture. Apply about 2 inches of water (measure it in a container placed under the sprinkler) once each week. If you have sandy soil, it will hold less and dry more quickly. Apply about an inch of water twice a week.

of the pot. If the soil becomes so dry that it has shrunk and pulled away from the sides, water several more times to be certain the soil is thoroughly moistened. (Sometimes water can just run down the sides and out the bottom of the container.)

Water-absorbing polymers can be mixed into potting soil to create an internal reservoir. These clear gelatinous granules swell to many times their size, holding water that is released as the soil dries. These products are good for hanging baskets, window boxes, and mixed planters that can't make it through a hot day without wilting. Be careful though; if you don't follow directions and use too much, the soil will expand and overflow. *Linda C. Askey*

Hot Plants, Cool Colors

There's a point in summer when even the thermometer begins to sweat. August heat hits its stride and many flowers wilt or refuse to bloom. There are plants that thrive as the mercury rises, and if you choose colors carefully, your planter can appear cool as a cucumber.

Radiant red and dayglow orange blooms make a colorful statement, but this big splash of color also visually translates into heat. With white and pastel blossoms, even though the temperature is the same, the colors make a cooler appearance.

Summer bloomers that love heat are mandevilla, lantana, plumbago, and pentas. Colors range from hot pink to blinding yellow. Look a little further and you'll find selections with pristine white, soft rosy pink, peach, and pale yellow flowers.

Mandevilla provides a good example of color perception. The eye-popping, seriously pink selection Alice du Pont makes a flashy show in full sun. The paler selection called Leah is equally heat hardy, but has a cooler look. Another frosty choice is soft pink to nearly white Summer Snow.

Lantana is also available in cooler hues. Clear White is a weeping form good for a container's edge or hanging basket. Denholm White is a compact, heavy-flowering selection. Instead of blazing Golden Yellow Mound, try buttery Lemon Drop for soft-color blooms. Lady Olivia is a pastel bicolor with gentle pink-and-yellow flowers.

ABOVE: *Blue plumbago, light pink pentas, white lantana, and tricolor potato vine fill a pot with cool color.*

RIGHT: *Leah mandevilla is a heat-loving plant with refreshing, soft pink flowers. Pair it with blue plumbago for the perfect summer duo.*

PHOTOGRAPHS: JEAN ALLSOPP

Plumbago sports ice blue blooms that are the coolest of them all. Use it alone to fill a container or paired with other heat-lovers to add airy texture along with a refreshing hue. For more on plumbago, see page 163.

Pentas come in a pastel rainbow of colors. Look for soft pink, lavender, and white selections. There are few named selections, so choose based on what you see in bloom. For more on pentas, see page 177.

Ellen Riley
(For sources turn to pages 250–251.)

BEAT THE HEAT TIPS FOR COLORFUL CONTAINERS

There are a few things you can do to keep your flowers in top form during summer's dog days.

■ Water daily until liquid runs from the pot's drainage hole. The best time is morning.

■ Feed your plants weekly with a water-soluble fertilizer. Use one, such as 15-30-15, with a high middle number.

■ Clip off old blooms once a week.

■ Place the container on pot "feet" to add an inch of air space between the container and the hot surface underneath.

RIGHT: The view of the garage end of the house shows a much more inviting landscape.

BEFORE

PHOTOGRAPH: JEAN ALLSOPP

New Home, New Yard

If only new houses could come with old yards. But unless you've demolished an old house and built another one in its place, chances are your new home is surrounded by a flat lawn and a few too-small-to-see baby plants.

Don't despair. Just as you picked out wallpaper, carpet, and paint colors, you need to pick out trees, shrubs, and ground covers to give your yard personality. Take a look at what Randy and Jeannie Dawson of Watkinsville, Georgia, have done by working on their landscape in stages over the past seven years.

Their first step was to turn to a professional for advice. Horticulturist Ron Deal of Classic City Gardens in Athens, Georgia, met with the Dawsons and sketched out a plan to direct their do-it-yourself efforts. Ron designed a simple retaining wall to separate the lawn area by the street from a smaller planting area three steps down. The multilevel yard makes the front more interesting.

Planting for privacy was the next priority. Quick-growing Leyland cypress, Japanese anise, and yaupon hollies frame the house and block the view of a water tower looming on the horizon.

One of the best ways to avoid the plopped-down look of a new house is to plant a tree that gets big fast. A river birch planted beside the garage quickly grew above the roof. Now that the house is no longer the tallest thing on the property, its size seems appropriate for the yard. The birch's leafy canopy also adds much-needed shade to the landscape.

Colorful low-maintenance plants show off against the house's light facade. Gold Mound spirea contrasts with a bed of Crimson Pygmy barberry. Lavender spikes crown a lilac chaste tree each summer. Other plants, such as wax myrtles and Zabel cherry laurels were chosen because they stay green year-round.

"The barberries are my favorite," says Jeannie. "I also love the Kwanzan cherry underplanted with spreading yew."

Jo Kellum

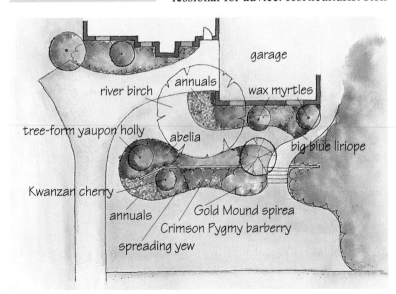

garage

river birch

annuals

wax myrtles

tree-form yaupon holly

abelia

big blue liriope

Kwanzan cherry

annuals

Gold Mound spirea

Crimson Pygmy barberry

spreading yew

For the most impact, mass a single color rather than planting one of each.

Easy to grow and a favorite of hummingbirds and butterflies, this flower blooms nonstop in colors of red, pink, lavender, and white.

PENTAS
At a Glance

Size: 2 to 3 feet tall and wide
Light: sun or light shade
Soil: moist, fertile, well drained
Pests: spider mites in hot, dry weather
Propagation: seeds, cuttings
Hardiness: perennial in Coastal and Tropical South; annual elsewhere
Expect to pay: $2 to $5, depending on size

Pentas Does It All

Are you a shameless creature of habit? Have you been setting out marigolds and scarlet sage ever since the Beatles disbanded? Then it's time you tried something new. And I have just the thing. It's a flower called pentas that simply does everything well.

It blooms nonstop in warm weather. It attracts hummingbirds and butterflies. Its cut flowers last a long time in water. Its cut stems root easily in soil or just plain water.

The point is, this is one terrific plant. Native to Tropical Africa, pentas *(Pentas lanceolata)* grows 2 to 3 feet tall and wide. Flat clusters of red, pink, lavender, or white starlike flowers appear atop dark green, deeply veined leaves. Perennial in the Coastal and Tropical South, it's an annual elsewhere. Of course, if you're a real cheapo like me, you can pot it up and take it indoors to a sunny window for the winter.

Although some folks prefer to mix the colors, mass plantings of a single color show up better in flowerbeds. Pentas makes an excellent container plant too. Periodically removing spent flowers and shortening stems keeps this champion performer bushy and floriferous.

You'll find pentas at most good nurseries and garden centers. I wish I could say you'll find the Beatles there too. But Paul still refuses to garden with George and Ringo. *Steve Bender*

*Having a place
to plant makes all
the difference.*

Just Enough Garden

While many apartment dwellers revel in the freedom from yard work, others languish without a garden. By recognizing that need in many of their residents, Post Properties, Inc., keeps their apartments full and their tenants happy.

Although not all of the Post Developments have garden plots for their residents, many do. They are located throughout the South, from Tampa to the outskirts of D.C. But within that stretch of corporate holdings lies a philosophy that is as personal as a gardener's seed order. Residents may have only a square yard or two to plant a few tomatoes, zinnias, or collards, but that bed is an entrée to the community, a link to a personal past, and a way to put down roots—both real and psychological.

Rick Matczak lives in the Post Collier Hills community in Atlanta, and the availability of a garden plot was key in

his decision to live there. "This is the area where I want to live, and I can have a garden too," Rick says. "I normally wouldn't like to live in an apartment, but I can have a plot of ground here."

The way these gardens are constructed and managed would make many homeowners happy as well. Raised beds reduce strain on backs and provide deep, loose soil for the plants. There is a convenient source of water and an area to wash vegetables to avoid a

RIGHT: *Rick Matczak chose to live here because of the community garden. Raised beds and a convenient source of water make gardening more pleasure than work.*

There's nothing like picking a few radishes or fresh lettuce leaves for supper's salad.

A table with an expanded mesh top makes washing the daily harvest easy.

Shawn McKinney at Post Crest Apartment Homes in Atlanta enjoys coming home and spending time in her garden after work.

kitchen sink full of soil. Tool storage is nearby, and the entire garden is fenced to keep out lettuce-munching bunnies.

But in some ways—namely the camaraderie of gardeners and the know-how provided by the staff of Post Properties—these apartment dwellers have the advantage of homeowners. Gardeners such as Shawn McKinney at Post Crest Apartment Homes check the bulletin board for upcoming workshops or advice from the garden staff. The joy of shedding work clothes at the end of the day and heading to the garden in the comfort of blue jeans shines in her eyes. There's nothing like picking a few radishes or fresh lettuce for supper's salad, or taking a few minutes to sow some seeds to ease that transition at the end of the day.

Regular workshops are scheduled to teach gardeners who are just starting out. According to floriculture manager Todd Link, "About 95% of our gardeners are beginners." He sees the appeal going far beyond the harvest. The garden becomes a social outlet.

While the size of the bed may sound restrictive, many enjoy a little opportunity that can't grow into an obligation. "Some residents call it a 'one martini garden,'" laughs Post apartment management senior vice president John Hooks. *Linda C. Askey*

KEEP ON
BLOOMING

The wind blows hard across the landscape and disperses seeds from old, dried flower heads. This is the way Mother Nature plants trees, shrubs, and flowers on the earth's floor.

We as gardeners are able to select seeds and throw them where and when we want quick, colorful displays. Most gardeners put out seeds in the spring or in autumn, but by sowing seeds now you will have summer flowers in the fall. Last August, I planted seeds and had blooms until the first hard frost.

Direct sowing seeds is the easiest way to get inexpensive color. It's a simple process of taking seeds and throwing them on top of the ground. However, you should do a little soil preparation beforehand (see photos at far right). The soil should be loose, well drained, and fertile.

Plants that may be seeded late in the summer include cosmos, zinnia, celosia, cleome, and tithonia. These plants should be up and flowering in 6 to 10 weeks. You can scatter the seeds by hand if you have a small area. Large areas may require a seed distributor or spreader. Small hand-held spreaders are perfect for most homeowners.

Some seeds need warmth and moisture to germinate quickly. In August

Direct sowing seeds now is an easy way to get inexpensive color into fall.

there's plenty of warmth, but moisture can be scarce except for the humidity. Make sure you have the ability to water.

These seeds are so small there is no need to cover them with soil. Use a water wand with a fine-mist setting to settle seeds into the ground. During germination, keep the seed bed evenly moist. Begin feeding with 20-20-20 water-soluble fertilizer at half strength when seedlings first appear. Feed once a month with a full strength solution after the first true leaves appear. There's no time for a second crop, so make sure you take care of your seedlings and pamper them.

If some of the areas come up sparse, transplant seedlings from thicker areas to make the planting more even. As summer changes to fall, nighttime temperatures turn cooler and flowers hold up longer. Late in the fall when your plants decline or are killed by frost, you can simply cut them down with a nylon-string trimmer or lawnmower.

While all your neighbors are complaining about how they need to pull up their rough-looking summer annuals, you can smile with pride and enjoy your seeded summer annuals into the fall. And, if you seed now, you'll be able to cut flowers for Thanksgiving. ◇

BY CHARLIE THIGPEN / PHOTOGRAPHY VAN CHAPLIN

Add organic matter, such as leaf mold or mushroom compost, to poor soil.

A small tiller works well for turning and mixing soil in flowerbeds.

Use a hard rake to remove any debris and to smooth the surface of the bed.

QUICK FLOWERS FROM SEED

Cosmos—Bright Lights, Early Wonder
Celosia—Flamingo Purple, Pink Candle
Cleome—Rose Queen, Violet Queen
Tithonia—Goldfinger, Torch
Zinnia—Cut and Come Again, Envy, Giant Double, State Fair

Brazilian verbena (See page 195.)

September

Checklist for September

EDITORS' NOTEBOOK

Famous writers seldom look to insects for inspiration. But when Sir Walter Scott penned, "Oh, what a tangled web we weave, when first we practise to deceive!" I think he was talking about bugs. Just look up into your hardwood trees right now. You'll see silken webs wrapped around the ends of branches. Fall webworms hiding inside are eating all the leaves. The damage is, in the evocative words of my cousin Harley Poteet, "uglier than a bathroom with a polka-dot pink commode." There are three things you can do about webworms. First, cut off and burn the branch. Second, break up the web, and then spray it with carbaryl or malathion. Third, break up the web, and then spray it with apple cider. Yellow jackets love apple cider and will eat the webworms just for spite. Sounds mean, but Walter and Harley say that's what webworms get for being so sneaky. *Steve Bender*

☐ **Avocados**—In the Coastal and Tropical South, enjoy fall-ripening selections this month. Pick the fruit when it reaches full size, and let it ripen off the tree. Most types cannot be tree-ripened.

☐ **Coconuts**—In the Tropical South, it is time to prune older fronds and fruit from coconut trees in preparation for the most active months of the hurricane season.

☐ **Flowers**—In the Coastal and Tropical South, dig old clumps of daylilies to separate into smaller portions that will be more vigorous. Gently divide crowded bulbs such as amaryllis, African iris, calla lilies, and Easter lilies; spread them out for a larger, more spectacular planting. ▶

☐ **Lawn renovation**—After a playful summer, your fescue lawn may have some thin spots. Lime and fertilize as recommended by a soil test. If the soil is compacted, loosen it using an aerator or tiller. Choose a turf-type fescue or cool-season blend. Use a spreader for even distribution. Keep the lawn moist as you would a new lawn.

☐ **Spring-flowering bulbs**—In the Lower and Coastal South, prepare beds for fall planting by incorporating several inches of organic material along with 4 to 5 pounds of bonemeal or superphosphate per 100 square feet of bed area. Raise the beds several inches above surrounding areas to facilitate good drainage because most bulbs rot easily in wet areas.

◀ **Watering**—The best time to turn on your sprinkler is in the morning. It is still cool enough that water won't evaporate before it hits the ground, yet the leaves will dry as the sun rises higher in the sky. If you water in the evening, the leaves will remain wet all night, encouraging the growth of foliage diseases. And if you water at midday, you'll lose a lot of water to evaporation.

☐ **Bluebonnets**—In the Middle, Lower, and Coastal South, sow seeds of bluebonnets on lightly cultivated soil, and rake gently. For best results, cover the seeds with ¼ to ½ inch of soil. Water well weekly until rains are sufficient. Bluebonnets are drought tolerant, but they require moisture to germinate.

☐ **Fall annuals**—Plant zinnias, marigolds, and impatiens for fall flower color. These warm-weather favorites gain new vigor as they enter the shorter days and cooler nights of fall. ▶

☐ **Heat-tolerant annuals**—For color that can take the heat, try Madagascar periwinkles, zinnias, portulaca, globe amaranth, celosia, melampodium, coleus, and impatiens in your garden.

☐ **Herbs**—There's still time to sow seeds of dill and cilantro (coriander). You can also set out transplants or sow seeds of parsley.

☐ **Overseeding**—Sow annual or perennial ryegrass seed over Bermuda lawns late this month or early next month for green all winter long. Apply about 5 pounds per 1,000 square feet, and water daily until germination. The rye will overtake the Bermuda this fall, and then they will trade places next spring.

☐ **Perennials**—In the Upper and Middle South, shasta daisies, daylilies, iris, peonies, and purple coneflowers may be set out now for spring bloom. Arrange them in elongated masses of at least 7 to 10 individual plants spaced about 12 to 18 inches apart. ▶

◀ **Vegetables**—Set out fall vegetables now in the Middle and Lower South. Sow seeds of spinach, lettuce, radishes, mustard, collards, kale, and corn salad. Plant sets of garlic and onions. You can also set out transplants of cole crops (cabbage, broccoli, and their kin) if you get them in early.

PRUNE

☐ **Perennials**—It is time to cut back tired stalks and faded flowers of veronica, verbena, artemisia, canna, salvia, and other perennials. Feed with a liquid fertilizer such as 20-20-20 for renewed growth and fall blooms. ▶

CONTROL

◀ **Roses**—The hot, wet days of summer and early fall promote the development of black spot disease on rose leaves. Spray every 7 to 10 days with a fungicide, such as Funginex, labeled for black spot on roses.

☐ **Weeds**—Apply pre-emergence weed control if annual bluegrass was a problem this past spring. Although it is most visible in spring, the coming weeks when night temperatures drop into the 50s will be the prime time for these seeds to germinate. Apply Treflan (Preen), Dimension, Balan, or pendimethalin as directed on the label.

FERTILIZE

☐ **Camellias**—In the Lower and Coastal South, fertilize camellias for the last time this year. Later feedings may encourage new growth, which is susceptible to freeze damage later in the year. Select and apply an acid-forming fertilizer that lists azaleas and camellias on the label.

☐ **Citrus**—In the Coastal South, it is time to stop fertilizing citrus trees. Let the trees begin to go dormant, building cold hardiness in case a freeze later occurs. ▶

☐ **Lawns**—Feed warm-season lawns for the last time this season. Apply a product such as 16-4-8 or 15-5-10 at the rate recommended on the bag, or use a winterizer that has extra potassium such as 22-4-14.

September notes:

BEAUTIFUL BUTTERFLIES

56 PLATES IN FULL COLOUR

Butterflies' f r i e n d

Starlings to the left of you, swallows to the right—what's a butterfly to do? In Thomasville, Georgia, the best plan by far is to head for the glorious garden of Julie Neel, as butterflies have been doing for the last 40 years.

Julie began featuring butterfly plants in her home garden to increase the butterflies' chances to propagate in safety. Then, as she explains, "Our daughters became interested. It was fun for them as children. They're still involved, and now I get to take my granddaughter, Eliza, out to count butterfly eggs in the garden."

Julie was asked to select the state butterflies for both Georgia (Tiger Swallowtail) and Florida (Zebra Longwing), basing her choices on the criteria that a state butterfly must not be harmful to agriculture and must occur throughout the state so all residents can enjoy it.

Her current project involves working with the Joseph W. Jones

BY LIZ DRUITT / PHOTOGRAPHY JEAN ALLSOPP

Plants that attract butterflies include tithonia, verbena, lantana, porter weed, summer phlox, and purple coneflower.

them. I feed the birds, even though they're the greatest predator of caterpillars, and I put in plants to attract other sorts of predators. Everything just balances out—really. I sure have got scads of butterflies this year!"

Two things Julie does do are scatter her larval host plants apart and mass the groups of nectaring plants together. The first gives the caterpillars a natural edge over the birds and avoids having tattered skeletons of caterpillar-chewed foliage turn her beautiful wrap-around-the-house garden into a ragged mess. Grouping the fragrant, nectaring plants, on the other hand, saves energy for butterflies seeking supper. And that part is easy too. As Julie points out, "Lantanas and porter weeds

Butterflies can see the full spectrum of colors, but they'll be most attracted to yellows, oranges, purples, and reds.

Porter weed

Ecological Research Center in Newton, Georgia. She's helping to establish both a butterfly garden and an outdoor classroom for teachers who want to share the butterfly experience with their pupils. Julie also gives special slide programs on butterflies for kids and adults.

In addition to being generous to wildlife, this expert is generous with information for the beginner. "If you have a small garden or are just getting started," she says, "put in some nectaring plants first. Butterflies will come to eat, and once you identify your butterflies, you'll know which larval host plants to add. For example, passionflower vine supports Gulf Fritillary caterpillars. And you can put in plants for butterflies to lay eggs on. Feed the adults first; then you can go on to support their whole life cycle." The best of all nectaring plants, in Julie's experience, are butterfly bush (*Buddleia* sp.), lantana, verbena, and pentas.

"It's very important not to use pesticides—very important. And I've found out through the years that you don't need

[*Stachytarpheta* sp.] that grow 6 feet across truly provide their own mass!"

Planting the right flowers is a start, but Julie has even more advice for making a butterfly haven out of your garden. It takes very little work to provide a "puddling place" for butterflies to drink. Julie's puddling place is a simple plastic container filled with builder's sand and aquarium gravel to make it shallow. She keeps a watering can nearby so she can sprinkle it whenever she passes. Butterflies aren't looking for deep water—just a little moisture. They're also looking for nutrients and salts. Adding a small amount of pure mushroom compost to the damp gravel gives the ideal flavor, and then all you need are a few nice basking rocks where your butterflies can enjoy the sun on their wings.

Color, fragrance, sunny rocks, and a salty puddle. Paradise enough. ◇

Pentas

Simple plantings, just enough color, a deep green lawn, and an attractive fence create that all-important curb appeal.

Walk on By

"I like this idea for the birdbath"

Folks in Lorenda Stetler's Tulsa neighborhood like to walk their dogs up and down the sidewalk. Trouble is, the pooches often wander onto neighbors' lawns and do unspeakable things. So Lorenda asked landscape architect Cynthia C. Patton to design a solution that would give her front yard privacy, enclosure, and curb appeal, while requiring minimal maintenance.

Step one involved the construction of a handsome picket fence and gate. "I stole the fence design from Hawaii," confesses Lorenda. "My husband and I were driving through a gated community in Maui when I spotted it. I said, 'There's my fence!' So I jumped out and sketched the fence on the back of my airline ticket folder." Placing the fence about a foot back from the sidewalk left room for flowers.

To reduce maintenance, Cynthia planted low-growing evergreens in front of the house and mixed shrub borders along the sides of the yard. Two narrow beds of annuals in front of the evergreens add the right amount of sparkle but don't take much time to water. A Zoysia lawn is small enough that mowing is a relaxing chore.

Because the front yard is shallow and the house is tall, Cynthia decided shade trees were necessary to soften the transition from house to curb. "The trees make the lot look deeper and the house look shorter," Cynthia explains. "This gives the yard a more human scale." Plus, their leaves help screen the house from the street.

Thanks to the fence and well-thought-out plantings, Lorenda's yard is now the prettiest on the street. And the dogs and their owners just walk on by. *Steve Bender*

RIGHT: *This bench and stone terrace on one side of the yard serve as a focal point. Mixed trees and shrubs on either side block views of an adjacent driveway.*

PHOTOGRAPHS: ALLEN ROKACH

Placing the fence about a foot back from the sidewalk leaves room for flowers. A red oak planted behind the fence screens the house from the street, providing privacy and helping the shallow lot appear deeper.

BEFORE

Smart Makeover

It takes just a few changes to give a house a little charm.

BY JO KELLUM
PHOTOGRAPHY ALLEN ROKACH

Tucked in between cuter, more expensive houses are occasional diamonds in the rough. If you like the neighborhood, the floor plan, the lot, and the price, don't worry about a boring facade. Gather your ideas, set a budget, and get ready to pour on the curb appeal. Need inspiration? Take a look at the makeover of this house in Birmingham.

BEFORE
The original awning was attached too low, blocking the view of the front door. Overgrown shrubs gave a forlorn look. Black wrought iron rails hemmed in the small stoop. The odd front face may have been the result of a zoning dispute; the house is built right on the setback line. Perhaps original plans for a front porch were abandoned, leaving the architecture looking unbalanced.

AFTER
A new color palette of black, white, and terra-cotta was selected. The front door, a dark blue-gray, was re-painted a deep copper. A new brass knocker, kick plate, and mail slot add sparkle. Glossy white trim sets off the new door color and separates it from the taupe siding. Before, the front steps and the front door were painted the same color. Repainting the steps with a neutral warm gray made the door stand out.

Mounting the new bubble awning above the overhang helped establish a taller vertical line at the front door. The new black awning cost about $390 installed.

The house still needed presence, so a 7½- x 4½-foot landing was designed to replace a broken bottom step. The new landing was framed with exterior-grade pressure-treated

lumber, stained to match the steps. A bed of crushed limestone fills the frame; mitered corners keep the limestone in place. The raised landing and some additional soil added around the steps eliminated the need for rails, so those were removed with a reciprocating saw.

Eighteen-inch-square concrete pads were used for the surface of the landing. They cost about $4 each and can be set without mortar. Staining every other square black created a checkerboard pattern.

A lattice trellis near the front door repeats the black-and-white square theme. The trellis balances the asymmetrical facade and frames the off-center door. A pair of 4 x 4 posts set in concrete footers supports the trellis. The posts attach to the home's overhang at the top.

The planting plan is simple. First, existing masses of nandina were used to fill in gaps. Curving in front of the nandina around the landing, low-growing Helleri hollies add year-round greenery. Southern shield fern contributes a lacy texture. Room for perennials right around the door allows color where this house needs it. Black-eyed Susans, Queen Anne's lace, joe-pye weed, and Powis Castle artemisia will come back each year.

Supplementing the color beds with annuals such as marigolds and Gold Mound lantana is a quick way to dress things up. A Natchez crepe myrtle planted near the triple front window balances the landscape. The result: a fresh new look for a previously overlooked house. ◇

(For sources turn to pages 250–251.)

BEFORE

LANDSCAPE ARCHITECT: JO KELLUM

ABOVE: *A new awning and trellis makes the difference. Fresh paint on the door helps too.* RIGHT: *Before, the house's unfriendly entry left an unfortunate first impression.*

SQUEEZING LEMONS

Turn quirks into perks. The odd overhang formed a narrow recess above the front door. This became an opportunity to fix another problem: lighting. The old wall-mounted fixture was removed and replaced with can lights set in the recess above the door. Now light shines from inside the awning directly on the front door.

Chalk Up a Win Over Alkaline Soil

Do your oak trees sport sickly yellow leaves? Do the leaves of your azaleas and gardenias turn yellow between the veins? The culprit may be alkaline soil.

What exactly is alkaline soil? It's soil with a pH above the neutral point of 7.0 (a pH below 7.0 is considered acid). It typically occurs in regions with sparse rainfall, such as West and North Texas and west Oklahoma. But it also occurs where beds of ancient limestone lie just beneath the soil surface. This is why alkaline soil is often referred to as "limy" or "chalky." Limestone deposits can be found in every Southern state except Louisiana. Major deposits exist in Texas, Missouri, Kentucky, Tennessee, Alabama, and Florida.

Alkaline soil affects plants by increasing the availability of some soil nutrients, while holding back on others. For example, alkaline soil supplies plants with plenty of calcium and magnesium. But it's stingy with zinc, manganese, and sulfur. These shortfalls stunt certain plants. The nutrient most commonly deficient in high pH soil is iron. Lack of iron causes chlorosis (leaves yellowing

Live oaks like limestone just fine. Their wide-spreading canopies and sculptural trunks are common sights in most of Texas.

between the veins). Severe chlorosis eventually kills affected plants.

To determine whether you have alkaline soil, get a soil test kit. You'll find simple test kits at garden centers, nurseries, and home-center stores.

Having alkaline soil isn't a problem if you select plants adapted to it. There are many native ones that are carefree and drought tolerant (see chart below). There are also a few popular plants that should never be planted in

alkaline soil: American holly *(Ilex opaca),* azalea, blueberry, camellia, flowering dogwood *(Cornus florida),* gardenia, ixora, Japanese andromeda *(Pieris japonica),* mountain laurel *(Kalmia latifolia),* pin oak *(Quercus palustris),* rhododendron, and willow oak *(Quercus phellos).*

So save yourself some toil and torment. If your soil is limy, choose plants that like it. You'll wonder where the yellow went. *Steve Bender*

TREES FOR ALKALINE SOIL

Common Name	Botanical Name	Mature Height	Range	Special Features
Caddo sugar maple	(Acer saccharum Caddo)	40-50 feet	US, MS, LS	brilliant fall color
chaste tree	(Vitex agnus-castus)	10-15 feet	US, MS, LS, CS	blue summer flowers
Chinese pistachio	(Pistacia chinensis)	30-40 feet	US, MS, LS, CS	excellent fall color
crepe myrtle	(Lagerstroemia indica)	6-30 feet	US, MS, LS, CS	showy flowers, fall foliage, bark
live oak	(Quercus virginiana)	40-80 feet	LS, CS, TS	magnificent, wide-spreading tree
redbud	(Cercis sp.)	10-40 feet	US, MS, LS, CS	beautiful spring flowers
Shumard's red oak	(Quercus shumardii)	40-60 feet	US, MS, LS, CS	red fall foliage
sweet gum	(Liquidambar styraciflua)	60-75 feet	US, MS, LS, CS	outstanding fall color
Texas mountain laurel	(Sophora secundiflora)	10-25 feet	LS, CS	fragrant, deep purple flowers

SHRUBS FOR ALKALINE SOIL

Common Name	Botanical Name	Mature Height	Range	Special Features
creeping juniper	(Juniperus horizontalis)	1-2 feet	US, MS, LS, CS	tough, prostrate ground cover
firethorn	(Pyracantha sp.)	3-12 feet	US, MS, LS, CS	red, orange, or yellow autumn berries
flowering quince	(Chaenomeles sp.)	6-10 feet	US, MS, LS	spectacular spring flowers
Indian hawthorn	(Raphiolepis indica)	4-6 feet	LS, CS, TS	showy spring flowers
Japanese pittosporum	(Pittosporum tobira)	3-15 feet	LS, CS, TS	handsome, evergreen foliage
mock orange	(Philadelphus sp.)	8-12 feet	US, MS, LS	fragrant, white spring flowers
nandina	(Nandina domestica)	6-8 feet	US, MS, LS, CS	showy, bright red berries
spirea	(Spiraea sp.)	3-10 feet	US, MS, LS, CS	showy spring or summer flowers
yaupon	(Ilex vomitoria)	10-20 feet	MS, LS, CS	shiny red berries, evergreen leaves

US=Upper South, MS=Middle South, LS=Lower South, CS=Coastal South, TS=Tropical South

Rain lilies are sometimes called summer's crocus because they look similar and are about the same size. August and September rains trigger starry white blooms.

As summer's heat takes its toll on the garden, plants curl, crumple, and give in to the searing sun. Few plants thrive late in the season, but one tiny flower shines.

Rain lily *(Zephyranthes candida)* usually begins to bloom in late July. This tough little bulb grows naturally in the marshes of South America. Its common name refers to the blooms that magically appear after rains. It may bloom several times during the season, and it peaks in August and September. The white flowers are sometimes edged in pink. Bright yellow stamens spring from their centers.

Rain lilies look small and delicate, but they are extremely tough. Most pests leave them alone. A site with rich, moist soil is preferred but they will also grow in heavy-clay soils. The bulbs suffer if the soil around them becomes completely dry for prolonged periods. Keep bulbs moist during summer droughts.

You can sometimes find bulbs growing in containers at nurseries, but you may have to mail-order them. Once established, rain lilies will multiply at an alarming rate. Small offshoots form on bulbs,

Tiny Blooms

making new plants. They also propagate by reseeding.

Rain lilies look great planted in irregular-shaped drifts. As they multiply, they will appear as if they are native plants that have formed loose colonies. The versatile little bulbs look at home edging a small pond, sprinkled through a woodland garden, or in a formal border. They even work well in containers.

Plant a few of these delightful bulbs. Their goblet white blooms will perk up your garden in the heat when many plants are melting. They're easy to grow, and after a summer shower you can watch your garden rain lilies. *Charlie Thigpen*

(For sources turn to pages 250–251.)

RAIN LILIES
At a Glance

Size: 10 to 12 inches tall
Light: sun to partial shade
Bloom time: late July through September
Flower color: white with yellow stamens
Comments: will grow in boggy as well as heavy-clay soils

Cool as Can Be

It looks icy all summer and never melts. That's why Powis Castle artemisia is one of the South's hottest perennials.

Named for the famous Welsh castle in whose gardens it likely originated, Powis Castle artemisia does all of the good things we like artemisias to do. Its delicately filigreed foliage, frosted in silver, shines as brightly as a polished chrome bumper. Its fine texture blends well with coarser-leaved plants, such as iris, daffodil, hydrangea, hibiscus, and coneflower. Its calm, refreshing color allows it to mediate between potent reds, oranges, and pinks in the border. And when you pair this plant with deep green leaves or blue or yellow flowers, it's a match made in horticultural heaven.

Just as importantly, Powis Castle avoids pitfalls common to other artemisias that drive Southerners batty. While other types melt during

Powis Castle artemisia fills mixed borders with cool, silvery foliage.

POWIS CASTLE ARTEMISIA
At a Glance

Size: 30 to 36 inches tall, twice as wide
Light: full sun
Soil: well drained, acid or alkaline
Pests: none serious
Prune: early spring after new growth starts
Range: Upper, Middle, Lower South
Expect to pay: $5 to $7

a typically sultry summer, this one keeps its cool. And while others submarine through the soil, surfacing everywhere, this one stays in place.

Given plenty of sun and well-drained soil, Powis Castle forms a dense, compact mound, 30 to 36 inches high and often twice as wide. It's a good gap filler in a border, easing its way into voids left by other plants. By early fall, it gets a little leggy, but don't cut it back then. Wait until early spring, when you

see new growth sprouting near the crown of the plant, to prune straggly stalks. According to my colleague, Ellen Riley, who has grown this plant for years, "If you cut it back in fall, Powis Castle is surely history."

This perennial belongs in the present, not the past, so take care to prune it correctly. You'll ensure a bright future for your garden, even where summers sear the shade.

Steve Bender

(For sources turn to pages 250–251.)

No Ordinary Joe

In the fall, the tall dusty pink clusters of joe-pye weed along the sides of roads in the South are sure to catch your eye. Rooted in damp drainage ditches, stems that grow until the flower clusters open up, measuring at least 8 to 12 inches in diameter.

But unlike some vigorous roadside plants that gallop in your garden, joe-pye knows how to behave. Placed in the back of an irrigated border or in moist areas, the plant makes a dependable show that attracts a parade of migrating butterflies.

Don't be intimidated by its potential height of 7 to 10 feet. You can cut the stems in half early in the season to reduce its height at bloom, or you

OWNERS: MOLLY AND SCOTT KISCADEN, ABINGDON, VIRGINIA

From Summer to September

This perennial savors summer long into fall. Clusters of tiny purple flowers held stiffly by gawky green stems last through hot weather until heavy frost. The blossoms hold their color after cutting, making them a favorite in arrangements.

Growing Brazilian verbena *(Verbena bonariensis)* is easy. It thrives in full sun and poor soil, and once in bloom, it stays that way. This verbena is a faithful reseeder; make sure you want to see it reappear each year before you sow. Plants will spread, especially if you scatter seeds while pulling out old plants in late fall. To control their rampant spread, collect seeds when flowers fade, and then sow them in spring after the last frost.

The hardest part about adding Brazilian verbena to your garden is knowing where to put it. Plants regularly reach heights of 4 feet or more. Each plant requires about 2 feet of bed width to accommodate its wiry, shrubby shape.

The pretty little blossoms don't make planting decisions easy either. Purple tends to recede in the landscape, disappearing against dark backgrounds. You can take the guesswork out of growing Brazilian verbena by following some pointers from the professionals at North Carolina's Biltmore Estate.

They've figured out a few ways to make this sparse-leafed plant show off. First of all, Biltmore gardeners never plant just one Brazilian verbena. Something about its airy form makes a single plant look awkward, but a grouping looks great.

For the best display of flowers, try this Biltmore trick. Pair the verbena's purple blooms with yellow ones for an eye-catching combination. Patrinia *(Patrinia scabiosifolia)* has the same cultural requirements as verbena, so it's easy to grow the two together. Patrinia grows even taller than Brazilian verbena and sports bright yellow flowers, making it a perfect background companion. Both plants flower into fall.

But don't fret if you don't have room for patrinia. Double your color yield by underplanting Brazilian verbena with French marigolds. The taller plant's open structure allows plenty of sunlight to reach the bright little annuals. "Marigolds add interest to the bed early in the growing season when the verbena is just getting started," says Suzanne Habel, landscape supervisor at the Biltmore Estate.

And, like a purple cloud hovering over a miniature yellow meadow, the two plants bloom in unison from summer through the waning warmth of autumn. *Jo Kellum*

The purple flowers of Brazilian verbena stand out against the background of yellow French marigolds.

BRAZILIAN VERBENA
At a Glance

Size: 4 feet tall
Light: full sun
Soil: any well drained
Range: all South
Expect to pay: about $2 per seed packet

PHOTOGRAPH: TINA CORNETT

can buy a shorter growing selection such as Gateway, which grows about 5 feet tall.

Upper South gardeners can grow any of the three species: *Eupatorium maculatum, E. fistulosum,* and *E. purpureum.* However, Middle and Lower South gardeners should always opt for the more heat tolerant *E. fistulosum* or *E. purpureum.* ◇

(For sources turn to pages 250–251.)

Joe-pye weed is a roadside perennial worthy of a place in the garden. Because it grows at least twice as tall as black-eyed Susan, plant it toward the back of a border where it can shine in late summer and autumn.

JOE-PYE WEED
At a Glance

Light: sun to partial shade
Soil: moist or even wet
Size: 5 to 10 feet tall
Comments: native plant, attracts butterflies

(For sources turn to pages 250–251.)

The Biggest Room in the House

Presented with a useless deck and a empty yard, a Dallas couple created outdoor living space that has become the envy of their neighbors.

The enclosed former porch was bland and boxlike, and the accompanying deck was too small to be useful.

Buying a house often means having to fix previous owners' mistakes. That's exactly what Doug and Polly Urquhart faced when they moved into their 50-year-old Dallas home. Several years ago a porch on the back of the house was enclosed, creating a facade with all the charm of a plastic milk jug. To make things worse, they'd also added a redwood deck skinnier than the legs of a fashion model.

Polly wasn't thrilled. "The white part of the house bugged me," she recalls. "I was always asking my husband if we could do something to break it up."

It didn't take long sitting outside in the hot Texas sun to figure out what that "something"

might be. An arbor attached to the house would provide cooling shade, while also visually dividing the rear wall into separate planes. To design the structure, as well as an entirely new garden, they called upon Dallas landscape architect Naud Burnett.

"Breathtaking" is how Polly describes the transformation. "People gasp when they walk through the back gate," she says proudly. Gone is the awful redwood deck. Instead, you step up onto a painted concrete terrace spacious enough for tables and chairs. Amble across the terrace and you arrive at a new wooden deck, stained to match the terrace.

The deck serves several purposes. It acts as steps leading from French doors down to the terrace, and the textural contrast between wood and concrete adds interest. The deck also safely covers the base of a large tree at a corner of the house

BEFORE

A cedar arbor breaks up the rear wall, while shading windows and a new terrace and deck below. The concrete walk edges a curving lawn now bordered by shrubs and perennials.

without disturbing the tree's roots.

Overhead, an arbor of Western red cedar, stained to match the terrace and deck, runs the length of the house. It shades the terrace, deck, and lower windows, while breaking up the rear wall. Ceiling fans mounted to the arbor keep the air moving on warm days. Hanging baskets supply color from spring through fall.

The arbor and terrace are only a prelude to the garden that awaits beyond. Naud took advantage of a slight grade change between the old deck and the lawn and constructed a two-level, recirculating waterfall and fishpond next to the new deck. Perennials, shrubs, and small trees soften the edges of the pond, giving it a natural look. In addition, the plantings lightly screen the deck from the yard, adding privacy.

The transformation didn't end there. Naud reshaped the boring, featureless lawn into a gracefully curving space bordered by masses of shrubs and perennials. A concrete

Hanging baskets watered by thin irrigation lines give color from spring through fall. Beyond the elevated deck sits a former garage, now used as a toolhouse and workshop.

walk lines the lawn's entire perimeter. The walk keeps the lawn neatly edged, simplifying maintenance. It encourages visitors to experience the entire garden as well. "If you have a walk, people will go out and stroll through the garden," explains Naud. "If you don't, they'll stand on the terrace, stare out, and say, 'Isn't that nice?'"

Delighted with the results, Polly declares, "We no longer have a yard; we have a garden." She and Doug especially enjoy the additional living space. "When we first sat on our new deck," Polly recalls, "my husband looked out and said, 'This is the biggest room in our house!'"

Steve Bender

This small fishpond next to the deck adds the calming element of water. The foliage of shrubs, trees, and perennials flowing over the stones gives the pond a natural look.

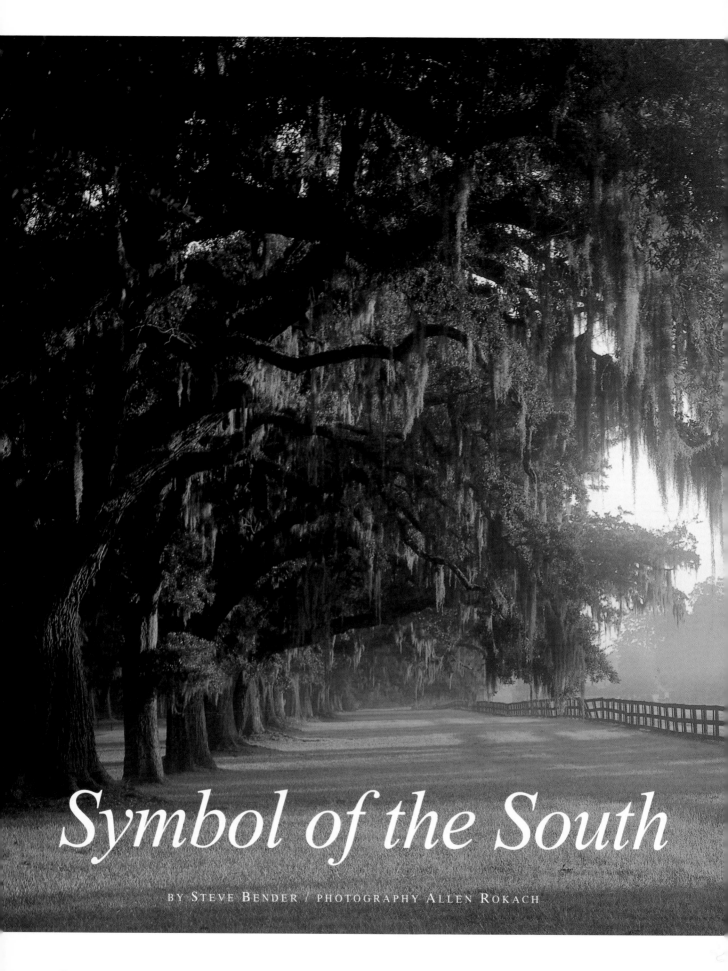

Symbol of the South

BY STEVE BENDER / PHOTOGRAPHY ALLEN ROKACH

Its flowers are puny, its foliage dull, and it lies upon the landscape like a boy in his hammock. Yet this indolent plant, this Spanish moss, sums up all that is Southern. Watch its listless sway, and in the cobwebs of its being you will smell fried okra, tread sugar-sand beaches, cuss no-see-ums, and keep time to a gospel choir.

Neither Spanish nor moss, Spanish moss *(Tillandsia usneoides)* acquired its name through an exchange of ethnic insults. Early French explorers counseled native Americans to call it *"barbe Espagnol"* or "Spanish beard." Greatly offended, the Spanish countered that the proper name was *"cabello francés"* or "French hair." Native Americans apparently thought better of the French, so "Spanish beard" won out. Political correctness finally prevailed in the 18th century. Swedish botanist Carolus Linnaeus named the species *usneoides,* which means "looks like moss." Thus "Spanish moss" was born.

Spanish moss occurs primarily in mild Coastal Plains from the Carolinas down to Louisiana and Texas and as far south as Argentina and Chile. Although it tolerates drought and brief stretches of cold, it flourishes in the Lowcountry, where humidity hangs like wash on a line.

An epiphyte, Spanish moss relies on trees only for support. Chlorophyll allows it to turn sunlight, water, and carbon dioxide into nourishing carbohydrates. Grayish scales, called "trichomes," covering the leaves also trap minerals and nutrients that flow down from tree canopies following a rain.

The plant propagates in two ways. Birds and the wind carry moss fragments from tree to tree, where they lodge and grow. In addition, tiny yellowish green or blue flowers produce wind-borne seeds that snag in the fissures of tree bark. Live oak is

a favorite host, but the plant also targets bald cypress, pond cypress, black gum, water tupelo, pecan, and red cedar. Individual strands may stretch 25 feet.

Through the years, people found many practical uses for Spanish moss. Early settlers mixed it with mud to caulk their cabins. Doctors took advantage of its antibacterial qualities and also prescribed extracts to treat diabetes. Because it "breathes" well and stays cool, it was a favorite material for stuffing mattresses in the hot, humid Lowcountry. It is still prized today for filling fine upholstered furniture. Spanish moss is also a popular decorative mulch for pots. Zapping freshly gathered moss in the

Spanish moss defines our region with filaments that span both branches and time.

microwave for three minutes before using it kills the chiggers it often harbors.

No matter how we choose to picture the South, Spanish moss insinuates its way into every image. It is, says writer James J. Kilpatrick, "an indigenous, indestructible part of the Southern character; it blurs, conceals, softens, and wraps the hard limbs and hard times in a fringed shawl." ◇

autumn's foliage (See pages 204–206.)

October

Checklist for October

EDITORS' NOTEBOOK

I think my mother invented the term "home economist." She bought only bent cans before grocery stores wised up and stopped discounting them; she routinely made a 2-pound roast last four days for five people; and for dessert my brothers and I could have either one double cookie (such as an Oreo) or two singles (such as a Lorna Doone). So you'll understand my genetic aversion to buying a plant if somehow I can get it for free. This brings me to Southern magnolias. They're extremely easy to grow from seed. All you have to do is harvest the seeds in fall, scrape off the red coating, and sow them in containers filled with moist potting soil. They'll sprout in about four months. I don't think you can grow trees any cheaper than this. But my mother does. She thinks that I should start with bent seeds.

Steve Bender

◀ **Cuttings**—Take cuttings of tender annuals such as coleus, salvias, begonias, New Guinea impatiens, Cuban oregano, and double impatiens. Dip each cutting in rooting hormone, and plant it in a pot of moist soil. Keep watered and out of direct sun. Place in a greenhouse or sunny window through the winter until it is time to plant next spring.

☐ **Mulch**—Supplies are plentiful now for creating an organic mulch of pine needles or ground leaves. While keeping soil moist and weeds down, mulch slowly decomposes to improve the soil and nourish plants.

☐ **Perennials**—If you weren't happy with the look or performance of your perennials this year, now is the time to do something. Dig established plants, and divide them if clumps are old and large. Replant divisions at the same depth they were originally growing, but spread them out or give some away.

☐ **Pumpkins**—Store your holiday pumpkins out of direct sun, and don't carve jack-o'-lanterns until a few hours before trick-or-treaters arrive. Cut pumpkins will shrivel and rot in the October heat.

☐ **Save seeds**—If you've harvested seeds of a favorite old-fashioned plant, allow them to air-dry, and then place them in an airtight container. Label each container with the name and year and store in the refrigerator.

☐ **Start composting**—It's a good time to begin collecting leaves and other garden waste for the compost pile. Be sure to have extra soil available to cover each 6-inch layer of leaves with several inches of soil. Wet the leaf layer thoroughly before adding the soil, and add about 1 pound of any formula fertilizer to each layer of leaves to provide the necessary nitrogen for decomposition.

☐ **Water**—In the Coastal and Tropical South, this month marks the end of the rainy season, so be sure the garden gets adequate water. A deep soaking twice a week is better than a light watering. ▶

☐ **Annuals**—Set out cool-weather annuals this month for flowers this fall, winter, and early spring. Pansies and violas are the hardiest, flowering through winter when the weather is mild. Other good bets in the Lower and Coastal South include calendulas, English daisies, snapdragons, nasturtiums, and sweet alyssum.

◀ **Bulb time**—Spring blossoms await in plain brown wrappers at your garden center. Daffodils, tulips, hyacinths, crocus, Dutch iris, and more are only a few months away. Buy now and plant anytime during the next couple of months when night temperatures start dropping below 50 degrees.

☐ **Perennials**—In the Lower South, oxeye daisies, daylilies, Louisiana and bearded iris, purple coneflowers, yarrow, and Louisiana and prairie phlox do best when divided every one to three years. Now is a good time to divide them. Set individual divisions or transplants 8 to 10 inches apart in groupings of five or more. Water them well every three to five days until fall rains thoroughly moisten the soil. (See "Divide and Conquer" on page 211 for tips on dividing and transplanting perennials.)

☐ **Vegetables**—In the Coastal South, plant cold-tolerant crops, such as cabbage, collards, carrots, snap peas, and beets. Gardeners in colder areas can sow crimson clover to enrich vacant beds this winter.

PRUNE

☐ **Birds**—Don't cut down the seedheads of purple coneflowers and black-eyed Susans until the migratory birds have flown through and dined on the seeds.

☐ **Roses**—Roses will benefit from a light tip-pruning now. Remove no more than one-fourth the height of the bush. This will stimulate a strong fall bloom flush.

☐ **Trees and shrubs**—Limit pruning to cutting out dead or diseased limbs or light pruning of an errant sprout or two. Severe pruning encourages the plant to sprout new shoots that may not mature before the first frost. Be sure to delay cutting plants back until late winter. ▶

CONTROL

☐ **Camellia scale**—Yellow splotches on the foliage are good clues to an infestation of this insect; the undersides of the leaves will have crusty, white deposits. Spray according to label directions with a systemic insecticide, or apply a dormant oil spray to the underside of the foliage. The oil coats the pests so they suffocate.

☐ **Mildew**—As night temperatures decrease, powdery mildew may become a problem on grapes, roses, crepe myrtles, mangoes, and other susceptible plants. Prevent it with a fungicide such as Funginex for ornamentals and wettable sulfur for fruits and vegetables. You can also wash the foliage frequently with water. Fortunately, you'll find that unlike most fungi, powdery mildew doesn't like getting wet.

FERTILIZE

☐ **Bed prep**—Prepare new soil by adding 3 to 4 inches of organic material such as peat, pine bark, or compost along with 1 to 2 pounds of balanced

fertilizer such as 10-15-10 per 100 square feet of bed. First till to a depth of 8 to 10 inches to loosen the soil; add the amendments and till again.

☐ **Lawns**—Apply 1 to 2 pounds of a complete fertilizer such as 16-4-8 per 100 square feet of lawn. Use a spreader to avoid the streaked appearance of hand-strewn fertilizer.

◀ **Trees, shrubs, and roses**—Most trees and shrubs should not be fertilized again until spring, but roses will benefit from a feeding now to promote high-quality fall blooms. You can use 1 cup of 12-4-8 or similar formulation per bush.

TIP OF THE MONTH

During a very rainy gardening year, I found I was spending time almost every day cleaning mud from my shoes. So I tried pulling a plastic grocery bag over each shoe and tying the bags around my ankles. Mud didn't stick to the bags, and my shoes were clean and dry every time.

ELLEN BRIDGES
HUNTSVILLE, ALABAMA

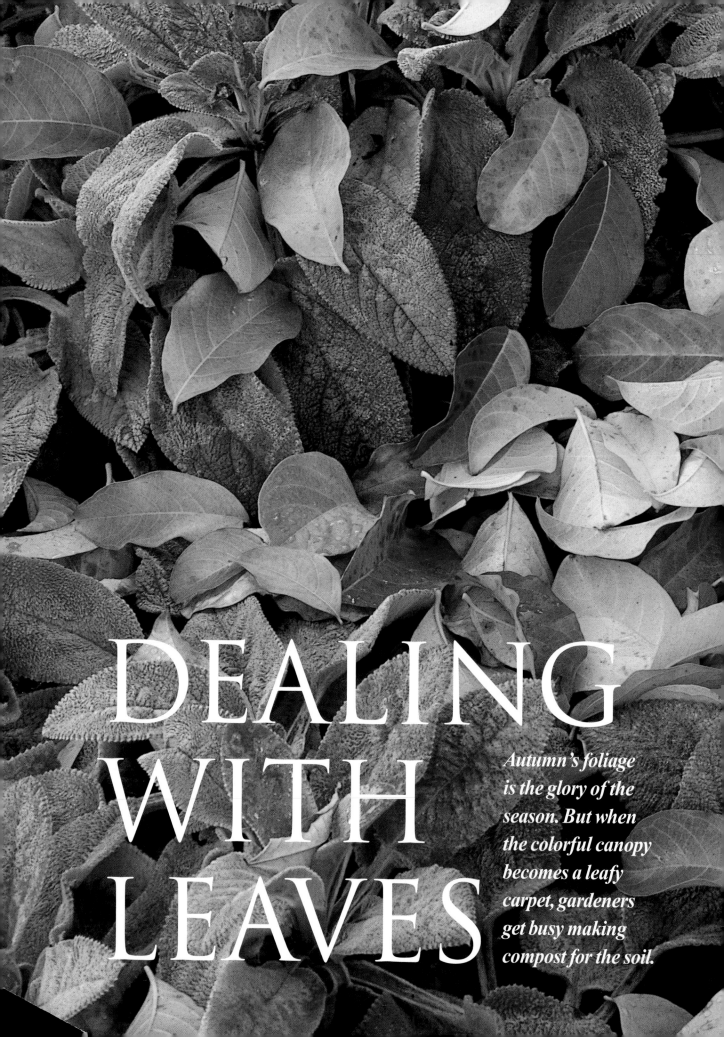

DEALING WITH LEAVES

Autumn's foliage is the glory of the season. But when the colorful canopy becomes a leafy carpet, gardeners get busy making compost for the soil.

Sunlight streaking through coral and gold foliage is the finale of the garden season, like a big burst of fireworks at the end of a well-paced display. But when the party is over, it's time to clean up the mess that's left behind.

Leaves left lying on the lawn and in beds of perennials and ground covers will form a mat of decaying foliage and smother all that lies beneath. This is helpful if you are trying to create a new bed. Just pile on the leaves, and let them rot.

But if you have worked on your lawn all season and made the effort to establish beds, you don't want a week of neglect to spoil it all. It's time to get outside and gather the fallen leaves before an ill-timed rain makes the job much harder.

Rakes have been the tool of choice for generations. Who can forget helping their parents rake them into a pile only to throw down the rake and jump in?

BY LINDA C. ASKEY / PHOTOGRAPHY VAN CHAPLIN

BELOW: Blowers make quick work of dry leaves. Choose the one that best suits you and your garden.

BOTTOM: Rakes comb leaves out of mondo grass and turf. Getting to them before a rain while they are dry and fluffy makes the job easier.

Stiff bamboo and metal leaf rakes have largely been replaced by flexible, lightweight plastic- and rubber-tined heads. Even with the newer models, you can get an incredible upper body workout without ever darkening the door of the gym.

A bagging lawn mower is an excellent way to gather leaves and grind them for mulch at the same time. There are other alternatives as well. A light covering of leaves on the lawn, a newly seeded lawn, or an accumulation on hard surfaces such as a deck, terrace, drive, or walk can be quickly cleared using a leaf blower.

One trip to the garden equipment aisle, and you realize that choosing a blower takes some study. In addition to obvious choices such as gas powered versus electric, there are options in power, comfort, and price.

Electric blowers are less expensive, quieter, and lighter. Some models are as powerful as handheld gas models, and many come with a vacuum option. However, they have the disadvantage of a cord, which limits their effectiveness to smaller yards. Cordless, rechargeable models are ideal for townhouse gardens and clearing hard surfaces such as decks, walks, and driveways.

Gas-powered models offer equal or better power and cord-free use ideal for large properties. However, they weigh more, are louder, and require fuel. The heavier backpack models are preferable because the weight is not in your hands. Before you buy, hold the blower to judge if the handles are in a convenient place and the side-to-side motion used to blow leaves is comfortable.

To assess power, read the manufacturer's nozzle air speed and air volume. (A minimum air speed of 150 m.p.h. seems to give adequate performance.) Obviously, the more powerful the better, but weigh power against the other criteria and choose what suits your needs best. Remember, always wear ear protection when operating blowers or any noisy equipment.

> Given the cooler days and the crisp air, raking is not a bad way to spend a Saturday afternoon.

Beds of broad-leafed ground covers and perennials can be injured by a rake, and a blower only lodges the debris within the stems. A blower with a vacuum option can lift out the leaf litter cleanly and without damage. One advantage is that these tools grind the leaves, so they will quickly compost in a bin or as a mulch.

Things to consider when selecting a blower/vacuum include amount of power, size of nozzle, how securely the nozzle attaches, the convenience of switching from blower to vacuum, size of the bag that holds the leaves, and how comfortable the weight of the tool is as the bag fills. You want the maximum power and a fairly large nozzle to accommodate large leaves such as sycamore. ◇

As Pretty As Its Name

Few plants boast botanical names prettier than their common names. But here's one—*Nyssa sylvatica,* otherwise known as sour gum, black gum, or tupelo. Nyssa (pronounced "nissa") sounds so classically Southern that one woman I went to horticulture school with dreamed she gave birth to a daughter and named her Nyssa. (Luckily she woke up when she did or she might have named the next one Sylvatica.)

This native tree looks every bit as lovely as Nyssa sounds, especially in fall. Depending on the individual tree, the lustrous, dark green leaves may turn brilliant scarlet, burgundy, orange, or yellow. It's one of the first trees to color in autumn, often changing with the dogwoods and sumacs. Though it grows as far south as Florida, it reserves its finest autumn raiment for the Upper and Middle South.

Sour gum may be male, female, or a mixture of both, making it the arboreal equivalent of Dennis Rodman or RuPaul. Such sexual ambivalence matters only if you plant non-males near paved or sitting areas. Small, bluish-black berries, prized by birds and squirrels, rain down for weeks in autumn. But as there's no way to tell a tree's sex until it's too late, your best bet is to plant sour gum out in the yard where its gender makes no difference.

A long taproot and sparse root system make sour gum notoriously hard to transplant from the wild. The largest trees I've dug successfully were barely 3 to 4 feet tall. Instead, go to the garden center and ask for a container-grown tree. Plant it at the same depth as it's growing in the pot. Fall and spring are good times.

And maybe someday you'll name your very own daughter for this beautiful tree. Just think—she'll be the only girl in school who answers to "Sour Gum." *Steve Bender*

(For sources turn to pages 250–251.)

Sour gum, also known as black gum and tupelo, is a handsome shade tree native to the Southeast. Among the most dependable trees for bright fall color, it turns scarlet, burgundy, orange, or yellow in early autumn.

PHOTOGRAPHS: JEAN ALLSOPP, SYLVIA MARTIN

SOUR GUM
At a Glance

Size: 50 to 60 feet tall
Light: full sun or light shade
Soil: moist, acid, well drained
Growth rate: slow to moderate
Pests: none serious
Areas adapted: all except Tropical South

Four- to five-inch pointed green leaves, orchidlike flowers, and the arching habit of its stems are the outstanding characteristics of this fall-blooming perennial for shade.

A Prince of a Perennial

TOAD LILY
At a Glance

Light: full to partial shade
Soil: rich, moist, well drained
Bloom time: September and October
Propagation: by division in spring or self-sown seedlings
Range: Upper, Middle, Lower South
Cultivation: Water regularly and add compost every year.

While a frog is not a toad, the toad lily is not a typical lily. This perennial is a great addition to your shade garden. Blooming in the fall in full to partial shade, it fills a real need for more plants in this particular category.

Flowers occur singly at the stem tip and in the leaf axils of gracefully arching 1- to 3-foot stems. They are funnel shaped, about an inch in width, and most have heavy speckling on the tepals (petals). Bloom time—about six weeks—is in September and October, although some species bloom until frost.

Garden designer Edith Eddleman grows toad lily *(Tricyrtis hirta)* successfully in her shady front yard in Durham, North Carolina. Because she has sandy soil, she provides extra water for it. "Toad lily, which in its many species flowers during summer and throughout fall, deserves to be grown more often. It's a perfect choice for the Southern garden's long growing season," Edith says. "It needs good, bold-textured companions like hostas." She also grows a purple-speckled, lavender-flowered type *(T. macropoda)* under a pink crepe myrtle tree.

Its flowers are what make toad lily so unusual. The prominent stamens are reminiscent of those of a passion flower, but smaller. A heavy sprinkling of purple, red, or brown spots, depending on the species, adorns the flowers.

The foliage of the toad lily shown here is covered with downy hairs; however, some other species have shiny green foliage. You may see a number of these other species in the trade, including the pure white of *T. hirta* Alba.

Golden toad lily (*T. formosana* Gates of Heaven) has striking golden leaves and purple flowers, while *T. formosana* Amethystina has white flowers with blue tips and tiny red spots. *T. macrantha* Macranthopsis is a yellow-flowered species dusted with raspberry spots.

In the shade garden toad lily needs moist, rich soil. It can be planted in the spring or fall. And it looks good in the foreground of a border where its stems can arch over the path and its unusual flowers can be viewed up close. Divide them in spring while they are still dormant. Besides hostas, other good companion plants include hardy begonias and ferns. ◇

(For sources turn to pages 250–251.)

Landyn and Caitlin Scudder don't need to swim to have fun. This arbor by their pool is perfect for playing board games or visiting with friends.

Making a Private Space

Just because you're by the pool doesn't mean you have to be onstage.

You see them all the time—dreary motels with nearly deserted swimming pools sitting in full view of the highway. It's hard to imagine less comfortable places for swimming and sunbathing.

Now you know why interior designer Kim Scudder built her arbor. Not that she lives in a dreary motel. On the contrary, she and her family reside in a very nice house in Ocala, Florida. But she didn't like the fact that the only thing that came between her backyard pool and her neighbors was her lawn. The pool was just too exposed.

Kim also recognized the need to integrate the pool into the rest of the yard. "I just hate it when you go to someone's house and there's just the pool and the grass," she says. "There needed to be an end to our pool area to separate it from the rest of the

Slats in the built-in benches allow water to drain freely. Planting mondo grass and impatiens between concrete pavers gives a soft, natural look.

yard, so that your eye would stop there instead of continuing on."

The answer? A painted arbor, flanked by crepe myrtles and planting beds, that sits just off the pool deck. The structure's rafters and beams provide filtered shade that buffers the glare from the pool. Built-in benches with narrow slats permit water from rain or wet bathing suits to drain. Concrete pavers divided by ribbons of mondo grass and impatiens supply firm footing and good drainage too.

The arbor and planting transformed the pool area into an inviting outdoor room. "I like to divide the yard into a series of spaces," Kim explains. "This gives the pool its own separate space, a very private one. It's a place where you can just relax or read and get away from everything."

Steve Bender

Mexican bush sage brings fall glory to a San Antonio border composed by John Troy. Blending their flowers into the autumn scene are lazy daisy, narrowleaf zinnia, native lantana, Mutabilis rose, Indigo Spires salvia, plus herbs, ornamental grasses, and the graceful silvery trunks of a Texas persimmon tree.

The Second Season

After months of summer heat so thick and heavy that the clouds of mosquitoes can barely pierce it, fall in the South is an exquisite relief. The whole garden shows it too. Just a few nights of temperatures below 70 degrees and a cool rain or two to freshen the parched ground, and suddenly we're full swing into the heart-stopping second season of bloom.

One of the biggest mistakes made by recently transplanted Northerners is to assume spring and summer are the whole show in Southern gardens. Those of us raised with 9-, 10- or even 12-month growing seasons can't wait for the fall color.

The flowers of fall are larger and more richly tinted than those of spring, due to cooler temperatures. With a little effort in plant selection and basic garden maintenance at the end of summer, you can have two or three months of major performance.

Choosing plants for stunning fall displays isn't difficult. Just check your local nursery for ideas and recommendations on what's easiest to grow. Landscape architect John Troy of San Antonio takes the second season even further by focusing on exciting color combinations.

"It's the highlight, the summit—fall to me is the culmination of the year in the garden," enthuses John. "We have some summer performers with spectacular colors, but when the cool weather comes back, it's like 'Oh, you're alive again, after all that heat!'

"Fall is cooling. Some people like blues just in the summer, but I love to bring those cool shades into the fall. Pale yellows and whites (you have to have white for nighttime!) complement the blues, but you also need the rich autumn tones of maroons and reds," he says.

All summer long we Southerners must earn—with sweat, weeding, and watering—every blossom we receive. Come fall, it's time to just enjoy the easy glory. *Liz Druitt*

BEST OF THE BLUES

To bring the best of easy fall color to your own garden, John Troy recommends starting with some summer-blooming blue flowers, trimmed back in mid- to late-August (a light or heavy trimming depending on horticultural and climate conditions), that will carry the garden from one season into the next. These include Indigo Spires salvia, Victoria mealycup sage, Longwood Blue spirea, Sunny Border Blue or Goodness Grows veronica, and even old-fashioned plumbago in pale or darker blue. Then the stage is set for the best blue of the fall season as Mexican bush sage hits its stride.

Divide
And
Conquer

Nancy Goodwin shows us her foolproof method for dividing many perennials. Those with crowns that can be pulled apart are featured.

Knowing the cost of perennials, thrifty gardeners are always looking for ways to multiply their favorites without having to subtract money from their checking accounts. It's simple to divide the perennials you already have. (See photos for step-by-step instructions.) After you have divided your plants, you may have enough to start another bed or to swap with a neighbor who is dividing other perennials. Either way, it stretches your plant budget, as the only cost is your own labor.

Nancy Goodwin of Montrose Garden in Hillsborough, North Carolina, demonstrates her method for dividing perennials in the fall. The plant illustrated is a primrose, but many other clump-forming perennials can be divided this way. A partial list would include stokes' aster *(Stokesia laevis),* black-eyed Susan, purple coneflower, bleeding heart *(Dicentra* sp.), lamb's-ears, and liriope. As a general rule, you should divide spring-blooming perennials in the fall and fall-blooming perennials in the spring. *Orene Stroud Horton*

Divide clumps of spring-flowering primroses in the fall for even greater impact in seasons to come.

Dig up the perennial and break it into smaller, rooted plants by pulling or cutting apart. Then prepare a hole, and amend the removed soil with compost.

*Place the new plant against the side of the hole, and add a portion of the amended backfill. Water it in. (This is often called "muddying in" or "puddling.") Then add the remainder of the amended soil and water again. This gets water to the roots and eliminates any air pockets. It also means you won't need to water again as soon. **Note:** The reason for placing the new plant against the side of the hole is to allow the plant to choose whether to grow into loose, amended soil or into tighter soil.*

Color is magical. Whether bold and bright or subtle and soft, it sets the mood and style of a garden. It can also be much more than flowers and foliage. A well-placed chair, for instance, painted to complement its surroundings can make a garden fairly sing.

Garden designer Edith Eddleman is queen of paint in her Durham, North Carolina garden. "A painted chair becomes a focal point. It gives your eyes a place to rest, and draws your eyes to it," she says. "It's something different, and different is fun."

The where to begin question can be intimidating. Edith's theory of color without fear is helpful. "Simply choose a color that pleases you, one you really like. That's the most important thing. Chances are, that color will already be reflected in your choice of plants in the garden as well," she says.

Paint in the Garden

Edith's chairs change locations with the garden's bloom cycles. "My red chair has moved around since early spring. It started out by my quince and almost perfectly matched it with reddy-orange color. Next, I moved it close to the apricot foxgloves. It looked great with the pastel flowers. Now, it's in a mostly green garden. It has maximum impact because it's with complementary colors," Edith says.

Whether to move a chair or not is purely choice. Left in one place, color relationships still change. "Different elements come into play with a painted chair. At one point in the season the chair may be in color harmony with the garden, and at other times it may change to a complementary situation," she says.

TOP: *This autumn-orange bench lights up a dark space. The framed acrylic mirror bounces light back into the garden.* RIGHT: *The red chair, flanked by matching gazing balls, is surrounded by swamp sunflowers, maiden grass, and the foliage of Marguarita sweet potato vine and red-leafed coleus.*

BY ELLEN RILEY / PHOTOGRAPHY VAN CHAPLIN

ABOVE: *Green is brilliant amid fall leaves and mums. Two different colors of paint were used for added play.*
LEFT: *A lavender chair, asters, and mums weave their colors in harmony.*

WHERE TO BEGIN

"You have a space in mind that is perfect for two chairs; it's a cool, appealing place where you can sit in the evening, have a drink, and chat. Look at the elements in that space, and work with the colors that you like. If the garden is full of blue phlox in the spring and you love that color, find paint that matches so you can have it year-round on your chairs," Edith says.

If you do not have a special place in mind, paint the chair a favorite color. "Then, move the chair around until you find the perfect place for it," she says.

Edith has found an easy way to choose paint colors. "You can go to a paint store and ask for color fans. Walk around the garden with them spread out until you come upon a color you like," she says.

And finally, Edith's last edict on paint: "Remember, it's not permanent. Anytime you want, just change it." ◇

This Sorbet mix of violas blankets the garden. Using large masses of small flowering annuals gives lots of impact.

Don't be misled by the dainty looks of this tough little flower.

Bright, Tiny Faces

Violas are like children. Their small, round faces are delightful, and they bring us great joy. The colorful blooms seem to smile and light up the garden. They may look little and vulnerable when first planted in the fall, but they're tough.

They will endure a cold winter and show their resilience by bouncing back in the spring to become a mound of showy blooms.

Violas come in many shapes and sizes and can be found in most nurseries. *Viola cornuta* and *V. tricolor* have much smaller blooms than pansies, which are their close relative. Although the blooms are smaller, they can add a refreshing touch to the garden. They also take the cold of winter and the

BY CHARLIE THIGPEN / PHOTOGRAPHY VAN CHAPLIN, ALLEN ROKACH

heat of summer better than pansies. Last year when all the pansies had fizzled, violas were still flowering.

To get the most out of your violas, plant them in the fall. If set out in autumn, the plants have time to develop an established root system that will give them a good foundation on which to grow. If winters aren't too severe violas will bloom throughout, but spring is when they peak.

Violas have become more popular recently as new selections are now readily available. They usually come in cell packs but sometimes can be found in 4-inch pots. These larger plants mature fast, so if you want a quick show, pay a little extra. But these don't usually last as long as plants in cell packs. If you have patience, buy cell packs; you get more bang for your buck with the smaller plants.

Some new selections of *V. cornuta* such as Lemon Chiffon Sorbet, Blueberry Cream Sorbet, and Lavender Ice Sorbet sound delicious, and they are edible. In fact many gardeners like to plant violas in herb gardens and kitchen gardens. The flowers may be used to garnish salads or dress up a dish.

Traditional violas, called Johnny-jump-ups *(V. tricolor),* have the blue-and-yellow faces with faint lines that look like cat whiskers, but some of the new selections have solid-colored blooms dotted with a tiny yellow center. They come in a wide range of colors from the satiny dark purple Bowles Black to the bright white Coconut Sorbet. Many people plant mixed colored violas. The Sorbet hybrid mix comes in a nice range of soft pastels.

Violas should be spaced about 5 to 10 inches apart, depending on selection. Ones that have more of a creeping habit, such as Alpine Summer

> Violas are like children. Their small, round faces are delightful, and they bring us great joy. The colorful blooms seem to smile and light up the garden.

hybrid, may be planted a little farther apart. Plants grown in 4-inch pots can also be spaced farther apart than ones in cell packs. Most violas purchased from reputable nurseries come tagged with information about growth and plant spacing. The distance between plants is critical, because if you bunch them too closely they will crowd out one another. But if they're spaced too far apart, your beds will look sparse. Positioned properly, your violas will grow together nicely and block out weeds.

Plant these easy flowers in a site with loose, well-drained soil. If you don't have flowerbeds, grow them in containers. They are also perfect for a flower border because their small blooms blend in nicely with other annuals and perennials.

If planted in full to partial sun, violas will stay compact and bushy. They will bloom even if neglected. But to keep them in tip-top shape you should give them a small dose of all-purpose fertilizer, such as 12-6-6, two weeks after planting. After fertilizing, water plantings thoroughly, washing any fertilizer off the foliage. Remove spent flowers every couple of weeks. By clipping old blooms you stop plants from declining prematurely and going to seed.

Violas are notorious for reseeding. No matter how hard you try to remove all the seedpods, you'll always miss a few. The seedlings will pop up throughout the garden. Remove them where they are not wanted, or you can leave a few here and there for a naturalized look.

If you're tired of planting the same old pansies, try violas. Their tiny faces will make your garden a happier place. And just like little children, violas will prosper if you give them plenty of TLC. ◇

OWNERS (INSET PHOTO ON PREVIOUS PAGE): THOMAS AND KAY MERRILL.

rosemary
(See pages 230–231.)

November

Checklist
for
November

EDITORS' NOTEBOOK

Hairless cats and brainless turkeys aren't the only living things on earth that suffer from scrambled genes. Plants also exhibit pretty weird properties as a result of their DNA. Take our native red maple *(Acer rubrum)*. You'd think a tree with "red" in its name would be a sure bet to turn red at some point in its life, right? Think again, young Skywalker. Red maple can turn red in the fall or else it can turn bright yellow. So if you want a red red maple, you need to buy a named selection such as October Glory, Red Sunset, Autumn Flame, or Yoda (this last one is rare, but very wise). Or at the very least, pick out a tree at the garden center that's showing red fall color. Why does red maple make things so hard for us? Like I say, it's probably genetic. On the other hand, there's an outside chance the tree has gone over to the dark side.

Steve Bender

☐ **Acid lovers**—If azalea, blueberry, or camellia plants are showing signs of iron deficiency (yellow leaves with green veins), apply iron sulfate to the soil at $\frac{1}{4}$ to $\frac{1}{3}$ cup per plant or sulfur at $\frac{1}{2}$ cup per plant. This will acidify the soil, making iron available to the plant. ▶

☐ **Citrus**—In the Tropical South, Sunburst and Robinson tangerines, Orlando tangelo, and most selections of pink and red grapefruit will be ripening this month. Because peel color is not always a good indicator of ripeness, taste fruit to see if it is ready.

☐ **Fruit**—Avoid watering mango and litchi trees for the rest of fall and winter in the Tropical South. They need dry conditions to stimulate flowering for next year's crop.

☐ **Power equipment**—Now's the time to winterize your mower, gas string trimmer, edger, and any other tools by running them until the tank is empty. Plan to use up all fuel in gas cans because it will age and foul your equipment in spring.

☐ **Seeds**—Take time to sit down with the seed catalogs that have been stacking up. Order the flower and vegetable seeds that you will need for spring, summer, and fall gardens.

☐ **Slow down**—As growth slows and most plants start to go dormant, you can stop fertilizing and cut back on irrigation, watering just enough to prevent wilting.

☐ **Start composting**—Begin collecting leaves and other garden waste for the compost pile. Have some extra soil available to cover each 6-inch layer of leaves with several inches of soil. Wet the layer of leaves thoroughly before adding the soil, and add about 1 pound of any formula fertilizer to each leaf layer to provide the necessary nitrogen for decomposition.

☐ **Water gardens**—Remove accumulated leaves from your pond, especially if you have fish. The decomposition will rob them of oxygen. You can prevent the leaves from getting in by suspending a net over the pond while they are falling.

☐ **Winter**—Bring in sprinklers and drain garden hoses in the Middle and Upper South where freezing water can destroy these summer essentials. Also bring in clay pots, or empty them and turn them upside down in a dry shed or basement.

◀ **Annuals**—Plant seeds of sweet peas, poppies, larkspur, dill, and forget-me-nots (myosotis) now for flowers next spring.

☐ **Berries**—In the Coastal, Lower, Middle, and Upper South, plant shrubs—such as possumhaw, dwarf Burford holly, Nellie R. Stevens holly, and yaupon—to attract birds and add color during the winter. All thrive in the area and provide color until birds remove the fruit in the spring. Water during dry spells to ensure a plump, colorful berry crop.

☐ **Bulbs**—Plant daffodils, hyacinths, Dutch iris, ranunculus, and anemones for spring color. Select a sunny area in the garden, or plant them in pots so they can be moved about the garden and home. Gardeners in the Coastal and Tropical South will need to prechill these bulbs.

◄ **Cuttings**—Many types of shrubs and herbaceous plants may be rooted from cuttings this month. Take a 4- to 6-inch stem with several leaves, dip the base in a rooting hormone powder, and plant in a pot of moist soil. Cover the cutting with a glass jar or plastic bag to maintain humidity and place in a shady spot until roots form.

☐ **Pansies and violas**—This is the time to plant masses and drifts of blooming-size plants for vibrant color during winter and spring. Remember to select a sunny area to plant these plants, be sure that beds are raised at least 4 to 6 inches above surrounding areas for good drainage, and use a slow-release fertilizer at planting. ►

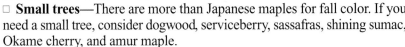

☐ **Perennials**—Continue to divide and replant Louisiana and bearded iris, daylilies, oxeye, and Shasta daisies, purple coneflower, columbines, Louisiana and prairie phlox, yarrow, and penstemons. Be sure to do this before the onset of cold weather.

☐ **Small trees**—There are more than Japanese maples for fall color. If you need a small tree, consider dogwood, serviceberry, sassafras, shining sumac, Okame cherry, and amur maple.

☐ **Spring seasonal flowers**—Set out transplants of snapdragons, stock, candytuft, Bells-of-Ireland, sweet alyssum, and sweet peas. Space the transplants 6 to 8 inches apart. Fertilize new plants with a water-soluble fertilizer, such as 20-20-20, or a slow-release fertilizer applied according to label instructions.

◄ **Vegetables**—In the Tropical South, plant seeds of tomatoes, peppers, eggplant, cabbage, broccoli, and collards in small pots now to be transplanted to the garden next month. You can always wait and buy transplants from a garden center, but it's fun to grow your own.

FERTILIZE

☐ **Bulbs**—Now's the time to feed established beds of daffodils with Holland Bulb Booster (9-9-6) and about ½ cup Epsom salts per 10 square feet of bed for magnesium. Bulbs have already sprouted roots and are ready to take up the nutrients. For more information on planting bulbs, see pages 222–224.

☐ **Lawns**—Turf-type fescues and cool-season blends in the Middle and Upper South will benefit from an application of 16-4-8 before the end of the month. Apply as recommended on the label, and water well if rain does not cooperate.

☐ **New beds**—Add several inches of organic material, such as soil conditioner (composted pine bark), sphagnum peat moss, or compost, along with 2 to 3 pounds of balanced fertilizer per 100 square feet of bed area. Till to a depth of 8 to 10 inches.

☐ **Roses**—In the Coastal and Tropical South, this is the best month for blooms. Keep plants watered and fertilized to maintain good growth. Apply 1 cup of 12-4-8 or similar formulation under the average size shrub; use more or less for larger and smaller plants. Remember to remove the flowers as they fade.

November notes:

TIP OF THE MONTH

When lifting and storing dahlias for the winter, it's important that each tuber in the clump have a piece of the mother stalk attached so it will sprout next spring. Store individual tubers in sawdust or dry sphagnum peat moss. Good tubers will sprout by spring, so you don't have to guess which ones will grow.

BOBBIE MAE COOLEY
BOWEN, ILLINOIS

BY LINDA C. ASKEY
PHOTOGRAPHY
VAN CHAPLIN

At this time of year gardening is like asking directions from a stranger. Do this, do that. We follow the described route with blind faith, and usually it works out. As gardeners, we set out our pansies and bulbs and leave them at the mercy of winter, trusting they will come through and bloom in spring.

Occasionally pansies are cut down by a cold snap or hungry deer. These are the calamities no gardener can prevent. But in the end, nature is our friend.

Most bulbs (such as daffodils) and biennials (such as foxgloves) require months of cold to enable them to bloom. Many annuals also benefit from fall planting in most areas of the South. As long as the soil is not frozen, their roots are growing, getting a head start on spring. If the weather is mild, they'll bloom all winter. So year after year, we plant for spring and hope for the best. The key to a spring garden is fall planting.

SPRING BEGINS IN FALL

First, choose a sunny place for a spring flower garden. Then prepare the soil by adding plenty of organic matter. Cover your bed several inches deep with compost, soil conditioner (composted pine bark), or leaf mold. Add a slow-release fertilizer such as Holland Bulb Booster (9-9-6) or Osmocote (18-6-12) at the rate recommended on the label. Then turn it all into the soil.

When you decide what to plant (see lists on page 224), try to create a parade of flowers from early to late spring. During the cool days of early spring, it only takes a few blooms to make a gardener glad. By planting pansies in the same bed where you have already set out bulbs, you will have something to enjoy this winter until the early bulbs push

Plant for Spring, Hope for the Best

Gardeners are optimists, always willing to try. Some ideas work and some don't. That is the fascination of a garden.

LEFT: *While nandina leaves are still burgundy, daffodils, and pansies are in full bloom. Daffodils are set back where foxgloves and snapdragons will hide their foliage.* ABOVE: *Fill out beds with flowers and greenery.*

through the soil. When the first daffodil raises its sunny head, you'll know that the fullness of spring is not far behind.

After you return from the garden center and unload your plants, bulbs, and seeds, spread them out in front of the freshly worked soil. Take transplants out of their containers, and lay them on top of the soil where you think they will look nice. Don't plant them yet. Then spread your bulbs around, remembering that they can come up between other plants.

Arrange the bed so that the taller flowers of mid- to late-spring will be at the back. For example, if you are growing sweet William and foxgloves, put the foxgloves in back. Early bulbs can go anywhere, even in the middle or background where taller, later-flowering plants will grow to hide their foliage.

Use your imagination to visualize the sweeps of color, the blooming

Due to a warm winter, the pansies went to seed early, and the foxgloves were sporadic in their blooming. So we pulled the pansies early and replaced them with Homestead Purple verbena, which will provide color into summer.

The snapdragons and larkspur filled the back of the bed with color. Parsley grew full and lush.

Meanwhile, our foxgloves just sat there, as if they were determined not to be in any pictures with those trashy pansies. The bloom spikes appeared erratically, if at all, probably due to insufficient cold weather.

Although not everything went as planned, the garden was very pretty. To keep it going we pulled out the pansies in late spring and set out Homestead Purple verbena to fill the front gaps and carry us into summer.

GARDENING ON THE EDGE

The South is a diverse region with great variation in gardening climates. Those who live in the coldest areas of the Upper South will probably do better to plant bulbs and biennials this fall and then set out annuals and seeds in early spring.

However, climates in the Coastal South are the other extreme. There isn't enough cold weather to even grow daffodils in many areas. But you can grow many cool-season annuals such as petunias and geraniums throughout the winter months. ◊

sequence, and the plant heights. Make adjustments as needed. Then work your way across the bed with trowel in hand, planting as you go. Sow any annual seeds, such as larkspur or poppies, after setting out transplants.

ANNUALS TO TRANSPLANT

pansies
violas
*sweet alyssum
*dianthus
*calendula
*ornamental
  cabbage
*ornamental kale
*geraniums
*petunias
snapdragons
*will only survive winter in the Lower or Coastal South

COUNT ON SURPRISES

Because so much is dependent upon the weather, you could plant the same garden every year and get different results each spring.

Our garden plan worked well, particularly in early season. The daffodils and pansies were spectacular, but the peak of spring was very warm and the pansies grew smaller and their stems drooped. Closer examination revealed that they were developing seedpods. Cutting these off, as well as pinching and fertilizing, sustained them a while, but not as long as we had hoped.

ANNUALS TO SOW

myosotis
poppies
larkspur
Johnny-jump-up

BIENNIALS**

foxgloves
sweet William
wallflower
stock
parsley
**plants that
need cold
weather before
blooming in
spring, seeding,
and dying

Young Tree, Big Dreams

In life, great accomplishments start with a simple idea. In your garden, the grandest tree begins the same way, with a seed or young plant and the gardener's vision for it.

Planting a tree is not difficult, but to ensure success, there are a few essential steps to follow.

Determine the correct location for your tree. This crepe myrtle is to be planted on sloping ground. Rocks were used to prop it up while the planting hole was outlined in marking paint. Use the shovel handle as a measurement. Ideally the hole should be at least twice the width of the container.

Dig the hole to a depth equal to the height of the root ball. That way tree roots are resting on the undisturbed bottom and their upper surface is level with the existing soil. Because this tree is on a slope, that level is determined by laying a shovel handle across the slope. Digging a hole deeper than the root ball and backfilling can result in the tree settling too deeply as the freshly worked soil compacts.

Add a soil amendment such as composted pine bark, compost, sphagnum peat moss, or other organic material. If you have soil that is heavy clay or sand, it's a good idea to use equal parts amendments and native soil. If your soil is naturally rich, you may need to add very little.

Before setting the tree in the planting hole, score the sides of the root ball with the shovel blade. This severs any encircling roots and encourages them to branch into the surrounding soil.

A topping of mulch—such as pine needles—will help keep the soil moist for your newly planted tree.

Once the tree is placed in the ground, backfill the hole around the root ball. When doing this, you may find it helpful to create a water well, particularly in a sloping situation such as this one. The "life preserver" of soil mounded on the edge of the planting hole on the downhill side holds rainwater in place longer so it has a chance to soak in.

Editors' tip: When you dig the hole for your new tree, place a tarp on the ground and shovel the excavated soil on top of it. That way the grass around your tree will be as good as new when you are finished planting.

Linda Askey

The seedpods, which look remarkably like butterflies, appear at all stages of ripeness at the same time as the vivid yellow flowers.

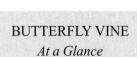

Blooming With Butterflies

Spattered with yellow from bright little orchidlike flowers and splashed with big chartreuse-green or tawny-brown butterfly-shaped seedpods, butterfly vine is one of the most entertaining climbers for the warm-climate garden. Flowers and winged seedpods in every stage of maturity all happen at once on an established plant, and the whole show keeps going all season.

Butterfly vine *(Stigmaphyllon ciliatum)* is a tropical American native with wide applications in Southern landscapes. The bright green, glossy leaves and clear yellow flowers look at home in a Florida or New Orleans garden full of banana trees and plumbago. The twisting brown stems and tan seedpods tone it down just enough, however, to fit in equally well in a Central Texas limestone landscape. Fortunately, butterfly vine is lackadaisical about soil quality and pH. In most garden situations the plant will grow a vigorous 10 to 20 feet without any fussing.

For the Lower and Coastal South, butterfly vine is reliably evergreen, so it's a good choice for decorating a trellis that screens a driveway or pool or hides the neighbor's yard. It looks particularly stunning against pale stone or stucco, where various interesting aspects of the graceful plant show up clearly.

Middle South gardeners can also enjoy growing butterfly vine by planting it in a sheltered location and mulching the roots heavily. It should be hardy to 10 degrees under most conditions. Come spring, just cut out any damaged portions that become noticeable as new growth begins.

Butterfly vine does its best to entertain from spring until fall, and some of the mature brown butterfly pods may cling to the vine over winter. These seedpods last for months in dried arrangements indoors as well, allowing butterfly vine to stay in the spotlight—outdoors, indoors, and always. *Liz Druitt*

BUTTERFLY VINE
At a Glance

Range: reliably evergreen in Lower and Coastal South; usually root hardy with protection in Middle South; treat as a tropical when temperatures fall below 10 degrees in winter
Light: sun to partial shade
Soil: not choosy, though extreme alkalinity will cause some chlorosis; best in well-drained organic soil
Moisture: Water thoroughly, once a week.
Bloom season: late spring until frost
Size: 10 to 20 feet
Expect to pay: $25
Propagate: by cuttings

(For sources turn to pages 250–251.)

These Evergreens Make Good Neighbors

ABOVE: *Some screens aren't meant to hide views completely, but just define borders and provide a sense of enclosure. That's exactly what Japanese anise does here.*

RIGHT: *Florida leucothoe is one broadleaf evergreen that deserves wider use. Its long, arching stems form a soft fountain of foliage from 8 to 12 feet tall.*

Good fences may make good neighbors. But they don't always make City Hall happy. Local ordinances sometimes prohibit you from putting a fence where you need it. So if you want to block an unpleasant view or you need some extra privacy, consider planting an evergreen screen instead. You'll get the added privacy and a softer look, too. Plus, a city inspector won't pay a surprise visit. Here are some candidates to consider for tall, dense screens.

There's a good reason more people don't plant Florida leucothoe *(Agarista populifolia)*. They can't pronounce its name. (For the record, it's loo-COE-thoe-ee.) But folks should give this handsome shrub a chance. Native to the Southeast, it grows 8 to 12 feet tall with long, arching branches and glossy, rich green leaves. Small, creamy white blossoms dangle beneath the leaves in early summer.

Given minimal pruning, Florida leucothoe naturally forms a soft, leafy fountain. It likes the same growing conditions as its cousin, the azalea. This means moist, acid, well-drained soil containing plenty of organic matter. The shrub also prefers light shade provided by tall pines or hardwoods. It grows well in the Middle, Lower, and Coastal South. To get a thick screen, space plants 3 to 4 feet apart.

Japanese anise *(Illicium anisatum)* gets its name from the distinct, aniselike scent you smell when you crush a leaf. But that's not the only thing worth noting about this shrub. It holds its younger foliage upright, nearly flat against the stem. As the leathery, light green leaves mature, they relax and point outward, resembling the foliage of rhododendrons.

Adapted to the Lower and Coastal South, Japanese anise grows 6 to 10 feet tall (sometimes taller). It tolerates full sun or light shade and prefers fertile, moist, well-drained soil. To make a dense screen, you'll need to prune it occasionally. Use hand pruners, never hedge trimmers. Prune individual branches back to a leaf or side branch. For a natural look, cut major branches at slightly different heights—don't flat-top the shrub. Space plants 4 to 5 feet apart.

More hollies are used for screening than just about any other plant. And for good reason—they are easy to grow, accepting of sun or shade, tolerant of most well-drained soils, and adorned with showy, red berries in fall and winter.

Arguably the finest holly for screening is the Nellie R. Stevens. A cross between English holly *(Ilex aquifolium)* and Chinese holly *(I. cornuta)*, it grows quickly into a small, pyramidal tree from 15 to 25 feet tall. Bright red berries (set without cross-pollination) accompany glossy, deep green leaves. Like most hollies, this one tolerates heavy pruning, which results in a denser screen. It grows well everywhere except for warmer parts of the Tropical South. Space plants 4 to 6 feet apart.

Many other hollies will do the trick though. For a dense screen up to 6 feet tall, try dwarf Burford holly *(I. cornuta* Burfordii Nana). For screens up to 25 feet tall, try Savannah holly *(I.* x *attenuata* Savannah), Foster's holly *(I.* x *attenuata* Foster #2), and yaupon *(I. vomitoria)*. *Steve Bender*

A Perfect Place

When Kevin Young first stepped into the foreclosed townhouse that would become his Atlanta home, he looked past the mess indoors to the view from the dining room window. It was a paint-spattered concrete slab surrounded by a brick wall. The sun beat down and the heat was trapped by the masonry, making the area unlivable for people or plants. Most of us would have turned and run. Kevin's first thought was "It's the perfect place for a fountain."

In the five years since, Kevin has proved himself to be as energetic as he is optimistic. By investing a few weekends and a do-it-yourselfer's budget, he has transformed this concrete void into a shaded nook.

Soon after buying the townhouse, Kevin found a concrete lion's head fountain at an antiques shop for $18. "The evolution of the garden's design was based upon the placement of the lion's head as it would be viewed

Tin-and-glass lanterns are lit with short strands of Christmas lights, giving the garden a romantic glow that was missing with the existing floodlights.

from inside the house," he says. Below it would be a pool of water.

Because the area measured only 13 x 19 feet and was concrete from wall to wall, Kevin had nowhere to go but up. "The fountain is basically a big box with water in it," he explains. It was constructed of dry-stacked concrete blocks arranged in a rectangle with a stuccolike surface to hold them in place. A black pond liner, pump, and terra-cotta-colored concrete pavers finished the project.

"The pond was the first thing," Kevin says, "but a close second was to get some shade and screening to block both the sunlight and the view of the condos that back up to this one." His quick fix consisted of big pots of bamboo inside the courtyard on each side of the fountain and East Palatka hollies planted in the ground outside the wall.

Because Kevin's courtyard is totally paved, all plants have to be grown

In a space only 13 feet wide, Kevin Young has created an idyllic spot for enjoying the outdoors in privacy, in spite of the closeness inherent in townhouse living.

in containers. However, sun and heat dictated the type of pots he used. "Out of necessity, I went to using plastic pots. I love terra-cotta, but for me it was not practical," Kevin says. "As it turns out, plastic pots are a good choice. The newer ones look amazingly like terra-cotta and can stand up to extreme hot and cold temperatures. Also, they are inexpensive compared to clay and concrete."

To help create a reservoir of moisture in the smaller pots, Kevin uses kitchen sponges to cover the drainage holes. The excess water can drain out, but the sponge holds a lot of moisture that would be lost otherwise.

Kevin has also figured out that when he wants to use terra-cotta, lining the pots with plastic garbage bags (with holes cut in the bottom for drainage) also reduces moisture loss. Mixing real clay pots with plastic pots designed to look like clay enhances the illusion.

Of course, the little courtyard would not have been complete without a decorative floor treatment.

Planned to offer an appealing view from the dining room, the leafy canopy admits light but filters the blast of sun that used to bake the courtyard and the dining room.

The look of an old tile floor was achieved with paint. While covering the spilled paint of a previous resident, Kevin gave the courtyard character.

Kevin bought a can of red paint, cut out a 12-inch-square cardboard template, centered the pattern on the fountain, marked the squares in sidewalk chalk, and went to work with a kitchen sponge. The result is a delightful checkerboard pattern.

The final touch was evening lighting. Kevin chose glass lanterns from a local discount store. Although designed to hold a candle, each lantern is filled with a short, coiled strand of white Christmas lights. The effect is reminiscent of a jar that a child has filled with fireflies. It's just another wonderful detail in Kevin's courtyard, a quiet retreat outside his charmingly restored townhouse. *Linda C. Askey*

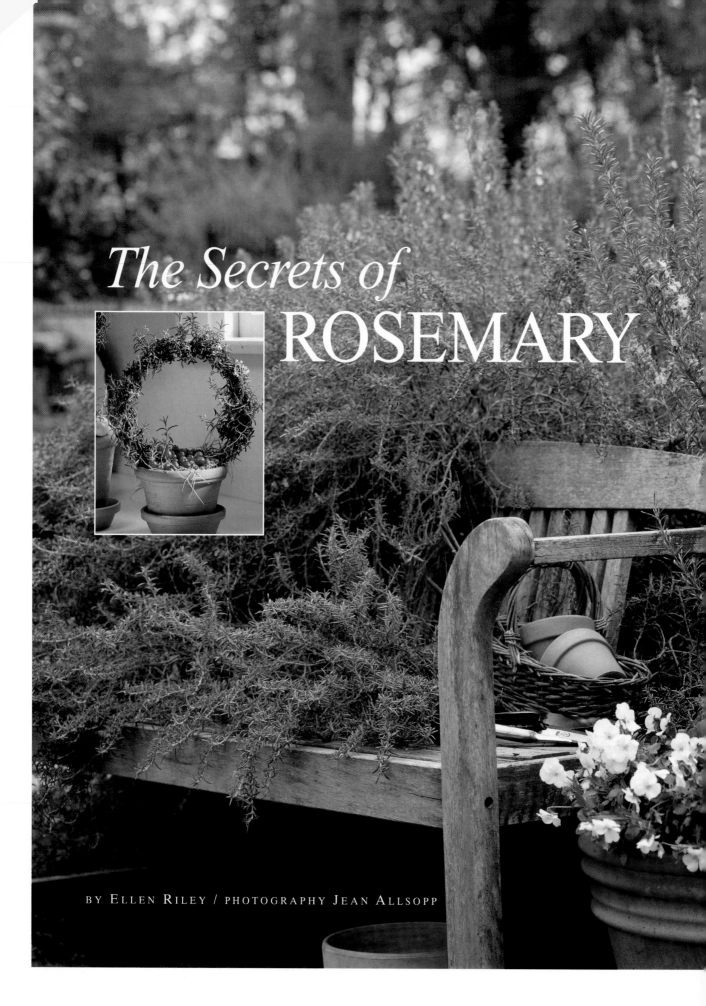

The Secrets of
ROSEMARY

BY ELLEN RILEY / PHOTOGRAPHY JEAN ALLSOPP

Rosemary, the herb of remembrance, is too often recalled for its short life span. If you've loved and lost this aromatic herb, take heart. We'll dispel a few myths, and Libby Rich, owner of Plant Odyssey in Birmingham, will give you tips for success.

Myth #1: Rosemary is an easy-to-grow houseplant.

Truth: This woody herb enjoys life outdoors. It prefers full sun and can grow anywhere from 3 to 5 feet tall and wide. "I never recommend rosemary be grown indoors for any length of time. Period. This is a very rigid statement, but it is rarely grown successfully indoors," Libby says. "If you have a porch that stays about 50 degrees or an unheated area with relatively high humidity, then you *may* have a chance at success. But for most of us, rosemary is strictly an outdoor plant."

For success: Libby says, "Keep your rosemary topiary outdoors. Bring it inside for a party; certainly no longer than 24 to 48 hours."

Myth #2: Rosemary is a Mediterranean herb, so it should not require much water.

Truth: When potted rosemary dries out, it rarely recovers. But too much water causes root rot. "The number one killer of outdoor plants during winter is lack of water. Check plants in containers every five to seven days," Libby says. If the container is small, check more often. "Never put a saucer under potted rosemary," she says. "If the plant stands in water, that is as damaging as dryness."

For success: Outdoors, check the need for water every five days.

Myth #3: Rosemary has no disease problems.

Truth: Outdoors, this is true. "Indoors, rosemary is very prone to powdery mildew and spider mites," Libby says.

For success: If white powdery fungus appears on the foliage, mix 1 teaspoon baking soda in 1 quart of water and spray the foliage weekly.

One other tip from Libby: "Winter winds are a critical factor. When bitter winds kick up, wrap the plants in burlap, or move them into a protected, unheated area," she says. Then, when calm returns, unwrap them or move them back outdoors.

"I think hope springs eternal in the hearts of gardeners," Libby says. "You might be one of the very few people who can successfully grow rosemary indoors, but if it doesn't work, don't take it personally. Try again, and grow it outdoors." ◇

hollies cut for Christmas decorating (See page 243.)

December

Checklist
for
December

☐ **Annual color**—In the Lower and Coastal South, encourage branching with snapdragons, candytuft, Bells-of-Ireland, and stock by pinching out their central leader when plants reach about 6 inches tall. Thin larkspur, bluebonnet, and poppy seedlings to 6 to 8 inches apart. Extra plants may be transplanted if dug with a small ball of soil and watered every day for 7 to 10 days. ▶

◀ **Christmas cactus**—If you're moving your plants inside for the holidays, try to avoid late changes in their environment. To prevent flowerbuds from dropping, duplicate as close as possible to the water and light levels they had outdoors.

☐ **Citrus**—Navel oranges, grapefruit, and most tangerines are ready this month in the Coastal and Tropical South, even if their peel color is still rather green. Taste them if you have any doubt. ▶

☐ **Freeze protection**—When a freeze is predicted, cover tender plants with blankets, rugs, or newspaper. Don't use clear plastic, which gives little protection. Sprinkling plants with water is also helpful, but if ice builds up on large trees and shrubs, the weight may break the limbs.

☐ **Holly**—In the Lower and Coastal South, use selections of *Ilex* x *attenuata*, such as East Palatka or Savannah, as substitutes for American holly. They're better adapted and can produce a good crop of red berries without a male tree for pollination.

☐ **Living trees**—Before you invest in a tree to plant outdoors after Christmas, consider the type of evergreen that will be hardy in your area and suit your overall garden plan. Then buy a small one; they are heavy. Your tree shouldn't be indoors more than a week. Keep the roots moist, but not wet, until you have time to plant.

☐ **Mulch**—This is a good time to mulch roses and other flowerbeds. Popular materials include pine bark, pine straw, and oak leaves. A mulch layer 3 to 4 inches thick will discourage weed growth.

◀ **Orchids**—Among gift plants available at Christmas, don't overlook orchids. When you consider how long they last, they are a good buy. Lady's slippers (*Paphiopedilum* sp.) and moth orchids (*Phalaenopsis* sp.) are easy to rebloom in years to come.

☐ **Poinsettia**—If you accidentally break a branch, sear the end of the stem with the flame from a match. Then place in water. It will last as long as any cut flower.

☐ **Prevent breakage**—Turn clay pots upside down, and drain your garden hose to prevent the water inside from freezing and cracking it. Better yet, bring them into a shed, garage, or basement.

EDITORS' NOTEBOOK

When you want a living Christmas tree that you don't have to lug back outside right away, look no further than to Norfolk Island pine. You know this plant—you've seen one dying in almost every apartment in America. The reason it usually looks so awful is that to thrive indoors it needs high humidity and lots of light. People typically forget about this. And then there's the height problem. In its native tropical habitat, Norfolk Island pine grows 100 feet tall—slightly higher than the average ceiling. So eventually you have a choice of cutting a hole in your roof or donating your scraggly, giant tree to the botanical gardens. Well, I have some bad news. After receiving approximately 10,000 Norfolk Island pines from the public last January, the botanical gardens are onto you. They know you're coming, they've turned off the lights, and they're not answering the door. *Steve Bender*

□ **Storage**—Left in a damp basement or shed, an opened bag of granular fertilizer can turn into one big lump. Seal it or put several bags into a sealed plastic trash can. Just remember to keep your fertilizers, as well as your pesticides, in their original containers.

□ **Water**—Evergreens continue to need moisture even during the dormant season, and irrigation is essential for newly planted trees and shrubs. Be sure to water regularly during dry spells.

PLANT

□ **Amaryllis**—These big bulbs will entertain the family during the holidays. You can actually see them grow taller from day to day. Plant a bulb in a pot about 2 to 3 inches wider than the bulb so that the neck is sticking up an inch or two. Water and keep moist in bright light. (Leggy flower stems result when the light is low.) Stake to prevent the stalk from falling over and breaking. You'll have flowers in a few weeks.

□ **Gifts**—Plant pots of bulbs for gifts this month. A single amaryllis or a half-dozen paperwhite or leucojum bulbs in a 6- to 8-inch pot make a lovely present. Recipients can set them in the garden later. ▶

□ **Peonies**—In the Upper and Middle South, select a site that receives some afternoon shade away from competing tree roots. Dig a hole 2 feet deep and 3 feet wide. If existing soil is poor, bring in sandy loam and mix in about a cup of superphosphate and several buckets of compost. Set the "eyes" or crowns at about ground level. Choose early or mid-season selections, such as Festiva Maxima, that bloom before hot weather in the spring.

□ **Planting holes**—Prepare planting holes for roses, grapes, fruit, and nut trees later in the season. Improve the soil by digging holes about 2 feet wide and 18 inches deep. Mix the removed soil with about one-third as much compost, rotted manure, or peat moss. A half-cup of fertilizer such as 12-6-6 may be added. Replace the mixture in the hole, and allow it to weather. Planting will be easy and quick when your plants arrive.

◀ **Vegetables**—Don't overlook cool-weather greens for the interest they add as winter annuals. Lower and Coastal South gardeners will particularly enjoy the bronze leaves of Red Giant mustard. Others include the blue frills of Dwarf Blue Curled Scotch Vates kale and the chartreuse of Black-seeded Simpson lettuce. Coastal and Tropical South gardeners can plant cabbage, broccoli, carrots, peas, and collards for pot greens. Tomatoes and peppers can also be planted, but protect if a freeze is predicted.

PRUNE

□ **Perennials**—Cut back chrysanthemums, salvias, Mexican mint marigold, asters, and other perennials after the first hard frost. Remember to leave only 1 to 2 inches of stem growth above ground.

□ **Roses**—In the Tropical South, give roses their main, heavy pruning this month or next. First, cut out all dead wood as well as thin, twiggy growth. Then cut back the remaining thick, healthy canes by at least one-third of their height—or even more if you need to reduce the size of the bush. It's also wise to remove all of the leaves at pruning time to get rid of black spot and mildew spores.

December notes:

❧✗❧

TIP OF THE MONTH

After frost has killed my potted annuals on the patio, I stick 8-inch cuttings of boxwood into the containers and keep the potting soil moist through winter and spring. I enjoy the greenery all winter. By summer, the cuttings have rooted and are ready to transplant.

JUDY H. TUCKER
JACKSON, MISSISSIPPI

SCENTSIBLE Solution

Grow these fragrant flowers outdoors, and gain a little breathing room.

Paperwhites are a paradox. Modest in appearance, their snowflake-white flowers add refreshing simplicity to the busy holiday season. On the other hand, these unpretentious blossoms are also endowed with extravagant fragrance. If the aroma leaves you cold, grow this flower outdoors where it's perfectly at home in cool December temperatures. The flowers last longer than if they were kept inside, and the scent has room to air.

There are two ways to have paperwhites outdoors. One method is to grow the bulbs in pebbles and water indoors. Keep them in a cool, bright location so the change in temperature and light will not be shocking when moved. Once they are tall and budded, place them outside in a decorative container.

In the Lower and Coastal South bulbs may be planted directly in the garden. They will bud and bloom in about the same time as forced bulbs. If a freeze comes while they are still tightly budded, no harm will be done. But once they are in bloom, a freeze will damage flowers. Rather than lose them all to the cold, cut a few stems to bring indoors.

MERRY WAYS WITH FLOWERS

From dormant bulb to full-fledged flower in only a few weeks, paperwhites' rush to bloom is as fast paced as the holidays. Fill your birdbath with pebbles or black river rocks, and add water to barely cover. Place bulbs on top with only the bottoms getting wet. Roots will grow in time, and flowers will appear in jusr several weeks. Ours bloomed almost two and a half weeks.

Set on the front steps, our decorative mailbox is filled with surprises. We grew bulbs in pebbles and water until ready to bloom; then we put

BY ELLEN RILEY
PHOTOGRAPHY JEAN ALLSOPP

them in plastic sandwich bags filled with damp moss. Set inside the mailbox, the top-heavy paperwhite stems gain support from their container. They flowered for about 10 days.

Even if you're too busy for gardening, press your boots into action. Place close-to-bloom bulbs in plastic sandwich bags lined with moist moss. Stuff the boots with newspaper about halfway up, and snuggle the paperwhites down inside. A fluffy cuff of sweet alyssum, violas, and ivy in plastic bags softens the edges. Every four to five days add a little water to each pouch.

Our lunchbox special is for the birds. Peanut butter-and-birdseed sandwiches with a froth of sweet alyssum on the side is the day's menu. The aluminum foil-lined lunchbox is filled with pebbles, water, and bulbs. The paperwhites will last about two weeks. The sandwich will last about 15 minutes. ◇

(For sources turn to pages 250–251.)

*In the Lower and Coastal South, plant paperwhite bulbs
directly in the garden for fragrant winter blooms.*

Certain houseplants can forgive a little neglect. My son's first ones met the test. Here's our story.

TOUGH GUYS

BY ELLEN RILEY / PHOTOGRAPHY JEAN ALLSOPP

It was music to my ears: "Mom, I think I need some decorating help." My son, Owen, freshly graduated from college, was in his first apartment. With minimal funds for furniture, he was trying to make his new home comfortable and stay within a budget. "Once I had my furniture arranged, the place still felt empty," Owen says. "I knew my mom was waiting for an invitation to come help. I also suspected that her solution would be plants."

Houseplants add life to sterile surroundings. I knew it would take only a few well-placed pots of sturdy foliage to make his apartment inviting. I also knew maintenance was not Owen's strong suit. The task was to choose tough, low-care houseplants for big impact.

We headed to Moore & Moore West, a local garden center in Nashville, to get expert advice from Marty DeHart. "When low maintenance is a priority, look for plants that don't require much light and can survive erratic watering," she says. "Some people water too much, others too little. Choose a plant that will withstand extreme treatment.

"Look for plants with sturdy, thick leaves. They are usually more

RIGHT: *Cacti are some of the toughest of the bunch.* TOP, RIGHT: *The large leaves of rubber plant contrast with the pointed leaves of Warneckii dracaena. A bromeliad is also low maintenance.* BOTTOM, RIGHT: *A corn plant, snake plant, and pothos fill in a blank corner.*

Owen's success is due to the moisture meter. He gets a reading on when plants are dry and doesn't fall into the trap of overwatering.

pest resistant and less affected by low humidity during winter months. Home heat creates an almost desert-like atmosphere; plants with tough leaves have an easier time in this environment."

So a variety of plants were gathered that Owen liked and Marty knew would be survivors. We chose snake plant *(Sansevieria trifasciata)*, Warneckii dracaena*(Dracaena deremensis* Warneckii), corn plant *(Dracaena fragrans* Massangeana), rubber plant *(Ficus elastica),* and pothos *(Scindapsus aureus).* "Snake plant is probably one of the toughest plants available. You can leave it for a month and a half without water and it will be fine. It's astonishing," Marty says. "Pothos is a terrific vine. It can really look lousy from neglect and be brought back to health," she says.

For a dark corner, Marty rec-ommended a Chinese evergreen *(Aglaonema* sp.). "This is a good variegated low-light plant. There aren't many choices when you're looking for an interesting leaf, and this is one of the best," she says.

To add variety to the middle of the room, we decided to put a cactus assortment on Owen's coffee table. "Cacti require more light than the other plants we chose, but they're certainly drought tolerant," Marty says. "During winter months, water them every three to four weeks. In spring, increase it to every two weeks." Remember, when plants are in tiny pots water them more often. For extra light, occasionally rotate the plants to a window.

HOME, SWEET HOME
Back at his apartment, Owen's first question reinforced the need for tough plants: "So, how many weeks

> ### Owen's first question reinforced the need for tough plants: "So, how many weeks can they go without water?"

can they go without water?" Water requirements are based on several factors. If the plant is near a window or heat vent, it may dry out quickly and need water fairly often. If it is in a dark corner, the necessity for water lessens. Marty says, "There's no rule. What you need to do, even with tough plants, is spend a couple of weeks figuring out how fast or slow they dry out."

Marty assesses dryness by pot weight. "Water it, and then lift it. Teach yourself what it feels like when it's full of water; then lift it every day. When it feels light, it's time to water." With large plants, use a moisture meter. Place the probe at least 2 to 3 inches into the soil. When the dial is bordering between moist and dry, it is time to water.

HOUSECLEANING
Like everything else, houseplants get dusty. "It's a good idea, once during the winter, to put your large plants in the shower. Give the leaves a gentle lukewarm wash, and let the pots drain well," Marty says. "You'll be amazed how much good it will do to remove dust and give plants a boost in humidity," she says.

Owen has had his plants for about nine months. To my amazement, they are thriving. These plants are true survivors. ◇

TOUGH LOVE
Bachelors aren't the only ones to benefit from low-maintenance plants. People who travel a lot and busy homemakers will also find success. Follow these tips.
■ Establish a pattern for watering, and stick to it. Pick a specific day of the week for plant maintenance.
■ Never allow water to stay in the saucer under a houseplant more than 20 minutes.
■ Remove damaged or yellow foliage from plants regularly.
■ While insect problems are rare, occasionally check stems and leaf backs for pests.

Guide to the Holiday Harvest

Most gardeners think of pruning as a loathsome chore, at least for 11 months of the year. But it's a different story in December. Trimming trees and shrubs provides coveted leaves and berries for indoor decorations. Here are guidelines to help with the holiday harvest.

Beautyberry—This native shrub (*Callicarpa* sp.) loses its leaves by December, so the gaudy purple berries are your target. Clip berry-laden branches back as far as you want, but don't remove more than one-third of them. No need to place the branches in water; the berries last a long time without it.

Bittersweet—Like beautyberry, this rampant vine (*Celastrus* sp.) loses its leaves early on. Clip long lengths of the berried stems. No need to place them in water; the red berries last for months indoors. But handle the branches gently—the showy yellow husks attached to the berries are brittle and break easily.

Boxwood—Reach inside the shrub and cut sections 6 to 8 inches long. Prune from various spots around the plant to maintain the natural, billowy appearance. Always cut back to green growth. Condition the cuttings by immersing them in cold water for 24 hours prior to use.

Holly—By far the best evergreens for decorating, American, Burford, English, Foster #2, Nellie R. Stevens, and Savannah hollies offer glossy, green foliage and bright red berries. (Yaupon is an exception. Its berries drop soon after cutting and make a mess.) Clip branches of any length to shape up the plant. The remaining branch will sprout again from the point of the cuts. Immerse cut branches in water for 24 hours to condition. Discard them when berries start dropping.

Japanese aucuba—This shrub is prized for its yellow-and-green variegated foliage. As with holly, prune to shape the shrub. Cut back to a crotch or a dormant bud. Immerse in water for 24 hours to condition. The foliage lasts

Hollies respond well to pruning and offer beautiful foliage and berries for holiday decorations.

about a week out of water. If you place the cuttings in a water-filled vase, they'll last much longer and even root.

Nandina—Huge berry clusters atop this shrub can't be beat. Cut leggy stalks back to foliage lower down in the plant. No need for conditioning; the bright red berries will last months without it.

Pyracantha—Not a good candidate for decorating, this shrub has thorns to contend with and orange and red berries that drop almost immediately.

Southern magnolia—The large, glossy, deep green leaves of magnolia will last for weeks indoors. Selectively prune outer branches to shape up the tree. Always cut back to a side branch. Immerse in water for 24 hours to condition.

Thorny elaeagnus—This large, aggressive evergreen shrub thrives on pruning. Cut long, arching branches back to a leaf or bud. Immerse in water for 24 hours to condition. *Steve Bender*

Deck the halls with boughs of holly, boxwood, and magnolia. This is the season to make the most of the task of pruning.

Magic
FOR YOUR MANTEL

While you're trimming the tree and decorating the front door, make the mantel a highlight of your holiday adornments. You can easily create variety and interest by working some of your favorite containers, boxes, and other objects into the fireside scene you set. Preparing your home for the holidays is more creative and fun when you use out-of-the-ordinary elements in imaginative ways.

Provide an element of surprise. Besides the sparkly ornaments and Christmas balls that you always use, import some choice accessories from other rooms. Use a pair of containers to hold moss-and-nut-covered topiaries trimmed with tiny stars and shimmering ribbon. Or choose a garden urn to hold seasonal greenery. Create surprise by your placement of a piece. Instead of hanging a wreath above the mantel, set it in the fireplace opening. This

Dress your fireplace in bright and beautiful seasonal adornments.

is a good idea when a fireplace no longer operates or if the mantelpiece has been installed just for decorative use.

Create a sense of nature. Two weeks before you clothe your mantel in holiday garb, start a few pots of ryegrass. Space the containers along the length of the mantel, and nestle glittery ornaments in the grass. Use greenery, such as holly, magnolia, and boxwood, to make a simple cluster or swag arrangement. Insert greenery into felt stockings for a verdant look that Santa will love.

Wire lemons, limes, tangerines, and other fruit into wreaths and swags. Ivy topiaries and other houseplants will provide height to the arrangement; measure the depth of the mantel, and buy plants in pots that won't extend over the edge.

Add a touch of local color. Whether you choose pinecones or palmetto fronds, include elements characteristic of your locale. Shells from the beach, birdhouses acquired on a visit to the mountains, clay pots collected in Mexico—all will suggest places visited and times remembered. Let the mantel serve as a scrapbook of your family's activities for the year.

Give a twist to tradition. Instead of choosing lovely—and predictable—red poinsettias, use fresh flowers. Red roses cut short and inserted in an urn filled with florist foam provide the rich red color that's symbolic of the season. Candles are emblematic of joyous celebrations, and when purchased in unusual shapes and sizes provide a fresh take on the familiar.

Complement the surroundings. Use ribbon in colors that coordinate with your room. Emphasize a certain shade of citrus green or golden yellow with a pretty bow. Fashion small decorations for accessories that will remain at the fireplace. Make little clusters of boxwood or cedar, add a flourish of ribbon, and wire them to fireplace tools or to the painting above the mantel. ◇

BY JULIA H. THOMASON / PHOTOGRAPHY JEAN ALLSOPP

move
over,
MISTLETOE

*Kissing balls
made of ivy, roses,
seeded eucalyptus,
cranberries, or
boxwood and
baby's breath add tradition
and playfulness to the holidays.*

FROM LEFT TO RIGHT: *ivy
kissing ball, rose kissing ball,
seeded eucalyptus kissing ball,
cranberry kissing ball, baby's
breath kissing ball*
BELOW: *Fill a globe frame with
potting soil for an ivy kissing
ball that lasts past Christmas.*

BY ELLEN RILEY
PHOTOGRAPHY JEAN ALLSOPP

An eligible young lady in 18th-century England might have had her matrimonial fate determined under a kissing ball. If a peck on the cheek came her way, marriage would surely follow. But if things went amiss, without a kiss, wedlock was not to be. While finding true love is no more scientific at the close of the millennium, kissing balls are still a festive symbol of love's potential. Who knows? Under the kissing ball, your fate may be sealed with a smooch.

FRESH KISS
We chose a variety of fresh materials for our collection of kissing balls. Whether you use bicolored Leonidas roses, seeded eucalyptus, or boxwood and baby's breath, the assembly is the same. The base is a florist foam sphere. Add moisture daily to keep it fresh, or let the form and elements dry for an everlasting ornament.

Wrap the ball in florist tape as shown in the bottom photograph on the facing page. Use several layers for a good base. Wind plastic-coated wire on top of the tape, and make a loop to hang the globe. Thoroughly moisten the form with water, and suspend it with a strong wire to complete assembly.

Cut stems about 3 inches below the bloom or branch tip, and insert the ends into the foam. Blossoms should snuggle against the form, and foliage should be secure. Completely cover the form with your materials, leaving only a small space around the hanger to add water. Roses will remain fresh for about four days, while the eucalyptus and boxwood balls will appear fresh even if they have dried.

FIRMLY ROOTED ROMANCE
Keep your kissing ball through the year by planting a wire form with ivy. Our globe frame (see bottom photograph on facing page) is 6 inches in diameter, a perfect size to hang in a doorway. Begin at the bottom of the form, and line the inside about halfway up with sheet moss. Fill the inside with moist potting soil, and tuck roots of small ivy plants into the soil with tendrils

extending outside the globe. Add more moss, soil, and ivy up the sides until the ball is complete. Use enough ivy to cover the ball with foliage, and pin the tendrils to the moss with wire hairpins. Once complete, water it well, and drain before hanging.

Suspend the ivy orb with strong wire, covered with ribbon. Water it about every five days, and remember, indoors, ivy is susceptible to spider mites. Mist the foliage daily, or grow the ball outdoors until party time.

PUCKER UP WITH CRANBERRIES
Our cranberry kissing ball begins with either a florist foam or plastic foam sphere. Cover the form with green sheet moss, and wind plastic-covered wire around it to form a hanging loop. Attach cranberries to the moss with a low-temperature glue gun. Use only firm, fresh berries and your kissing ball will last several weeks.

Make a kissing ball to complement your home and holiday decor. It will add a touch of fun to a joyful season. ◇

(For sources turn to pages 250-251.)

Boxwood: *My boxwoods are too big and need trimming. How can I do this without producing a chopped-off look? When do I fertilize them after pruning?*

BETTYE C. KREH
ANNISTON, ALABAMA

Late winter, when plants are still dormant, is a good time to prune overgrown boxwoods. Don't use hedge trimmers—use hand pruners instead. To maintain a natural look, reach inside the plant and shorten branches to different lengths. Always cut back to a side branch or a sprig of foliage; don't leave large, bare stubs. Open up the center of the plant so that sunlight can penetrate. This encourages new foliage to sprout along the trimmed branches in spring. Sprinkle a cup or two of cottonseed meal around the base of each boxwood in spring.

Bermuda grass: *We recently sodded our lawn with bluegrass, then discovered that the sod contained lots of Bermuda grass. Naturally, the place where we bought our sod accepts no responsibility. Is there any way to remove the Bermuda other than spot treating it with Roundup?*

LINDA SPINNEY
BOWLING GREEN, KENTUCKY

Your letter shows the importance of buying only certified, weed-free sod. If your sod was certified (inspected by your state department of agriculture) and was nonetheless infested with Bermuda, somebody goofed and you're entitled to a replacement or refund. As to your question about removing Bermuda, our advice is to mow your bluegrass at 2 inches or higher. At this height, bluegrass will outcompete Bermuda in your area and should crowd it out.

Dogwood disaster: *I understand a new disease is killing our dogwoods. Is there any way to prevent it?*

CARROLL MCCARTHY
FAIRFAX, VIRGINIA

The disease is a fungus called dogwood anthracnose, which causes tan blotches on the leaves and sunken cankers on the twigs. Water from rainfall and sprinklers spreads the fungus. A badly diseased tree may lose its leaves and die. To protect dogwoods, plant them in the open where air circulates freely, not in tight groups. A lightly shaded spot beneath tall shade trees is fine. Don't wet the foliage when you water. Spray the foliage according to label directions with chlorothalonil (Daconil) in spring when leaf buds open and weekly until leaves fully expand. Rake up and burn all fallen dogwood leaves in fall. If you can, prune out and destroy cankered twigs.

Lawns: *We recently moved into a new house. The lawn out front is sparse and full of weeds. How can we have a healthy, green lawn?*

KELLY WALLS
OCEAN SPRINGS, MISSISSIPPI

It probably sounds drastic, but you should consider starting over. To do this, spray the lawn with glyphosate (Roundup) after it greens up. Follow label directions carefully. After the grass and weeds die, rake off the debris and lay St. Augustine, centipede, or hybrid Bermuda grass sod—all good choices for your area of the Coastal South. If sod costs too much, spray and kill the grass. Then rototill the area, rake it smooth, and remove debris. Apply slow-release, starter fertilizer, such as 12-18-10, according to directions on the bag. Sow either centipede or Bermuda grass seed (St. Augustine seed isn't available), and rake again to bury the seed about ¼-inch deep. Roll the soil to firm it, cover the soil with straw to prevent erosion, and water thoroughly. You should have a new green lawn within a month.

Bulbs: *My spring bulbs bloomed well the first year after planting. But this year, the tulips produced only a few leaves and no flowers. And the hyacinth blooms were very sparse. Any ideas why?*

MABEL SMOUSE
OAKLAND, MARYLAND

Hybrid tulips and large-flowered Dutch hyacinths are best treated as annuals in the South. They'll bloom well the first spring after planting, but produce fewer and fewer flowers after that. To get the best show, you need to plant new bulbs of these two each fall. If you want spring bulbs that perform well year after year with no replanting, try daffodils, Spanish bluebells (scillas), crocus, snowflakes *(Leucojum)*, and grape hyacinths *(Muscari)*.

Weeping willow: *Our weeping willow has a recurring problem with yellowing inner leaves, despite the fact that I've been fertilizing with iron and 12-6-6 fertilizer every three months. I'd appreciate any advice.*

SHELLIE KELLY
JACKSON, TENNESSEE

Lack of iron and other nutrients probably isn't the problem. More likely, the culprit is water stress. Weeping willow likes constantly moist soil, which is why it grows well on the banks of streams and ponds. But summer droughts can cause leaves to yellow and drop. The only solution is to give your tree extra water during periods of dry weather. (And given weeping willow's astonishingly fast growth rate, there's no reason to continue feeding it.)

Ant attack: *I like mulching my garden with hay, leaves, and pine straw to conserve water. But ants of all kinds build anthills under it. How can I get rid of them?*
BETTY ADAMS
FORT PAYNE, ALABAMA

Try spreading Diazinon or chlorpyrifos (Dursban) granules atop the soil before mulching. Then water thoroughly. Be sure to follow label directions carefully.

Crepe myrtle: *I have six crepe myrtles, three to four years old, growing in full sun. They look healthy, but only one has bloomed. Any ideas?*

T. G. DAVIS, JR.
PINEVILLE, LOUISIANA

Many selections of crepe myrtles exist out there and they vary greatly in their characteristics. Selections that grow very tall may spend much of their early years making new branches and leaves, rather than flowers. We suggest you be patient. If you take good care of your plants, they should bloom next year.

Bamboo: *We've tried and tried to get rid of bamboo, but to no avail. Is there anything that will kill it without harming the surrounding plants?*

A. M. RILEY
HAMPTON, VIRGINIA

Cut all of the bamboo to within 6 inches of the ground. Then paint the cut surface of each stump with undiluted triclopyr (Brush-B-Gon Poison Ivy, Poison Oak & Brush Killer₁) or glyphosate (Roundup). Follow label directions carefully. You'll probably have to do this more than once.

Wisteria: *I would like to plant wisterias around my house. Do you have any tasteful ideas?*

CONNIE ARENSBERG
MOBILE, ALABAMA

How about letting it shade an abandoned school bus? Seriously, the trick to using wisteria is not letting this rampant vine climb trees and bushes where it can escape cultivation. We suggest confining it to a sturdy arbor, wall, or fence where you can prune regularly. Don't let the bean pods form after flowering or you'll have wisterias coming up everywhere.

Christmas cactus: *This year my Christmas cactus didn't bloom very much. I put it in the dark in September and brought it out the week before Thanksgiving. Then I watered it, because the soil was dry. I'll appreciate any advice on its care.*

DORIS LAMBERT
VALDESE, NORTH CAROLINA

To get your plant to bloom well, you do need to give it about 14 hours of complete darkness per day for about a month in the fall. But don't leave it in the dark all day. Bring it into bright light for at least eight hours per day. Once flowerbuds appear, water so that the soil stays slightly moist. Make sure the pot has an open drainage hole. Feed every two weeks with a bloom-booster fertilizer. After the last flower fades, cease feeding until spring. From spring until fall, give the plant plenty of light. Let the soil go slightly dry between thorough waterings. Feed every other week with a general-purpose houseplant fertilizer diluted to half strength.

Mandevilla: *I purchased a mandevilla vine this summer but am not sure how cold hardy it is. Should I bring it indoors when frost is in the forecast or is it safe to leave outside?*

RENA CHRISTOPHER
CUMBERLAND, MARYLAND

Mandevilla is semitropical, which means it won't survive temperatures below 25 degrees. However, it will survive a brief frost when the mercury dips to around 30 degrees. In your area, you definitely have to take it inside for the winter if you want to save it. So pot it up now, cut it back if you have to, and move it inside to a sunny window. But because this flowering vine is relatively inexpensive ($5 to $10), readily available, and grows rapidly, you might just let it die with the cold and plant a new one next spring.

Houseplants: *My houseplants never seem to live very long. I could use some advice.*

KRISTINA JONES
MOBILE, ALABAMA

Well, the first thing to remember is never set them atop gas logs. After that, keeping houseplants alive is pretty easy. Choose plants that are easy to grow indoors, such as philodendron, snake plant, peace lily, grape ivy, pothos, and dracaena. Place them near bright windows, so they receive plenty of light. Water them whenever they start to wilt or the soil becomes thoroughly dry. But always make sure the pot has a drainage hole for excess water. Never let a plant sit in water. Next to gas logs, overwatering is the quickest way to kill a houseplant.

Saving hibiscus: *My Chinese hibiscus was beautiful this summer, but I've been told it won't survive the winter here outside. How can I save it for next year?*

LISA P. HURNER
SPOTSYLVANIA, VIRGINIA

Chinese hibiscus *(Hibiscus rosa-sinensis)* is semitropical and can't withstand freezing temperatures. So you'll need to take it inside to your brightest window. Dimmer indoor light will cause it to drop a lot of leaves, so it's a good idea to prune it back by half before you bring

it in. Then spray the remaining leaves, both upper and lower surfaces, with horticultural oil or insecticidal soap to kill any aphids and spider mites. Let the soil go slightly dry between thorough waterings. Feed monthly with water-soluble 20-20-20 or 15-30-15 fertilizer.

Confederate jasmine: *I just purchased a Confederate jasmine vine. Does it like sun or shade? Will it survive our Central Texas winter?*

ROSEMARY P. WHITE
SAN MARCOS, TEXAS

Confederate jasmine *(Trachelospermum jasminoides)* is a delightful evergreen vine with extremely fragrant, creamy white flowers in spring. It grows in sun or light shade and likes fertile, well-drained soil. It's winter hardy in the Lower and Coastal South and should do well in your area.

Deer: *We have a lot of deer near our home and wonder if you can suggest what kinds of trees, shrubs, and other plants deer won't eat.*

MARTHA HAYES
CHARLESTON, SOUTH CAROLINA

Oh no, not again. Every time we recommend a list of deer-resistant plants, we get bombarded by hate mail from irate readers whose deer-resistant plants were just gnawed to the ground. The fact is, hungry deer will devour almost any plant short of a pink, aluminum Christmas tree (and in a dry year, who knows?). But you may want to try barberry, boxwood, wax myrtle, yaupon, yucca, oleander, Asian star jasmine, or Southern magnolia.

January

THE CLASSIC CAMELLIA
Pages 20–23: **Camellias** available from Camellia Forest Nursery, Wintergarden. **The Illustrated Encyclopedia of Camellias** by Stirling Macoboy available from Timber Press.

February

ONE GREAT HOUSEPLANT
Page 31: **Clivia** available from Park Seed Company, Logee's Greenhouses.

MINOR BULBS
Pages 32–34: **Bulbs** available from The Daffodil Mart, McClure & Zimmerman.

BACK SAVERS
Page 39: **Medium garden cart** available from Gardener's Supply Company.

March

MERCY FOR FORSYTHIA
Page 49: **Minigold** available from Forest Farm. **Gold Tide** available from Wayside Gardens.

PORCH WITH PUNCH
Page 57: **Exterior wood columns** available from Hartman Sanders.

April

JUBILANT SPRING TABLE
Page 79: **Topiary form** available from The Ivy Elephant.

A BEASTLY BEAUTY
Page 83: **Primrose** available from Carroll Gardens.

May

REMEDIES FOR RHODIES
Pages 104–106: **Rhododendrons** available from Transplant Nursery, Roslyn Nursery, Pushepetappa Gardens.

NOTHING BUT A PORCH
Page 107: **Screened Garden House plans, SL-9905-264,** available from *Southern Living Plans.*

TANGERINE BEAUTY
Page 108: **Tangerine Beauty Crossvine** available from Roslyn Nursery, Wayside Gardens.

TIMELESS TOMATOES
Pages 112–113: **Tomato seeds** available from Southern Exposure Seed Exchange, Johnny's Selected Seeds, Seed Savers Exchange. **Tomato plants** available from Garden Smith Nursery.

FLOWERS AND A SMILE
Pages 114–115: For directions, call Blue Moon Gardens, Tallahassee Nurseries, The Greenery, Natchez Trace Gardens.

June

SUMMER BOUQUETS
Pages 140–141: **Flowers Are Almost Forever** available from Brandylane Publishers, Inc.

NO MYSTERY TO PINEAPPLE SAGE
Page 142: **Pineapple sage** *(Salvia elegans)* available from Story House Herb Farm, Dabney Herbs.

HYDRANGEAS
Pages 143–147: **Hydrangeas** available from Wilkerson Mill Gardens.

July

ANYTHING BUT COMMON
Page 161: **Common Purple phlox** *(Phlox paniculata)* available from Goodness Grows.

WINDOW DRESSINGS
Pages 164–165: **Metal hayrack** available from Kinsman Garden Co., Inc. **Sap buckets** available from Tricia's Treasures. **Boxwood pyramids** available from Monrovia.

August

SIMPLY GOURDEOUS
Pages 170–172: **Gourds** available from The Gourd Garden and Curiosity Shop.

MAKING THE POOL A PLUS
Page 173: **Landscape design** by Garden Gate Landscaping.

HOT PLANTS, COOL COLORS
Page 175: **Leah Mandevilla** and **Plumbago** (both available only in spring) available from Park Seed Company. **Summer Snow Mandevilla** available from Monrovia.

September

SMART MAKEOVER
Pages 190–191: **Paint** available from Sherwin-Williams. **Awning** was custom made. **Awning canvas** available from Sunbrella. **Fabric** available from Glen Raven Custom Fabrics LLC. **Concrete stain on landing** available from L. M. Scofield Company.

TINY BLOOMS
Page 193: **Rain lily** *(Zephyranthes candida)* available from Louisiana Nursery.

COOL AS CAN BE
Page 194: **Powis Castle artemisia** available from André Viette, Wayside Gardens, Crownsville Nursery.

NO ORDINARY JOE
Pages 194–195: **Joe-pye weed** available from Kurt Bluemel, Inc.

FROM SUMMER TO SEPTEMBER
Page 195: **Brazilian verbena** available from Plant Delights Nursery, Inc.

October

AS PRETTY AS ITS NAME
Page 207: **Sour gum** *(Nyssa sylvatica)* available from Carroll Gardens.

A PRINCE OF A PERENNIAL
Page 208: **Toad lily** *(Tricyrtis hirta)* available from Wayside Gardens, Plant Delights Nursery, Inc., Carroll Gardens, Singing Springs Nursery.

November

PLANT FOR SPRING, HOPE FOR THE BEST
Pages 222–224: **Foxgloves** available from Shop @ Southern Living.

BLOOMING WITH BUTTERFLIES
Page 226: **Butterfly vine** *(Stigmaphyllon ciliatum)* available from Shop @ Southern Living.

December

SCENTSIBLE SOLUTION
Pages 236–239: **Mailbox, adult garden boots, and lunchbox** available from Restoration Hardware.

MOVE OVER, MISTLETOE
Pages 246–247: **Floral globe frame** available from Kinsman Garden Co., Inc.

André Viette (O, R), (540) 943-2315, catalog $5.

Blue Moon Gardens (O), (903) 852-3897.

Brandylane Publishers, Inc. White Stone, VA, fax orders (804) 435-9812, E-mail orders brandy@crosslink.net.

Camellia Forest Nursery (O), (919) 968-0504, 125 Carolina Forest Road, Chapel Hill, NC 27516, catalog $2, $10 minimum shipping charge.

Carroll Gardens (O), (800) 638-6334, catalog $3.

Crownsville Nursery (O), (410) 849-3143, www.crownsvillenursery.com, catalog free.

Dabney Herbs (O), (502) 893-5198, catalog $2.

The Daffodil Mart (O), (800) 255-2852, spring catalog free.

Forest Farm (O), (541) 846-7269.

Gardener's Supply Company (O), (800) 955-3370, catalog free.

GardenSmith Nursery (R), (706) 367-9094.

Garden Gate Landscaping 821 Norwood Road, Silver Spring, MD 20905, (301) 924-4131.

Glen Raven Custom Fabrics LLC (M), Glen Raven, NC, (336) 227-6211, www.sunbrella.com.

Goodness Grows (O), (706) 743-5055, catalog free, minimum order $20; fall is the best time to ship.

The Gourd Garden and Curiosity Shop (R), 4808 East County Road 30-A, Santa Rosa Beach, FL 32459, (850) 231-2150.

The Greenery (O), (770) 228-3169.

Hartman Sanders, Atlanta, (800) 241-4303.

The Illustrated Encyclopedia of Camellias by Stirling Macoboy available from Timber Press (M), (800) 327-5680, $39.95.

The Ivy Elephant (R), 3300 Coleman Road, Anniston, AL 36207, (256) 237-8458.

Johnny's Selected Seeds (O), (207) 437-4301, catalog free.

Kinsman Garden Co., Inc. (R, O), (800) 733-4146, item #GFGS, www.kinsmangarden.com, catalog free.

Kurt Bluemel, Inc. (R, O), www.bluemel.com.

L.M. Scofield Company (M), (800) 800-9900 for a distributor.

Logee's Greenhouses (O), (888) 330-8038, catalog free.

Louisiana Nursery (O), 5853 State 182, Opelousas, LA 70570, (318) 948-3696.

McClure & Zimmerman (O), (800) 883-6998, spring catalog free.

Midwest Wildflowers (O), Box 64, Rockton, IL 61072, catalog $1.

Monrovia (M), (888) 752-6848.

Natchez Trace Gardens (O), (601) 289-2221.

Nichols Garden Nursery (O), (541) 928-9280, www.gardennursery.com.

Park Seed Company (O), (800) 845-3369, catalog free.

Plant Delights Nursery, Inc. (O), 9241 Sauls Road, Raleigh, NC 27603, (919) 772-4794, www.plantdel.com, free catalog.

Pushepetappa Gardens (O), Franklinton, LA (504) 839-4930.

Restoration Hardware (R, O), (800) 762-1005, www.restorationhardware.com.

Roslyn Nursery (O), Dix Hills, NY (516) 643-9347, catalog $3.

Seed Savers Exchange (O), (319) 382-5990, catalog free.

Sherwin-Williams (M), see www.sherwin.com for store locations.

Shop @ Southern Living, www.southernliving.com

Singing Springs Nursery (O), 8802 Wilderson Road, Cedar Grove, NC 27231, (919) 732-9403, catalog free.

Southern Exposure Seed Exchange (O), (804) 973-4703, catalog $2.

Southern Living Plans, send $55 to P.O. Box 830349, Birmingham, AL 35283-0349. Add $15 for shipping and handling. (Alabama residents add 4% sales tax; Tennessee residents add 8.25% sales tax.) Credit card orders call (800) 755-1122.

Story House Herb Farm (O), (502) 753-4158, $50 minimum order, catalog $2.

Sunbrella (M), (336) 227-6211, www.sunbrella.com.

Tallahassee Nurseries (O), (850) 385-2162.

Transplant Nursery (O), Lavonia, GA, (706) 356-8947.

Timber Press (M), (800) 327-5860.

Tricia's Treasures (R), 1433-5 Montgomery Highway, Birmingham, AL 35216, (205) 822-0004.

Wayside Gardens (O), (800) 845-1124, www.waysidegardens.com, catalog free.

Wilkerson Mill Gardens (R, O), (770) 463-2400, catalog $3.

Wintergarden (O) 415 North Maple Street, Fairhope, AL 36532, catalog $3.

Woodlanders, Inc. (O), 1128 Colleton Ave., Aiken, SC 29801, (803) 648-7522, catalog $2.

(M) Contact the manufacturer for a retail source near you. (O) Mail order. (R) Retail store. Unlisted items are one of a kind or unavailable.

Index